Teachers Taking ACTION

A Comprehensive Guide to Teacher Research

Cynthia A. Lassonde and Susan E. Israel

EDITORS

INTERNATIONAL
Reading Association
800 BARKSDALE ROAD, PO BOX 8139
NEWARK, DE 19714-8139, USA
www.reading.org

The International Reading Association attempts, through its publications, to provide a forum for a wide spectrum of opinions on reading. This policy permits divergent viewpoints without implying the endorsement of the Association.

Executive Editor, Books   Corinne M. Mooney
Developmental Editor   Charlene M. Nichols
Developmental Editor   Tori Mello Bachman
Developmental Editor   Stacey Lynn Sharp
Editorial Production Manager   Shannon T. Fortner
Design and Composition Manager   Anette Schuetz

Project Editors   Charlene M. Nichols and Christina Lambert

Cover   Design, Linda Steere; Photograph, © 2007 Jupiter Images Corporation

The publisher would appreciate notification where errors occur so that they may be corrected in subsequent printings and/or editions.

Library of Congress Cataloging-in-Publication Data

Teachers taking action : a comprehensive guide to teacher research / edited by Cynthia A. Lassonde & Susan E. Israel.
    p. cm.
Includes bibliographical references and index.
ISBN-13: 978-0-87207-463-7
1. Action research in education. 2. Education--Research. I. Lassonde, Cynthia A. II. Israel, Susan E.
LB1028.24.T44 2007
370.7'2--dc22

                                                                    2007038536

To my family, who make it all possible; Rose Marie Weber, my all-time favorite teacher; and Susan Israel, for having faith in me.

—C.L.

This book is dedicated to those who support teacher research at all levels: the institutional, the school, and the classroom.

—S.I.

CONTENTS

PART I
Understanding the Foundations of Teacher Research

PART II
Developing a Research Project

PART VI
Where Do We Go From Here?

ABOUT THE EDITORS

Cynthia A. Lassonde is an assistant professor of elementary education and reading at the State University of New York College at Oneonta, New York, USA. She teaches undergraduate and graduate literacy courses at SUNY Oneonta. A former elementary teacher and teacher researcher for more years than she'd like to admit, Cynthia's research interests include the teaching of writing and critical inquiry pedagogy. She has been published in educational journals including *Language Arts*, *Literacy Teaching and Learning*, *Support for Learning*, and *Youth and Society*. Two professional responsibilities she enjoys most are her positions as editor of the New York Association of Colleges for Teacher Education's journal *Excelsior: Leadership in Teaching and Learning* and chair of the Teacher as Researcher Subcommittee of the International Reading Association. But her life's joys are her daughters, Ann, Jill, and Kelly, and her husband, Mark.

Susan E. Israel is a literacy consultant and an assistant professor in the field of reading and educational psychology. Her research agenda focuses on reading comprehension and child–mind development as it relates to literacy processes in reading and writing.

Susan was awarded the 2005 Panhellenic Council Outstanding Professor Award at the University of Dayton, Ohio, USA. She was also the 1998 recipient of the Teacher as Researcher Grant from the International Reading Association, in which she has served and been a member for more than a decade.

Susan's most recent publications include *Using Metacognitive Assessments to Create Individualized Reading Instruction* (2007); an edited volume with E. Jennifer Monaghan titled *Shaping the Reading Field: The Impact of Early Reading Pioneers, Scientific Research, and Progressive Ideas* (2007); and an edited volume with Michelle M. Israel titled *Poetic Possibilities: Using Poetry to Enhance Literacy Learning* (2006), which features poems from *The Reading Teacher*.

Editor Information for Correspondence and Workshops

Cynthia and Susan would love to hear from readers, and they welcome questions or feedback. Cynthia can be reached at LASSONC@oneonta.edu. Susan can be reached at sueisrael@insightbb.com.

CONTRIBUTORS

Leanne M. Avery
Assistant Professor
Department of Elementary Education
    and Reading
State University of New York College
    at Oneonta
Oneonta, New York

James F. Baumann
Professor
Elementary and Early Childhood
    Education
University of Wyoming
Laramie, Wyoming

Amy D. Broemmel
Assistant Professor
Department of Theory and Practice
    in Teacher Education
The University of Tennessee
Knoxville, Tennessee

Peggy D. Cuevas
Visiting Assistant Professor
School of Education
University of Miami
Coral Gables, Florida

Barbara H. Davis
Associate Professor
Department of Curriculum
    and Instruction
Texas State University–San Marcos
San Marcos, Texas

Cheryl Dozier
Assistant Professor
Reading Department
University at Albany, State University
    of New York
Albany, New York

Elizabeth Carr Edwards
Assistant Professor
Department of Curriculum,
    Foundations, and Reading
Georgia Southern University
Statesboro, Georgia

Deborah Eldridge
Professor
Department of Curriculum
    and Teaching, College of Education
    and Human Services
Montclair State University
Montclair, New Jersey

Francine C. Falk-Ross
Associate Professor
Department of Literacy Education
Northern Illinois University
DeKalb, Illinois

Moira A. Fallon
Associate Professor
Department of Education and Human
    Development
State University of New York College
    at Brockport
Brockport, New York

Rebecca K. Fox
Assistant Professor
Advanced Studies in Teaching
    and Learning, College of Education
    and Human Development
George Mason University
Fairfax, Virginia

Mark A. Hogan
Associate Professor
Education Department
Bridgewater College
Bridgewater, Virginia

Susan E. Israel
Literacy Consultant
Assistant Professor
Fishers, Indiana

Nithya Narayanaswamy Iyer
Assistant Professor
Educational Psychology
    and Counseling
State University of New York College
    at Oneonta
Oneonta, New York

Cynthia A. Lassonde
Assistant Professor
Elementary Education and Reading
    Department
State University of New York College
    at Oneonta
Oneonta, New York

Susan Davis Lenski
Professor
Curriculum and Instruction
Portland State University
Portland, Oregon

Faith Maina
Assistant Professor
Department of Curriculum
    and Instruction
State University of New York
    at Oswego
Oswego, New York

Christine A. Mallozzi
Doctoral Candidate
Department of Language and Literacy
    Education
The University of Georgia
Athens, Georgia

Dixie D. Massey
Visiting Assistant Professor
Department of Teacher Education
University of Puget Sound
Tacoma, Washington

Daniel Z. Meyer
Assistant Professor
Department of Mathematics
    and Science Education
Illinois Institute of Technology
Chicago, Illinois

Nancy L. Michelson
Associate Professor
Department of Education Specialties
Salisbury University
Salisbury, Maryland

Sharon K. Miller
Codirector, Teacher Research
    and Inservice, Southern Arizona
    Writing Project
Department of English
The University of Arizona
Tucson, Arizona

Anthony J. Onwuegbuzie
Professor
Department of Educational Leadership
    and Counseling
Sam Houston State University
Huntsville, Texas

Alexandra Peña
Elementary Teacher
Elementary School 4
Fort Lee, New Jersey

Linda Pratt
Executive Director of Teacher
    Education, Dana Professor
    of Education
Department of Teacher Education
Elmira College
Elmira, New York

Taffy E. Raphael
University Scholar
College of Education
University of Illinois at Chicago
Chicago, Illinois

Janet C. Richards
Professor
Department of Childhood Education
University of South Florida
Tampa, Florida

Gail V. Ritchie
Coleader, Teacher Researcher Network
Fairfax County Public Schools
Fairfax, Virginia

Ilene R. Rutten
Assistant Professor
Department of Teacher Development
St. Cloud State University
St. Cloud, Minnesota

Neal Shambaugh
Associate Professor
Department of Technology, Learning,
    and Culture
West Virginia University
Morgantown, West Virginia

Kim T. Shea
Doctoral Candidate
Department of Childhood Education
University of South Florida
Tampa, Florida

Kathy G. Short
Professor
Department of Language, Reading,
    and Culture
The University of Arizona
Tucson, Arizona

Tracy L. Smiles
Assistant Professor
Division of Teacher Education
Western Oregon University
Monmouth, Oregon

Suzanne Wegener Soled
Professor and Chair
Department of Teacher Education
    and School Leadership
Northern Kentucky University
Highland Heights, Kentucky

Michelle Stein
Math Teacher
Hackensack High School
Hackensack, New Jersey

Elizabeth A. Swaggerty
Assistant Professor
Department of Curriculum
    and Instruction
East Carolina University
Greenville, North Carolina

Donna Ware
Literacy Coach
Whitehead Road Elementary School
Clarke County School District
Athens, Georgia

Alyson Wasko
Science Teacher
Montclair High School
Montclair, New Jersey

Starlin D. Weaver
Associate Professor
Department of Education Specialties
Salisbury University
Salisbury, Maryland

Jaci Webb-Dempsey
Assistant Professor
Department of Technology, Learning,
    and Culture
West Virginia University
Morgantown, West Virginia

Kenneth J. Weiss
Associate Professor
School of Education and Professional
    Studies, Department of Reading
    and Language Arts
Central Connecticut State University
New Britain, Connecticut

FOREWORD

As a teacher educator who has enjoyed both leading and participating in teacher research groups over the past few decades, I can appreciate how useful *Teachers Taking Action: A Comprehensive Guide to Teacher Research* is for today's educators. We are living in a time that demands evidence-based decision making at every level, a time that emphasizes articulating the research base underlying instructional decisions, and a time in which our field faces de-professionalization through emphasizing fidelity to commercial curriculum programs brought in through outsiders rather than teacher-constructed, coherent curriculum and instruction driven by students' particular needs. Thus, perhaps more than ever before, professional educators need tools and guidelines to understand existing research and to engage in research specific to their settings. *Teachers Taking Action* is a valuable resource for teachers and teacher educators—from preschool through higher education—who are committed to a rigorous examination of their own practices using established, relevant research approaches and methods.

The volume is user-friendly for both novice and experienced teacher researchers. I have taught graduate courses in teacher research methodologies as well as been a member of teacher research groups. Engaging in research in either of these settings leads the participants to consider a range of essential questions: Why would I want to do teacher research in the first place? What kinds of questions would teacher researchers want to address? How does a teacher researcher develop a project? What choices might I have for exploring a question and how do I decide what kind of evidence I will need to answer the question? Where do I get this evidence? What do I do with it once I have it? And what if I want to share what I've learned, how do I go about doing that? If I need supplies or equipment for the project I have in mind, how can I get some outside support so I can afford to do the project? And, the biggest question of all, how do I create time in my already overscheduled life to do the project justice?

These questions can be daunting even for teacher researchers and future teacher researchers who have the support of a professional learning community through study groups in their schools or professional organizations or through more formal settings such as graduate courses. This comprehensive guide provides much-needed information in an organized framework to build the confidence that the time committed to a teacher research project will be well spent. That is, the teacher researchers engaging in their projects will be confident that their efforts will result in significant learning about issues that are central to their professional lives. Further, the teacher researchers will have confidence that when they share what they have learned with colleagues, what they are sharing is based on rigorous examination of evidence that is both valid for the question they've asked and meets criteria of reliability.

Throughout the parts of the volume, vignettes provide concrete examples of teacher researchers in action and serve as jumping off points both for discussions as projects are being planned and for illustrations of how methods recommended are applied in the context of engaging in the teacher research process. Part I sets the stage for understanding the broad array of settings and questions ideal for teacher researcher methodologies and the "big picture" of what teacher research involves. For the novice teacher researchers, these two chapters are essential readings for basic understandings of the journey on which they are about to embark. Part II consists of excellent descriptions of the components of the project that, when thoughtfully addressed, ensure that time on the project will be well spent. These chapters provide essential information to help teacher researchers align their interests with a researchable question, align the question with appropriate methods, and plan their project so that it will result in answers to their questions. Part III guides teacher researchers in the actual process of what to do with what is typically qualitative evidence they have gathered: how to examine this data for trends and patterns and the value of working with colleagues throughout the analysis process. Part IV takes the readers into complexities, from how to overcome challenges and barriers—funding to access—to ensuring they are maintaining high standards for ethical behaviors since teacher researchers often have been granted access to confidential information about the lives of students, families, or organizations.

Frequently underdeveloped in the teacher research literature are the issues of audience. While many teacher researchers are engaging in the process to examine, cope with, or solve local problems of practice, it is important that the voices of those on the front line in educational practice are heard by those in the broader context: families, administrators, and policymakers. Part V provides a wonderful resource with many concrete suggestions for teacher researchers who would like to share what they have learned with this broader group, offering very specific guidelines for ways to go public with what they have learned—at conferences, within their local communities, in professional journals.

In summary, this text instantiates what it has promised to provide. It is, in fact, a comprehensive guide. It is a valuable resource for teacher researchers at all levels of experiences, as well as teacher educators and professional development leaders in schools, professional organizations, and higher education settings.

—Taffy E. Raphael
University of Illinois at Chicago

PREFACE

"We must find a way of bridging the
traditional divide between educational theory
and professional practice."

—*Jack Whitehead (as cited in* Action Research: Principles and
Practice *by Jean McNiff)*

Teacher research offers an effective opportunity to bridge the traditional divide between educational theory and professional practice. Educators who practice teacher research in classroom settings find they become more complete teachers as they study and analyze what they are doing in the classroom and integrate their findings with current readings and thoughts about teaching and learning.

A Book Is Born

Teachers Taking Action: A Comprehensive Guide to Teacher Research was derived from the charges of the Teacher Research Subcommittee of the International Reading Association (IRA) for the need to address its goal to disseminate information that supports and encourages teacher research. When the chair of the subcommittee, Cynthia Lassonde, communicated this goal to the members of the committee in the spring of 2006, one of the members, Susan Israel—a former recipient of the IRA Teacher as Researcher Grant—proposed a resource that focused specifically on effective tools teachers in the classroom can use to conduct their research. The idea of this comprehensive guide was born. Members of the Teacher as Researcher Subcommittee met at the IRA conference in Chicago, Illinois, in May 2006. All agreed that a book of this nature was needed in the field of teacher research to lead teacher researchers through the process of planning, developing, managing, funding, engaging in, analyzing, and disseminating the findings of their research. The insider view of learning is vital to our understanding of classroom practices and literacy education. Teacher research must be promoted, supported, and shared. *Teachers Taking Action* serves to demonstrate how to effectively engage in teacher research. Part of that engagement entails sharing your results with fellow educators through presentation and publication.

Contributors

This guide is unique in that it offers teacher researchers chapters written by a number of experts across many regions of the United States who represent practicing teacher researchers and teacher educators, who are passionate and supportive of the discipline, and who are well read on various aspects of current research. You need only to visit the Contributors page to note the wealth of experience and knowledge the chapter authors represent. We, the editors, are excited to share their expertise and research with you.

Organization

We have organized the volume into six parts that focus specifically on what you need to know when conducting research in your classroom and when sharing your findings. Each part is accompanied by an online case study that provides a contextualized example for understanding the real-life application of each chapter.

Part I, "Understanding the Foundations of Teacher Research," introduces key concepts that are the fundamentals of teacher research. First, teacher research terminology is "unpacked" or explored. Next, this part provides an overview of the procedures so you can get the big picture of what teacher research looks like from start to finish. The complete online case study shows application of the concepts introduced as well as multiple perspectives of the rationale behind why a teacher would and should want to participate in this type of classroom research.

Part II, "Developing a Research Project," gets into the specifics of shaping your teacher research study, beginning with the process of framing a researchable question and conceptualizing the project. Research methods are also described. Again, a corresponding online case study wraps up the part to help you synthesize learning.

Part III, "Engaging in Teacher Research Projects," helps you engage in the processes of organizing and analyzing data and collaborating with peers. The online case study for this part looks at the ways first-year teachers engage in teacher research to improve practice.

Part IV, "Supportive Strategies and Funding," takes a positive approach to managing stumbling blocks that might arise in the teacher research process. Strategies for dealing with a variety of issues that might develop, for example, with management and funding, are presented. The online case study for this part shares an elementary literacy coach's research and the stumbling blocks experienced along the way.

Part V, "Writing, Publishing, and Presenting Teacher Research," explains how to effectively write research reports, submit manuscripts for publication, and present at professional conferences. The final online case study reflects an example of collaborative writing on the part of two teacher researchers.

The final part of this volume, "Where Do We Go From Here?" synthesizes theoretical perspectives in relationship to teacher research in the classroom. Lessons for future teacher researchers, issues to think about as you begin your study, and possible literacy-related research directions are provided.

Distinctive Features

Several special features help to organize and clarify each chapter. First, chapter-opening questions help you organize your thoughts before reading or help you search for the answers to particular questions you might have. Second, listings of key terms at the beginning of each chapter allow you to see at a glimpse what topics will be highlighted, and, because the terms are boldfaced in the chapter as they are defined, you can also quickly scroll through a chapter when you need to locate a definition. Third, each chapter opens with a vignette. Throughout each chapter the vignettes are referenced to illustrate key concepts discussed within the chapters. Finally, visual representations such as diagrams, sample forms, and charts are inserted throughout each chapter to support or illustrate key concepts.

Content chapters close with several distinctive features, too. First, the "Synthesis and Concluding Thoughts" section provides more than a summary of the chapter and offers a synthesis that evaluates critically the research, ideas, or analysis of the significance of the findings. Then, the "Problem-Solving Vignette for Discussion" section includes literacy-related vignettes that pose a problem related to the chapter topic and prompt you to reflect on a solution. "What-would-you-do" questions are posed. Next, the "Tips for Teacher Researchers" section summarizes practical how-to's related to key concepts discussed in the chapter. Finally, "Questions for Reflection" provide three to four questions that prompt further thinking on the topic.

Two valuable appendixes appear at the end of the volume. Appendix A is an annotated list of favorite teacher resources that can be used to enhance professional development or extend your understanding of the topics in this volume. Appendix B offers a number of reproducible forms that may be duplicated for your use.

Although this guide leans toward literacy instruction and research in that case studies and examples focus on reading and writing practices, it is important to note that we view all teachers as teachers of literacy. Therefore, literacy instruction used to exemplify teacher research methods and strategies is integrated into a range of content areas across grade levels and institutions so that a variety is represented.

Written in an informal yet astute style, *Teachers Taking Action* is readily accessible as a class text for graduate students in research and education courses. It will also act as a guide to reading specialists, classroom teachers, administrators, supervisors, and curriculum coordinators investigating practice, learning, and program effectiveness. Readers with varying levels of knowledge and experience with teacher research or research in general will find the volume easy to follow yet full of practical knowledge about the how-to's of teacher research.

Through teacher research, educators can make ripples that can have far-reaching effects. If you find this guide provides you with the confidence to conduct teacher research in the classroom, helps you actualize your inquiries, and encourages you to share your findings with colleagues, then our goal for this volume has been achieved. We wish you well in your endeavor.

ACKNOWLEDGMENTS

Cynthia and Susan would like to acknowledge all the people they worked with at IRA, especially Corinne Mooney, Charlene Nichols, Christina Lambert, and all of the anonymous reviewers for helping to shape the book into the powerful resource it is. Thanks also to Kjersti VanSlyke-Briggs for her help and insight in organizing Appendix A and Sarah Fletcher for sharing her mentoring website. Susan would also like to acknowledge Dr. Judith Lysaker, the professor who encouraged her to pursue the Teacher as Researcher Grant through IRA.

PART I

Understanding the Foundations of Teacher Research

Part Opener: Becoming a Teacher Researcher
Linda Pratt, Kenneth J. Weiss, Faith Maina

Main Street Elementary School (pseudonym) is a high-needs, urban school with more than 400 pupils in prekindergarten through grade 5. For the last two years, the school's fourth-grade English language arts scores on standard state tests have fallen below the minimum requirements.

Kira, a fourth-grade teacher at Main Street Elementary School, is especially apprehensive about the language arts exams being administered during her tenure review period. The superintendent highlights teacher research as a possible productive way to help teachers meet their individual goals in the classroom as well as to help administrators attain their districtwide goals. Kira wonders, How does the superintendent expect me to do research on top of everything else I already do? I'm not a researcher. How do I become one?

Kira discovers teacher research as a workable way to be more successful in helping her students improve their literacy. Kira also learns that teacher research can help her sort out ways to improve students' learning by using effective teaching strategies, techniques, and lessons that are likely to yield positive outcomes. Kira's outlook becomes optimistic and enthusiastic once she sees how she can help herself become a more effective teacher and improve her students' learning by engaging in teacher research. (To read the complete case study, go to this book's link on the IRA website at www.reading.org and click on Case Study #1: Becoming a Teacher Researcher. You may find it helpful to first read the introduction that highlights the rationale for teacher research.)

As you continue to read part I of this book, you, like Kira, will learn more about the foundations and elements of teacher research. Specifically, in chapter 1 you will learn how to define and embrace teacher research and in chapter 2 you will examine the types of research design and the various methods for selection.

1

How Teacher Research Can Become *Your* Way of Being

*Cynthia A. Lassonde, Gail V. Ritchie,
Rebecca K. Fox*

KEY TERMS

Action research
Critical friends
Practitioner inquiry
Reflective teaching (or
critical reflective
practice)
Teacher inquiry
Teacher research
Teacher researchers

BEFORE-READING QUESTIONS

■ What is teacher research?

■ How has teacher research evolved historically?

■ How is the term *teacher research* distinguished from related terms?

■ What are the roles an educator may play in teacher research?

C ynthia is a fifth-grade teacher in a small, rural elementary school. One of her students, Matthew, is resistant to writing and frequently expresses his resistance in ways that distract the whole class. Cynthia is frustrated and is looking for ways to encourage Matthew to become an engaged writer. She thinks a systematic study of what is happening on a day-to-day basis might help her look at the situation with more clarity and objectivity. She decides to take a close look at her writing curriculum and instruction by conducting a teacher research study.

A week after starting the study, Cynthia mentions to a colleague that she finds it difficult to "wear two hats" in the classroom: the teacher in charge of managing the class and the researcher collecting data. Her colleague, an experienced teacher researcher asks, "Aren't all teachers researchers anyway...every day? They look at and analyze test scores and students' writing. They figure out what they're going to teach next based on how well students did. Isn't that what researchers do...collect data, analyze it, and state their findings?" This is a revelation to Cynthia. She decides to try to ease into the role of wearing both hats simultaneously rather than taking on one role at a time.

Teachers Taking Action: A Comprehensive Guide to Teacher Research, edited by Cynthia A. Lassonde and Susan E. Israel.
© 2008 by the International Reading Association.

Introduction

Teacher research takes many forms, from the individual teacher exploring his or her practice—like Cynthia—to groups of teachers working collaboratively, or educators recommending educational policy changes based on classroom findings. The benefits of reflective, systematic investigation of teaching and learning in the classroom setting are recognized in the field of education. Teachers who engage in inquiry into their practice gain knowledge about and insights on teaching and learning in their contexts. They develop proficiency in teaching their students and maximizing student achievement. By sharing the results of their inquiry, teacher researchers can also enrich the teaching profession. But, even more important, teacher researchers become empowered as they realize they are educational experts. In teacher research methodology, research is not something that is done *to* teachers. Instead, it is something done *by* teachers as they actively seek to improve teaching and learning and to add to the knowledge base about exemplary educational practices (Woodcock, Lassonde, & Rutten, 2004).

The opening vignette shares the idea that the ways we come to understand teacher research change as we experience it, become comfortable with it, talk with others, and read various sources. That first study happened years ago. Since then Cynthia's ideas about teacher research have changed quite a bit. The more she experienced and read about teacher research, her ideas about what it meant to be a teacher researcher developed. Her thoughts of all teachers being teacher researchers have flourished into a deeper understanding that teacher research includes, but is not synonymous with, reflective teaching.

What's important—if educators value teacher research as a knowledge-building paradigm—is that we patiently and persistently take time to learn about and practice teacher research techniques and continue to develop an understanding of teacher research.

Understanding Teacher Research

As defined by Cochran-Smith and Lytle (1993), **teacher research** is "systematic and intentional inquiry carried out by teachers" (p. 7). It is systematic in that it is planned and designed ahead of time and intentional in that a deliberate procedure is followed. Through teacher research, educators hold themselves accountable for their practices and students' learning as they take a close look at themselves as well as their philosophies and beliefs related to education. Bissex (1996) proposes that through teacher research, the practitioner becomes more complete.

In the past decade, the term *teacher research* has been used more and more frequently. However, there are specifics to consider about the terminology related to it and the roles a teacher researcher might play in the process. Therefore, before introducing the reasons, procedures, methods, and strategies for conducting and disseminating the results of teacher research that are discussed in the upcoming chapters of this book, we will take a moment to unpack, or explore, the concept and its possibilities, beginning with a short history lesson.

One of the earliest proponents of teachers making contributions to classroom research and educational reform was educator John Dewey. He is quoted as saying in 1929,

> It seems to me that the contributions that might come from classroom teachers are a comparatively neglected field...an almost unworked mine.... For these teachers are the ones in direct contact with pupils and hence the ones through whom the results of scientific consequences of educational theory come in to the lives of those at school. (Wallace, 1997, pp. 27–28)

It wasn't until the mid-1980s, however, that teacher research began to emerge as an alternate form of research in the field of literacy in North America (Lytle, 2000). A seminal edited volume of essays and teacher research studies by Goswami and Stillman (1987) portrayed teacher inquiry as a means of reform. Other work followed (e.g., Bissex & Bullock, 1987; Bullock, 1987). Largely these were collaborative studies based on relationships cultivated between classroom teachers and teacher consultants (Lytle, 2000). Teachers were perceived as not having the training to conduct research, so teacher research was largely seen as a collaborative effort among classroom and university-based researchers (Goswami & Stillman, 1987; Hubbard & Power, 1993).

It was in 1987 that Nancie Atwell's book about writing instruction, *In the Middle* (Atwell, 1987, 1998), was first published. This riveting book presented one of the first accounts of how a teacher embedded research in her classroom. It offered an alternative perspective to the teacher relying on another's more expert support. These volumes were the seeds that formed a grass-roots revolution of support for teacher inquiry as a means of promoting professional development (Lytle, 2000; Myers, 1987).

Today—with the assistance of local support groups; books such as the one you are reading; online listservs; and state, national, and international professional organizations—more and more teachers are turning to research to inform their teaching. In education today, teachers are held accountable for their students' learning in explicit and public ways. What better way to determine the effectiveness of your teaching than to perform a systematic study of your interactions with learners?

In the opening anecdote, Cynthia found that while observing and talking with students, reflecting on her journal entries, and looking at the other data in the study, what precipitated students' resistance was when they felt they weren't given choices. Teacher research provided an authentic, accountable, and meaningful way for her to learn from and about her students and herself.

Teacher Research by Many Other Names

Educational research is frequently associated with the U.S. government's current emphasis on the reliance on rigorous, scientifically based quantitative research and evidence to inform instruction (e.g., No Child Left Behind Act of 2001). Although the term *teacher research* does connote a scientific inquiry that is spurred by a researcher's question about teaching or learning—the teacher researcher's "puzzlement" (Jacob & Ruess, 2000)—it is the researcher's voice that drives the teacher researcher's study as he or she is in charge of constructing and generating knowledge and understanding within a specific classroom or educational context. As these new meanings are shared with other educators and researchers, they have the potential for leading to professional development and, in a broader picture, educational reform.

Teacher research typically follows a pattern, in broad terms, of forming a researchable question, designing the study, collecting data, analyzing and interpreting data, determining results and implications for teaching, and sharing the results. The process is both iterative and cyclical in nature. Figure 1.1 provides an example

FIGURE 1.1
The Teacher Research Process

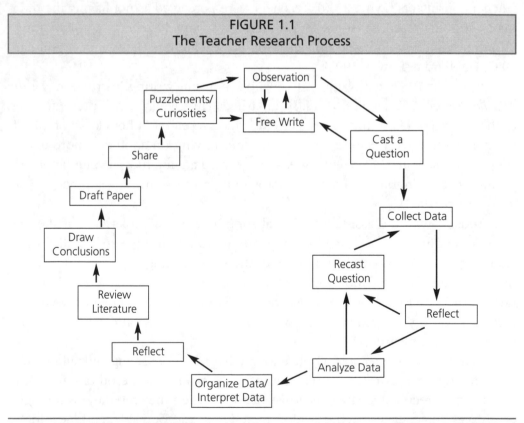

Created by Michelle Crabill and Gail V. Ritchie for use with teacher researchers in Fairfax County Public Schools, Fairfax, Virginia, and George Mason University, Fairfax, Virginia.

of how this progression might take place. Many of the procedures of research involve the same kinds of processes that are inherently part of managing a classroom. A teacher researcher does not have to necessarily (as described in the chapter-opening vignette) wear two hats as if he or she has two personas. Figure 1.2 shows how the roles of teacher and teacher researcher are interrelated.

Several terms are often associated with teacher research and in many cases are used interchangeably. They are *action research, teacher inquiry, practitioner inquiry,* and *reflective teaching* or *critical reflective practice.* Do all of these terms mean the same thing? If not, how are they distinguished from one another? Although all of these terms refer basically to educational research done in a learning context—typically a classroom—by the instructor, each emphasizes and represents a slightly different perspective of teaching and research. Teasing out these terms will provide insight regarding the entities of teacher research. Teacher research is a type of action research, is synonymous with teacher inquiry, shares many characteristics with practitioner inquiry, and incorporates reflective teaching and critical reflective practice (Brookfield, 1987, 1995). The next sections provide more information about those terms.

FIGURE 1.2
The Interrelated Roles of the Teacher and the Teacher Researcher

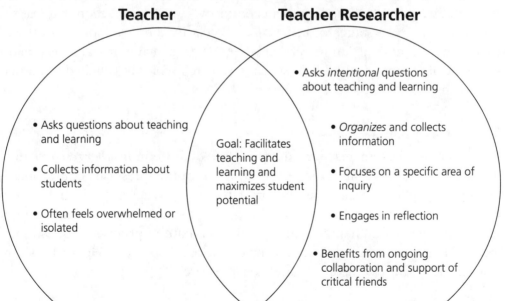

Created by Michelle Crabill and Gail V. Ritchie for use with teacher researchers in Fairfax County Public Schools, Fairfax, Virginia, and George Mason University, Fairfax, Virginia.

Action Research

Action research is "a disciplined process of inquiry conducted by and for those taking the action. The primary reason for engaging in action research is to assist the 'actor' in improving or refining his or her actions" (Sagor, 2000, p. 3). Action research has its roots in the social activism movements of the 1940s. The term was coined as a way of describing research conducted to improve social situations (Arhar, Holly, & Kasten, 2001). A stated goal of action research is "effecting positive changes" (Mills, 2000, p. 6).

Sagor (2005), who founded the Institute for the Study of Inquiry in Education in 1997, describes the steps of action research as

1. Selecting a Focus
2. Clarifying Theories
3. Identifying Research Questions
4. Collecting Data
5. Analyzing Data
6. Reporting Results
7. Taking Informed Action

The focus of action research is that the researcher will initiate informed action. By carefully analyzing data, the researcher uncovers a plan of action that leads to wisdom in the next stages of instruction. To clarify the terminology further, a teacher researcher or action researcher is the "actor" in action research as practice is continually refined (Sagor, 2005). Action research typically is linked to curriculum reconstruction (Noffke & Stevenson, 1995).

Teacher Inquiry

Those who use the term **teacher inquiry** in place of the term *teacher research* highlight the idea that classroom research draws from the questions educators ask about their practice by taking an inquiry stance as a teacher and a learner. Use of the word *inquiry* rather than the word *research* is sometimes less intimidating to novice teacher researchers in that it connotes a natural process of questioning and seeking answers rather than a technical, scientific process. Figure 1.3 shows how teacher inquiry compares to traditional research.

Practitioner Inquiry

A practitioner may be a teacher, administrator, community member, family member, tutor, counselor, or another stakeholder in the educational arena (Lytle, 2000).

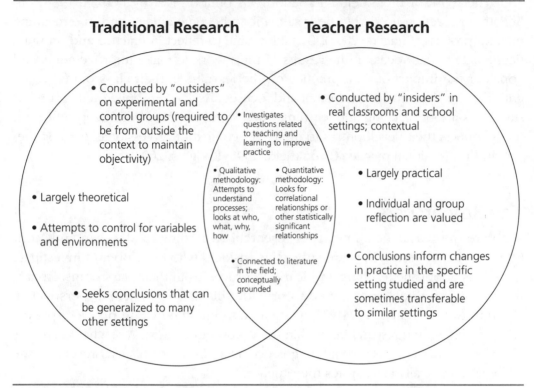

FIGURE 1.3
Similarities and Differences of Traditional Research vs. Teacher Research

Traditional Research

Teacher Research

- Conducted by "outsiders" on experimental and control groups (required to be from outside the context to maintain objectivity)

- Largely theoretical

- Attempts to control for variables and environments

- Seeks conclusions that can be generalized to many other settings

- Investigates questions related to teaching and learning to improve practice

- Qualitative methodology: Attempts to understand processes; looks at who, what, why, how

- Quantitative methodology: Looks for correlational relationships or other statistically significant relationships

- Connected to literature in the field; conceptually grounded

- Conducted by "insiders" in real classrooms and school settings; contextual

- Largely practical

- Individual and group reflection are valued

- Conclusions inform changes in practice in the specific setting studied and are sometimes transferable to similar settings

Created by Gail V. Ritchie for use with teacher researchers in Fairfax County Public Schools, Fairfax, Virginia, and George Mason University, Fairfax, Virginia.

Therefore, **practitioner inquiry** typically signals some type of contextual or setting-based teacher research collaboration initiated by these stakeholders.

Reflective Teaching and Critical Reflective Practice

Teacher research involves, and perhaps cannot exist without, **reflective teaching**, which is also referred to as **critical reflective practice** (Brookfield, 1987, 1995; Schön, 1983). Schön (1983) states that the best teachers actively incorporate reflection into their practice and take time to reflect in many ways, not only on their teaching but also on the results of their teaching on learners. However, the difference between reflective teaching and teacher research is that teacher research is an investigation of practice that is planned, designed, and carried out procedurally for an intended purpose. The National Commission on Teaching and America's Future (1996) states that teachers should be able to think systematically about their practice and learn from experience. They must be able to "critically examine their practice, seek the advice of others, and draw on educational research to deepen their knowledge, sharpen their judgment, and adapt their teaching to new findings and ideas" (p. 75).

The work of Brookfield and Schön was built on Dewey's (1933, 1938) beliefs that reflection needed to be systematic to become a deep and true meaning making process (Rodgers, 2002). By taking time to reflect in practice and on practice, teachers can focus on the results of their work to make improvements and consider the impact of their practice on the learners in their classrooms. To be critical, reflection must be consistent and focused. As teachers build on their understandings about teaching and learning, they stand to profit from deep reflection that connects their development to the larger context of professional learning theory and professional practice (Brookfield, 1995; Rodgers, 2002).

The Researchers

Who are the researchers in teacher research? According to MacLean and Mohr (1999), **teacher researchers** are subjective insiders who develop and investigate questions about the teaching and learning processes in their classrooms. In fact, teachers are uniquely positioned to provide this insider or "emic" perspective (Maykut & Morehouse, 1994). They are able to mix theory and practice (praxis) while teaching and researching within the classroom context. A teacher is curious about what, how, or why something is occurring in her or his classroom, so she or he systematically investigates the situation.

Teacher research is usually, but not exclusively, conducted by a classroom teacher in her or his classroom. In the opening anecdote, Cynthia was a teacher researcher in her fifth-grade classroom. However, Irene and Chrissie, the colleagues with whom she regularly talked about her research, took on roles as teacher researchers as well. As her **critical friends**, or research collaborators, they contributed to her analysis of data by talking with her about what was going on in the classroom and how she was interpreting it (Rodgers, 2002). Critical friends may help with all phases of research, such as collecting data, sharing and discussing current related literature, or simply reviewing a write-up of the results for publication as you'll see in chapter 7.

University- or organization-based associates often collaborate with teachers to support teacher research studies and act as critical friends. Sometimes this is done on site in the classroom, while at other times support may be provided through a collaborative discussion group meeting or even online networking. The concept has been broadened to include a variety of roles of participation, which are all aimed to encourage this "systematic and intentional inquiry carried out by teachers" (Cochran-Smith & Lytle, 1993, p. 7) and to compensate for many of the factors of this type of emic research that are frequently considered problematic. (See chapters 8 and 9 about barriers and issues related to teacher research.)

There are currently many networks varying in size and scope that support the work of teacher research, and more of such groups are springing up all over the country. Many resources for teacher research can be found in Appendix A.

Calling All Teachers

It is time to issue a call for all teachers to engage in teacher research as a means of proclaiming and sharing their knowledge about what works in actual classrooms. These days of high-stakes accountability might lead teachers to feel powerless in their classrooms; however, teacher research empowers teachers by providing them with classroom-based data as evidence of exemplary teaching and learning. Yendol-Hoppey (2006) refers to the "remote controlling" of teachers, meaning state and national testing and requirements are taking over classrooms and forcing teachers to focus on political mandates. Teacher research enables teachers to maintain a focus on what really matters—providing high-quality instruction for their students. Teaching requires both a high level of competency and a deep level of understanding our increasingly diverse society, child development, pedagogy, technology, and the subjects taught. Through the systematic, intentional processes of teacher research, teachers make instructional decisions and take action based on data rather than on mere perceptions.

Preservice, novice, and veteran teachers are all in prime positions to develop their powerful voices regarding educational issues. When educators participate in teacher research, they become active and informed decision makers as they analyze the evidence and generate new ideas. No longer do they have to rely solely on external perceptions of how theory relates to practice or be told the results of research. Teacher research empowers teachers to make a positive difference in terms of classroom practice; it enables them to provide relevant information about teaching and learning in actual classrooms. Most important, by engaging in reflective practice, the teacher researcher improves the lives of students by always seeking to develop more effective ways of implementing teaching and learning (Ritchie, 2000).

Synthesis and Concluding Thoughts

This chapter has provided an introduction to the terminology related to teacher research. By teasing out the differences among terms such as *teacher inquiry, action research, reflective teaching,* and others, we can begin to see how teacher research reflects our ideas of what it means to be a teacher and a learner in today's classroom. In Cynthia's anecdote about her first attempts at conducting research in her classroom, we saw how a teacher might struggle with refining an insider's perspective while being involved in the daily drama of the classroom.

Through practice and experience, her feeling of wearing the two hats of the researcher and the teacher matured into what Ritchie (2006) calls a "habit of mind" (p. 2), a way of thinking and acting, a way of being a more effective teacher.

Many teachers, already overburdened with curriculum requirements, accountability requirements, and all the day-to-day pressures of keeping a classroom running, wonder why they should take on one more thing. To them, teacher research is not an add-on; it is a way of being. When you look at your classroom from a stance of "How can I make teaching and learning better?" you are taking a teacher researcher stance. As stated earlier, teacher research is not something done *to* us; it is something done *by* us (Woodcock, Lassonde, & Rutten, 2004). The goal of teacher research is to put best practices about teaching and learning into actual practice in your classroom. And the person who does that is you, the classroom teacher (Ritchie, 2000).

PROBLEM-SOLVING VIGNETTE FOR DISCUSSION

Mark, a 10th-grade English teacher, was frustrated with always rushing through curriculum because he felt he had to prepare the students for the end-of-year test. He felt he was always "covering" the material but never giving students a chance to absorb and apply it. In short, he was frustrated with being told what to teach, how to teach it, and even by what schedule to teach.

Mark started to read about teacher research and decided to use it as a tool to investigate students' learning in his classroom. He collected students' writing samples, talked with students about their feelings and attitudes about the class, and kept a teaching journal in which he wrote about his observations and reflections each day. At the end of the semester, he wrote up his results and brought them to his department chair and the administrators in his building.

When the administrators read the results and talked with Mark, they realized that action was needed in the department, and perhaps in the district, to find methods that would help students not only do well on assessments but authentically apply what they were learning to real-life situations. Mark's research had made a difference. The systematic and organized way he had collected and analyzed his data couldn't be disputed.

How else could Mark use the results of his research in a proactive way to improve instruction and learning?

TIPS FOR TEACHER RESEARCHERS

As you begin to learn about teacher research, know that the terminology can be confusing. It may be helpful to begin a teacher research journal right away to document and reflect on how your ideas about the process and the concepts develop over time. Reflective writing can help you clarify your thoughts as you piece together ideas and think about the connections you are making between what you are doing and what you are reading. In this journal you might also want to organize a section to note terms you see as your keys to understanding as well as a section on lingering questions that develop.

QUESTIONS FOR REFLECTION

■ In what small ways and big ways could you start to make teacher research your way of being? Why would you want to or not want to?

■ How do you see teacher research changing in the future to follow developing trends in education?

REFERENCES

Arhar, J.M., Holly, M.L., & Kasten, W.C. (2001). *Action research for teachers: Traveling the yellow brick road.* Upper Saddle River, NJ: Prentice Hall.

Atwell, N. (1987). *In the middle: Writing, reading, and learning with adolescents.* Upper Montclair, NJ: Boynton/Cook.

Atwell, N. (1998). *In the middle: New understandings about writing, reading, and learning* (2nd ed.). Portsmouth, NH: Heinemann.

Bissex, G. (1996). *Partial truths: A memoir and essays on reading, writing, and researching.* Portsmouth, NH: Heinemann.

Bissex, G., & Bullock, R.H. (Eds.). (1987). *Seeing for ourselves: Case-study research by teachers of writing.* Portsmouth, NH: Heinemann.

Brookfield, S. (1987). *Developing critical thinkers: Challenging adults to explore alternative ways of thinking and acting.* San Francisco: Jossey-Bass.

Brookfield, S. (1995). *Becoming a critically reflective teacher.* San Francisco: Jossey-Bass.

Bullock, R.H. (1987). A quiet revolution: The power of teacher research. In G.L. Bissex & R.H. Bullock (Eds.), *Seeing for ourselves: Case-study research by teachers of writing* (pp. 21–27). Portsmouth, NH: Heinemann.

Cochran-Smith, M., & Lytle, S. (1993). *Inside/outside: Teacher research and knowledge.* New York: Teachers College Press.

Dewey, J. (1933). *How we think: A restatement of the relation of reflective thinking to the educative process.* Boston: D.C. Heath.

Dewey, J. (1938). *Experience and education.* New York: Macmillan.

Goswami, D., & Stillman, P. (Eds.). (1987). *Reclaiming the classroom: Teacher research as an agency for change.* Upper Montclair, NJ: Boynton/Cook.

Hubbard, R.S., & Power, B.M. (1993). *The art of classroom inquiry: A handbook for teacher-researchers.* Portsmouth, NH: Heinemann.

Jacob, E., & Ruess. K. (2000). Integrating technology and pedagogy in a cultural foundations course. *Journal of Computing in Teacher Education, 16*(4), 12–17.

Lytle, S.L. (2000). Teacher research in the contact zone. In M.L. Kamil, P. Mosenthal, P.D. Pearson, & R. Barr (Eds.), *Handbook of reading research* (Vol. 3, pp. 691–718). Mahwah, NJ: Erlbaum.

MacLean, M.S., & Mohr, M.M. (1999). *Teacher-researchers at work.* Berkeley, CA: The National Writing Project.

Maykut, P., & Morehouse, R. (1994). *Beginning qualitative research: A philosophic and practical guide.* London: Falmer.

Mills, G.E. (2000). *Action research: A guide for the teacher researcher.* Upper Saddle River, NJ: Merrill.

Myers, M. (1987). Institutionalizing inquiry. *National Writing Project Quarterly, 9*(3), 1–4.

National Commission on Teaching and America's Future. (1996). *What matters most: Teaching for America's future.* New York: Author.

Noffke, S.E., & Stevenson, R.B. (Eds.). (1995). *Educational action research: Becoming practically critical.* New York: Teachers College Press.

Ritchie, G.V. (2000). *The importance of teacher research to the classroom teacher.* Retrieved August 20, 2007, from gse.gmu.edu/research/tr

Ritchie, G.V. (2006). *Teacher research as a habit of mind.* Unpublished doctoral dissertation, George Mason University, Fairfax, VA.

Rodgers, C. (2002). Defining reflection: Another look at John Dewey and reflective thinking. *Teachers College Record, 104,* 842–866.

Sagor, R. (2000). *Guiding school improvement with action research.* Arlington, VA: Association for Supervision and Curriculum Development.

Sagor, R. (2005). *The action research guidebook: A four-step process for educators and school teams.* Thousand Oaks, CA: Corwin Press.

Schön, D. (1983). *The reflective practitioner: How professionals think in action.* San Francisco: Jossey-Bass.

Wallace, J. (1997). A note from John Dewey on teacher research. *Teacher Research, 5*(1), 26–28.

Woodcock, C., Lassonde, C., & Rutten, I. (2004). How does collaborative reflection play a role in a teacher researcher's beliefs about herself and her teaching? Discovering the power of relationships. *Teaching and Learning: The Journal of Natural Inquiry and Reflective Practice, 18*(2), 55–73.

Yendol-Hoppey, D. (2006, Summer). Understanding the complexity of teacher learning. *Teaching and Teacher Education, Division K Newsletter.* American Educational Research Association, pp. 9–11.

CHAPTER 2

Getting the Big Picture: An Overview of the Teacher Research Process

Francine C. Falk-Ross, Peggy D. Cuevas

BEFORE-READING QUESTIONS

■ What are the elements of teacher research?

■ What are the methods and materials teachers need to initiate a research study in their classrooms?

■ How does the teacher researcher organize a study?

KEY TERMS

Citation

Data

Data analysis

Field notes

Implications

Needs assessment

Reflection

Reflective journals

Research plan

Research questions

Results

Theoretical framework

As Mrs. Henderson's third-grade class reads a portion of a trade book in its science block, most of the children appear to enjoy reading about dinosaurs. However, the results of a short, multiple-choice assessment, which Mrs. Henderson designs to measure students' comprehension of the passage, indicates that many students did not understand what the author was attempting to communicate.

After talking with colleagues and looking through several professional journals, Mrs. Henderson decides on a plan of action to incorporate a new approach to teaching and assessing reading comprehension in her classroom. To determine the effectiveness of the new approach, she wants to do a systematic study using teacher research methods, but she will need support as she proceeds with a research plan.

Mr. Wheeler, an experienced teacher researcher in the building, has offered to help Mrs. Henderson along the way. He even offers to come into her classroom to take field notes while Mrs. Henderson is teaching. He explains how these field notes will act as part of the qualitative data Mrs. Henderson will code and analyze as part of her study. They will help strengthen the study by overlapping and triangulating the sources of information.

Teachers Taking Action: A Comprehensive Guide to Teacher Research, edited by Cynthia A. Lassonde and Susan E. Israel.
© 2008 by the International Reading Association.

Introduction

Teachers are constantly considering their classroom practices as they work through the everyday learning of literacy and content knowledge. They notice general trends in classroom members' attention, individual needs of struggling students, the ease of use of specific materials, and the effectiveness of assessment tools. Just as Mrs. Henderson did in her assessment of reading comprehension in the opening vignette, teachers make decisions each day based on what they know of their students and what they consider important to share and facilitate through instruction. This process is the important way they "think on their feet" as they challenge and engage students in learning activities. Mrs. Henderson's formalization of her observations and actions through organized forms of inquiry and documentation, such as Mr. Wheeler's field notes, constitutes the elements of classroom-based research projects. As we learned in chapter 1, teacher research is the clear documentation of the cycle of inquiry and close study that teachers use to learn about the effects of changing or adding new approaches to teaching in their classrooms.

In this chapter, we will provide the "big picture" of the organization that happens when initiating and conducting teacher research. This chapter will help you put into perspective what teacher research entails. In turn, upcoming chapters provide more detail and in-depth procedural descriptions on each of the components introduced here.

Steps of a Teacher Research Project

In general, teacher research studies include a series of steps or phases that build into an organized investigation of change within the classroom. The following steps help direct teachers' attention to learning about students' needs, self-directed inquiry for professional development, creation of a solution, and assessment of change for further decision making. The steps we include are

1. Identify the inquiry

2. Develop purposes and potential research questions for the study

3. Research the topic for a theoretical framework

4. Design and organize a research plan

5. Collect, organize, and analyze data

6. Determine the results of the study

7. Share the conclusions and implications

The following sections describe these steps. Each section includes a cross reference to the chapter in this volume that discusses the steps further. Also, see Appendix B for the Teacher Research Organizing Worksheet, a reproducible that provides a visual representation to support or illustrate key concepts described in this chapter. You may use this worksheet as a planning sheet as you work through the steps.

Identify the Inquiry

There are several ways to identify what you want to study or inquire about through teacher research. One is to conduct a **needs assessment** of the class. That is, use informal or formal tests, examples of classroom work samples, checklists, or surveys to determine a specific target task (i.e., for literacy achievement) that requires your attention. Your challenge is to find the nature and extent of the need and to describe it clearly.

To identify the inquiry, begin a teaching journal and write in it regularly. Take time at the conclusion of your teaching day to write in your journal. Reflect on your practice by asking yourself the following questions: What were your objectives for the day? Were they achieved? What specific instructional practices or approaches produced the desired effect? Were there practices or approaches you believe could be modified to produce a better outcome? Why do you think the students responded as they did?

After a week or more of journaling, reflect on your writing. Do you see patterns or trends in your instruction that you would like to investigate? Ask a colleague to visit your classroom to observe you and your students in action. He or she can take general notes on what was observed. However, you may want the observer to pay particular attention to students' responses to a specific approach or strategy. A second analysis of your journal notes with new insight and a review of your colleague's observation notes will help you identify areas into which you would like to make a formal inquiry.

Develop an overview of the specific inquiry. Explain the context of the situation: the task, the methods used, the strategies used, the classroom environment, and so on. Your intention is to situate the inquiry within the program and the daily events and to stress its importance. (See chapter 3, this volume, for more information on this topic.)

Develop Purposes and Potential Research Questions for the Study

State your overall goals and specific instructional objectives for the study. Specify any change you intend to create using active verbs (e.g., increase, define) and the area you will target (e.g., vocabulary, reading comprehension). Describe the behaviors that you will require the students to use in a classroom activity (e.g., summarize the main idea). You need to use simple and direct language to maintain an objective stance.

Set your expectations for any change and student performance you would aim toward. Designate a target number or range that you estimate to be indicative of success (e.g., increase by 10 points or respond with at least 3 synonyms). These numbers or amounts will be used as criteria for decision making regarding pre- and postintervention.

Develop **research questions** to guide your study. Formulate at least two questions to set your focus for resolution. Ask your questions in ways that leave room for multiple findings (e.g., What effects will adding think-aloud strategy models have on reading comprehension in third graders?).

Identify the standards that align with your study. Include benchmarks from as many levels of governing bodies as appropriate for your purposes. Suggestions for standards include those set by national, state, school district, and professional levels. (See chapter 3 in this volume for more information on this topic.)

Research the Topic for a Theoretical Framework

A **theoretical framework** is a collection of concepts that guide your thinking. These fundamental beliefs about learning affect how you approach your project. Identify research studies that offer informative knowledge focused on your topic. Search for representative approaches to teaching in the area of your focus so you have a number of choices for choosing one fitted to your students' needs. Consider peripheral topics to balance your search (e.g., vocabulary can be developed through morphemic analysis and from comprehension strategies).

Consider input from more than one area of study or discipline to support your study. This might include new information from journals of literacy, general education, psychology, and content area instruction. Find connections to your research inquiry questions. Organize the information into themes that will align with your students' needs and focus.

Look in professional journals, research journals, textbooks, and on websites to find key ideas. Consider that researchers choose different formats and forums in which to present their project findings. The variety and overlap of information will be beneficial to you in gathering foundational knowledge.

Identify guiding areas of research investigation and precedents. These will inform your approach and use of materials for instruction and assessment of your intervention or change. Clearly reference the resources and researchers' work through which you located your information so you can acknowledge the precedents for instruction using a citation. A **citation** is the proper form of crediting original research that focuses on, or quotes, supportive and theoretical information upon which the study is based. (See chapters 5 and 6 in this volume for more information on this topic.)

Design and Organize a Research Plan

A **research plan** includes specification of where and when you will conduct your project, whom you will include in the study, and the steps you plan to take to move through the investigation. Your research plan will require careful thought because it will organize the scope and sequence of your activities, and it will guide you through each part of your research. Be sure to consider the positive aspects and challenges of each choice you make so that you can reduce the number of any unanticipated questions or consequences that might occur. Base your choices on your knowledge of teaching theory and your teaching experiences.

Identify the participants and comparison groups, if necessary, for your study. Choose whether you will work with the whole class or a small group to conduct your teacher research. If you choose to compare groups, you will need to find a second set of students who closely match those to whom you will be introducing the new approach. You may decide to match students by achievement levels, background knowledge, or other variables.

Obtain permission forms and release of information protocols if you plan to share the results with other teachers, school districts, or at inservice meetings and conferences. The use of videotape and audiotape are often covered in general permission forms that parents or guardians sign at the beginning of the school year for district use. However, the confidentiality of students' information is a serious issue that teachers and all members of school districts must contemplate for research agendas to move forward.

Specify the context and time restraints for your observations and data collection. Set realistic blocks of time to observe and gather artifacts, such as work samples or test results. You will need ample time to teach, model, guide, and evaluate application of students' new learning. However, extended time periods of research may draw out learning periods, decreasing the visibility of learning gains. You will need to find an appropriate time period for your study to obtain optimal results. (See chapters 4 and 5, this volume, for more information on this topic.)

Collect, Organize, and Analyze Data

Determine what **data** or information you will need to answer your research questions and how you will gather that information for your investigation. The data may be specified as assessment (i.e., the types of tests and rubrics for scoring you will use to evaluate students' work), artifacts (i.e., the examples of students' work and materials that will be collected as evidence), instructional directives (i.e., the language you will use to introduce activities and to guide completion of the work), and permission forms (i.e., a written description for the family and student that clearly explains the activities in the project and secures their signatures). Forms of data that are commonly used include some of the following:

- Pre- and posttesting
- Surveys
- Interviews
- Rating scales

- Written reflections

- Transcriptions of meetings, tests, portfolio artifacts, and so forth

Plan the study so as to provide adequate reliability—a measure of whether a study is replicable with similar results by a different researcher or for a second time—and validity—the measure of whether a study assesses the concept development that it proposes to study.

Determine forms of **data analysis**, or the ways in which you will compare the results of informal or formal evaluations that were administered before and after your project is completed. Data analysis may include quantitative or qualitative methods, including rubrics, reports of scores, and reflective comments from students or from your notes. The qualitative notes will require development and assignment of a coding strategy. The use of at least three different forms of data will demonstrate overlap, or triangulation, of the data. Triangulation indicates the strength of the study's findings by overlapping evidence from several sources (e.g., teacher interviews, student scores, classroom observations). (See chapters 5 and 6, this volume, for more information on this topic.)

Determine the Results of the Study

The **results** of your study are the findings or the changes that occurred during your project. List scores and comparisons of pretesting and posttesting. Provide explanations of observations and behaviors that are repeated. These recurring themes in qualitative data indicate trends in new learning and require in-depth descriptions and examples in your results section. Numerical information may be checked for statistical significance and percentage of change.

Organize charts to show data, trends, and statistical analyses. These charts make visible the formative, or ongoing, and summative, or final, scores and ratings from data collection. Information is easily stored, retrieved, and transferred or shared when presented in such a concise form. (See chapters 5 and 6 in this volume for more information on this topic.)

Share the Conclusions and Implications

Explain the **implications**, or educational importance, of results for students, families, district and community members, and professional audiences. Take the opportunity to suggest the uses of this new knowledge for other educators in their classrooms or educational forums. Compare your results with those of other educators working on similar projects to initiate other possible research projects.

Qualify the limits and challenges of the study, as necessary. Information gained from a teacher research study is meaningful for the specific students and the teacher in the study. The new learning is informative for making instructional decisions for this same group of students and possibly for students in classes that follow. It is important to note in your conclusions and discussion what small steps or considerations were not included that would have improved the clarity of the results or to mention obstacles that might be avoided in future studies.

Suggest the areas of further research needs. Usually by studying one aspect of literacy achievement, other tangential areas of need become obvious. Ideas for the next steps to be taken need to be articulated so as not to miss timely opportunities for change. (See chapters 9, 12, and 13 in this volume for more information on this topic.)

Methods and Materials to Initiate Research

As empowering as teacher research can be for all classroom members, there are physical and temporal preparations that should be a part of the planning. For example, when we are conducting a study, we are sure to set aside time specifically designated for **reflection**, or reconsideration of our approaches, assumptions, and activities. Typical reflections consist of comments about the effectiveness of the intervention, thoughts about how the activity might be rearranged, and associations with theory and prior experiences that might have been triggered by the lesson. At each step of the study, it is important to provide for careful, purposeful reflection that will not overwhelm the other everyday teaching activities. Setting aside time to informally reflect on developments will ensure that valuable insights on the progress of the study are not lost. Although interruptions to this scheduled reflection may occur, having clear goals in mind will help maintain the focus on the analysis of the experience. This time will be used to determine the next steps and to note students' progress or challenges in journal entries.

There are different forms of journal entries that may be used for your research documentation. **Reflective journals** generally consist of subjective, personal responses to different elements of the project, such as suggested revisions or interpretive comments. Another form of journal entries, often referred to as **field notes**, consist of objective descriptions of action in the classroom as teacher researchers document through written anecdotes the nature of classroom lessons, students' responses, and the development of learning. Both types of journals are appropriate to use. Many teachers use reflective entries and field notes together in a double-entry method, writing descriptions in the body of the notes and comments in the margins; other teachers write the comments in a different color of ink.

A method we find helpful when conducting research is to get some help gathering data. One form of help is to audiotape or videotape the activities in the classroom to catch the often-missed nuances of students' behaviors in the larger context of the classroom. Teachers can only be in one place in the room at a time, leaving some important comments, actions, or body language unobserved. Another form of help is to allow another adult in the classroom to document the students' work along with you or as you teach to double the amount of information you can collect and to add another's perspective.

In addition to these methods, we find it essential to gather and organize standard materials that will help with our research. Setting aside a physical space for collection of materials will allow for easier access and will separate the study data from the piles of work students and teachers generate as a part of everyday literacy lessons. A drawer in a file cabinet or desk or a shelf in a closet will suffice to formalize the project. You must then decide how to organize and store the data you collect in your research study. One way is to use Microsoft Excel files to enter information on your participants, their pre- and postassessment scores, and other information that can easily be transferred to a spreadsheet format. You can also transcribe all or parts of interviews and oral responses, so that you can scan the written forms for information later.

Make sure to make back-up copies of all of your information. You may choose to keep the data in hard copy files. You must decide whether to categorize information by participant or by type of data. For example, you might store all of the assessment and subjective information in a separate file folder labeled with the name of the participant. On the other hand, you might label your folders by type of information, such as demographic information, pre- and postassessment, interviews, surveys, field notes, and so forth. The choice of organization and method of storage is an individual one and should be based on personal preference.

Some suggestions for organization, taken from our experiences, are to use color-coded folders to separate the different forms of data that we collect and to use tabs to separate information within a large binder. To keep track of the various tests and materials, a data checklist is almost essential. A list of the materials organized in the order you will collect them may be listed in rows, and then the entry and completion dates may be entered in columns so that you have a clear record of your collected information. Often more than one checklist can be used. A list of entries for each set of materials may be attached inside the binder or folder to clarify its contents, and another list of all the materials being used may be kept as an overview. The information in the smaller list(s) may be transferred to the larger list periodically as an update.

Of utmost importance is remembering that whether you store your data electronically or in hard copy, make sure to safeguard the confidentiality of information that could be used to identify students (possibly causing unintended repercussions) by assigning pseudonyms or numbers or letters to identify each participant. Keep the information safe and secure within a file cabinet or desk drawer that can be locked for privacy. Limit the number of people who may have access to the assigned drawer to limit the accidental observation of data by students or school personnel. Place data samples in the assigned files as soon as possible rather than leaving them on your desk or an open shelf, and view them for analysis when students and observers are not present in your classroom or office. As for electronic documents, you might even send them via e-mail to a colleague so they are stored on another computer. That way, a lost flash or disk won't end your research project prematurely.

Issues dealing with arrangements for supportive environments, such as an assistant for management of data or financial support for purchase of professional texts from administrators, are necessary considerations. For example, in the past we have written small grant proposals (see chapter 10, this volume, for more information on this topic) listing the reasons for and the nature of our research to obtain support from local service organizations. We have also made sure that any assistants we recruit are trustworthy and understand the need for confidentiality.

It is difficult to conduct teacher research without the full cooperation of administrators and colleagues. For example, one of our students initiated a well-designed research plan focused on the effectiveness of an instructional protocol with struggling readers. She obtained all of the necessary permissions from parents and verbal assent to the research plan from her school administration. She overlooked checking with supervisors and administrators in securing the necessary extra materials (i.e., tables, books, tape recorders, shelves, and other items) that were readily available but being used in other areas of the school. She was able to secure help from other teachers who helped her rearrange schedules and cart the materials to her classroom; however, it would have been much easier if she had considered this prior to implementing the activities.

Organizing a Study

Organizing a research study in literacy education, for example, assumes a purposeful and thoughtful approach to capturing an element of instruction for a careful, close look at its effectiveness in a program. Each step in the process of a research study is intertwined with those that follow, building to a final clear and defendable statement for using a teaching or learning strategy, method, material, or tool. Selecting the questions that will guide the research determines the methodology for study. Choosing the forms of data collection and analysis that will drive the investigation determines the strength of the results and teaching implications. Therefore, engaging in teacher research requires careful planning of research design and systematic implementation of data collection.

The development of research design and the particulars of methodically implementing changes in classroom practice require a series of transitions for most teachers as they focus on elements of their teaching. In many ways, there is an evolution of understanding that occurs. The process of creating views and studies for classroom research follows the systematic focus on declarative, procedural, and conditional knowledge proposed by Paris, Lipson, and Wixson (1983). Specifically, this approach would involve teachers deciding on an appropriate strategy or instructional approach (declarative knowledge) and determining the manner in which the strategy or approach could be implemented to address the needs of their students (procedural knowledge). The conclusion section of the teacher research report would provide evidence for when, where, with whom, and under what circumstances this strategy or approach is best applied for maximum positive change in the classroom (conditional knowledge).

Synthesis and Concluding Thoughts

There are many ways teachers can begin to look more carefully and formally at the important work they do in classrooms to teach students new approaches to developing literacy knowledge and applications. Whether looking at test scores for progress or written samples for reflection and connections, teacher research has a place in school classrooms (International Reading Association [IRA], 2000).

Mandates for using research-based instructional strategies for literacy education have been set by states, professional organizations (e.g., IRA, 2004; IRA & National Council of Teachers of English, 1996), and the U.S. government (e.g., the No Child Left Behind initiatives). Teachers can become comfortable with engaging in research projects in their classrooms. Focusing on the way in which their classroom practice can benefit others empowers teachers to view themselves as agents of change when they have substantive, firsthand evidence of the effectiveness of a particular instructional intervention. Although posing and answering a well-formulated question is important, acting on the knowledge gained from the answer is equally important. Because teacher research is usually the response to a particular problem context, students in the classroom, as well as the teacher, can benefit from the knowledge gained through such studies.

Teacher educators can explicitly present models of teacher research in teacher-preparation programs. Neubert (1989) asserts that knowledge of the various stages of systematic inquiry, an understanding of how to access current research, and professional support are all needed to sustain research activity among classroom teachers. Systematic inquiry includes gathering and reviewing information on the question to be investigated. In the course of a busy day teachers have little time to study the relationships between learners, the topic under study, and the way in which teachers can present and students can comprehend this information. Teacher research, guided by a seasoned researcher, allows the teacher to embark on a systematic review of those relationships. Administrators, families, and community members can help support teachers' efforts.

A last concern is how the role of researcher changes teachers' perspectives in the classroom and initiates an evolution in thought about literacy education.

After participating in their teacher research projects, teachers have a different view of the importance of reading and responding to current research. Instructional change and teacher renewal come from internal sources, such as wide reading of research and the teacher-initiated research that reading promotes. Classroom research facilitates the change and renewal by providing teachers with the tools and knowledge to enhance instruction.

PROBLEM-SOLVING VIGNETTE FOR DISCUSSION

There are six students in your third-grade classroom who are second-language learners. Their language participation in classroom discourse is lower than average in amount. You anticipate this is partly because they do not follow the quick pace of the question–answer interaction and partly because they are self-conscious about being misunderstood. These students' reading comprehension is affected by this situation. Their vocabulary knowledge is generally weak, and words with multiple meanings (e.g., *change*, *fly*, *point*) or multiple pronunciations (e.g., *read*, *close*) are misunderstood. More and more frequently, they show signs of frustration in the classroom.

How would you engage in a teacher research project to determine how to modify instruction to address these concerns?

TIPS FOR TEACHER RESEARCHERS

Based on our experiences as teacher researchers, we believe effective principles of time management include the following:

■ Understand what you can realistically achieve with your time.

■ Plan to make the best use of the time available.

■ Leave enough time for things you absolutely must do.

■ Preserve contingency time to handle the unexpected.

■ Minimize stress by avoiding overcommitment to yourself and others.

And effective principles of data collection include the following:

■ Keep field notes faithfully.

■ Look for incidents worthy of discussion each and every day.

■ Look for alternative explanations for observed classroom events.

■ Organize and store data for safekeeping.

■ Write down everything you observe.

■ Keep multiple copies of all assessments and notes.

QUESTIONS FOR REFLECTION

■ What are some preparations within your educational setting that would need to be in place before you embark on a teacher research project?

■ How will you explain the purpose and importance of teacher research to your colleagues, administrators, and students' families?

■ How will you go about conducting your research on the topic? To whom could you turn for help in this area?

■ Once you have completed your teacher research project, how will you inform colleagues of your findings?

Acknowledgments

We would like to thank the preservice and practicing teachers in our university classes and partnership activities whose work has helped us focus and refine the ideas presented in our chapter.

REFERENCES

International Reading Association. (2000). *Teaching all children to read: The roles of the reading specialist* (Position statement). Newark, DE: Author.

International Reading Association & National Council of Teachers of English. (1996). *Standards for the English language arts.* Newark, DE; Urbana, IL: Authors.

Neubert, G.A. (1989). Supporting teacher research. *The Teacher Educator, 25*(1), 2–9.

Paris, S.G., Lipson, M.Y., & Wixson, K.K. (1983). Becoming a strategic reader. *Contemporary Educational Psychology, 8,* 293–316.

Professional Standards and Ethics Committee, International Reading Association. (2004). *Standards for reading professionals—Revised 2003.* Newark, DE: International Reading Association.

PART II

Developing a Research Project

Part Opener: Moving From Reflective Practitioner to Teacher Researcher
Nancy L. Michelson, Starlin D. Weaver

Even though Alexis had approached her first day as an English language arts teacher with excitement, by the end of the first semester Alexis feels exhausted and overwhelmed. She vents to Belinda, her mentor, about her students' negative attitudes about literature and reading.

Belinda sets about helping her find a solution to her frustration. But when Belinda uses the term *teacher research*, Alexis balks. "I'm a language arts teacher. I can't do research!" Belinda persists, leading Alexis to an understanding of teacher research as a systematic form of reflection, which Alexis values.

Alexis hesitantly begins to develop a research question. With Belinda's guidance, she begins to refine her question, making it researchable, and she considers how it could lead to an appropriate instructional action. Belinda gathers books and journals relevant to Alexis's concern. Alexis is thankful, thinking that Belinda is providing specific techniques to help her students better appreciate literature! However, Belinda explains that the materials only provide background and that an essential reason to conduct teacher research is the unique and contextualized complexity of individual classrooms and teachers. "If one person could develop a recipe for all other teachers to follow and get the same results, teaching would be easy!"

Thus, Alexis follows Belinda's instructions to use the materials as a source for ideas for her research. She has taken a step toward a critical goal of teacher research—empowerment—as she takes charge of her professional knowledge. Belinda also outlines next steps for Alexis: deciding what data will give Alexis the information she needs about each of her students, analyzing the data, and reflecting on what it tells her about the effectiveness of her intervention. Alexis finds that she may have to modify the intervention, collect additional data, and maybe even reframe her question. (To read the complete case study, go to this book's link on the IRA website at www.reading.org and click on Case Study #2: Moving From Reflective Practitioner to Teacher Researcher.)

As you read on in part II, you, like Alexis, will learn how to develop a research project from framing a substantive and researchable question in chapter 3 and learning about research designs in chapter 4, to the process of designing an effective plan in chapter 5.

CHAPTER 3

Focusing the Study: Framing a Researchable Question

Neal Shambaugh, Jaci Webb-Dempsey

KEY TERMS

Data sources
Framing the study
Learning outcomes
Researchability
Research focus
Teacher knowledge
Teaching strategies

BEFORE-READING QUESTIONS

- What is researchable and what is not researchable?
- How do you frame a research study?
- How do you identify research questions from a research focus?

Jackie, a preservice teacher, is meeting with her university liaison about her teacher research project. Jackie explains to her professor that she is uncertain about her choice for the topic of her project but she thinks she might want to do something with visual organizers. Her professor prompts her to think about a pressing learning issue in her classroom and then about how visual organizers might be one of several teaching strategies used to address this learning issue. Jackie talks about how the first 90 minutes of the school day are spent on reading, and that her host teacher says that the students can't remember the story. Jackie's professor suggests that some of that reading time could be spent having students make personal connections with the story through talking about it or creating pictures. The professor urges Jackie to read about what influences reading comprehension and to talk with her teacher about this idea. Jackie seems interested and encouraged by this topic and says that her teacher has told her that she's interested to see what she comes up with. The professor suggests that Jackie discuss with her teacher the possibility of conducting the research together.

Teachers Taking Action: A Comprehensive Guide to Teacher Research, edited by Cynthia A. Lassonde and Susan E. Israel.
© 2008 by the International Reading Association.

Introduction

Many teacher education students are at a loss as to how to identify a focus for a teacher research study. Despite many hours of observation or teaching, they are unsure of an appropriate topic for teacher research. Research is increasingly becoming a part of the school-day conversation. Teacher research is viewed by some schools and states as a means to help teachers document and reflect on student learning. However, no agreement exists on what **teacher knowledge** is and how it develops. Researchers have characterized teacher knowledge and provided organizing frameworks in a number of ways (for a review see Cochran-Smith & Lytle, 1999; Munby, Russell, & Martin, 2001). These perspectives frequently differ based on the role of researchers and teachers in "who is asking?" and "who is being asked?" (Magliaro & Shambaugh, 2005).

This chapter addresses the challenging stage of developing one or more research questions to guide teacher research. Many educators experience a challenge at this stage if they have not had practice writing research questions. To begin, it helps to be clear as to what teacher research is about. Although teacher research can embrace many aspects of schools, we perceive teacher research as inquiry into the practical problems that teachers face in their practice. We address the different concerns preservice and experienced teachers face. Next, we address the theoretical and practical issues of framing a study by asking three questions: What is researchable? How does one frame a study? How does one identify research questions? The chapter-opening vignette illuminates some of the theoretical issues facing the teacher researcher: What counts as research and what methodologies are appropriate? Who should be studied? What is doable?

What Counts as Teacher Research?

Teacher research constitutes focused inquiry by teachers with the overall intent being to improve their teaching in schools (McCutcheon & Jung, 1990). Teacher education programs incorporate research to develop new teachers' reflective habits (Clark & Peterson, 1986) and the disposition to improve one's teaching through systematic inquiry (Shulman, 1988). As higher education and public schools operate in what are different professional worlds, what "counts as research" varies in each (Paul & Marfo, 2001). Many teachers, administrators, families, and even students, view research as an activity outside of teaching rather than as something teachers do. With this in mind, then, we ask what criteria are involved in forming a teacher research topic?

Through our experience working with teacher researchers, we have learned that selecting a teacher research topic involves four criteria (Shambaugh & Webb-Dempsey, 2003). First, teacher research is about personal, professional practice and should, therefore, help to develop a teacher's professional and reflective habits. We have conducted teacher research for more than five years. While working together to prepare preservice teachers to conduct their action research projects, we have conducted research on our own teaching. We have found the benefits of systematic reflection are evident when we see our students achieving learning outcomes with fewer struggles. Sometimes it is a small improvement in an assignment or the way we organize students to engage in an activity that has made the difference, while at other times it has led to major changes in the way we deliver instruction. Seeing our students reap these benefits makes the effort and energy we devote to this form of research worthwhile. However, it may well be the modeling aspect of our inquiry that is the most powerful outcome. In our experience, it is not uncommon for preservice teachers to be resistant and experienced teachers to be hesitant. This form of research is new and different from what they have been told is research. It seems unnecessary to their immediate concerns of learning to become a teacher or meeting the demands of their classrooms. If supervising teachers aren't doing research, how can the requirement be relevant for preservice teachers? And further, if as teacher educators we aren't doing teacher research, how legitimate are we as advocates? This has led us to conduct research on our teaching in teacher research classes and professional development initiatives and to make that process transparent to students and colleagues. We have spent a considerable amount of time working to make the relationship between teacher research and teaching explicit. We explain that while this reflective process requires some additional habits, more so it demands an open mind to the possibilities of how research informs their teaching.

The second criterion is that teacher research should focus on improving teaching practice at the classroom level and taking action to make improvements. Teacher research for new teachers, then, is not about testing theory, improving the work environment of teachers, developing school policy, or revising a school curriculum. Rather, teacher research is focused on teaching practice at the classroom level for the primary purpose of improving student learning. In our experience, teacher research—with its focus on all students—is not about experimental treatments in which one group of students receives an innovation while another group does not. Thus, teacher research appears to be in direct opposition to what is viewed as accepted social science research. However, teacher research can and should be conducted systematically and with integrity.

Third, teacher research provides an ongoing process of problem identification, systematic data collection, reflection, analysis, data-driven action, and problem redefinition. The essential features of this cyclical process are the trying out of ideas in practice as a means of increasing knowledge about or improvement of curriculum, teaching, and learning (Kemmis & McTaggert, 1988). The process differs in terms of the different variations of teacher research, action research, or teacher inquiry. For instance, as described in chapter 1, the one feature that distinguishes action research, at least in terms of a process, is the explicit action taken by the teacher based on the study conducted, action that is implemented in future teaching (Mills, 2007).

Finally, we have observed that teacher research frequently is derived collaboratively, involving preservice teachers, supervising teachers, university liaisons, and teacher peers in identifying an area of inquiry and the design of an investigation. Although it is often assumed that teacher research is "collaborative, supportive, democratic, and critical" (Hitchcock & Hughes, 1989, p. 29), in reality, such outcomes between teacher education faculty and university faculty may be problematic. (See chapter 7 for more on collaboration.)

What Is Researchable and What Is Not Researchable?

Based on the criteria for selecting a teacher research project described in the previous section, several contextual issues determine whether what the teacher is interested in investigating is researchable. **Researchability** is the potential for a topic to be studied and for conclusions to be drawn from inquiry.

One issue related to researchability is the level of complexity, ranging from too broad (e.g., What is the best method for teaching math?) or too narrow (e.g., Why won't the boys in the back of the room pay attention to me?). In our experience, new teachers tend to identify a broad question. This provides a starting point but requires some focus in terms of research questions for new teachers to actually collect data to answer the questions. Sometimes, a topic for teacher research begins with discussions on what happened in the classroom that day. Student challenges with content and behavior then provide the context for a research focus.

Another issue of researchability is the nature of the phenomenon to be studied; in most cases, the phenomenon is the classroom. Classroom research requires the use of "why" and "how" questions. These are more difficult to answer than "what" questions, which can be answered using empirical data. This issue provides the source for additional tension in new teachers because they want to frame a study that addresses "what" questions. The notion of "what works and what doesn't" is very pervasive in teachers, and particularly with new teachers. Teacher research helps new teachers experience the reality that not just one strategy produces results.

One contextual issue is the pressure that teachers are facing in terms of accountability from family expectations and from high-stakes testing requirements in schools. Embedded in this accountability issue is the tension between content-based standards—what others think students should know—and the education of the whole child—what practicing teachers have always viewed as important for children. What counts as teacher research may be dictated by "what counts" as content to be learned in that school. For example, when Jaci provided professional development for new principals who were required to lead and support an action-research project in their schools as part of their orientation, it was apparent that they and their teachers were initially solely concerned with standardized test results as they considered possibilities. It required substantial discussion with experienced teacher researchers and higher education faculty supporting these school-based teams and among new principals and teachers to negotiate the tensions around "what counts."

These perceptions become obvious to new teachers who have to negotiate a topic choice. In his mentoring of teacher research by new teachers, Neal has had to mediate between what supervising teachers see as research and the strategies preservice teachers want to try out. The new teacher hears one suggestion from a supervising teacher and quite a different suggestion from teacher education professors. In our experience in coordinating teacher research, we have to spend considerable time and energy on educating new teachers, experienced teachers, and teaching educators on the nature of teacher research.

A second contextual issue is internal to the school and classroom and involves what is in the teacher's control. Issues of schoolwide behavior, family involvement, and curricular change may be outside the control of the new teacher. These broad topics of concern are frequently studied by groups of experienced teachers who are motivated by social justice, diversity, and teacher voice. New teachers have limited experience in making accurate judgments on how teacher research components, such as data collection, can be accomplished during the school day. Mentoring from other teachers and university faculty is usually needed to assist the new teacher in setting adequate boundaries on what can be studied and what is reasonable given the teacher's experience and scope of work.

A third contextual issue to consider is deciding whether to conduct teacher research solo or collaborate with peers in one's school or across schools. For experienced teachers, peer collaboration usually triggers such studies. We have found that negotiating a topic across different schools can be problematic from the viewpoint of supervising teachers. Any comparisons across schools should be done carefully, and the contexts and realities of different schools must be described in the methodology and be addressed in the results. The predominant concern of new teachers is working with people they trust in terms of sharing the work and the logistics of working across different schedules and physical locations. Another reality is that the context for one collaborator may change in ways different from the other collaborators, and the whole focus of the research may need to be revised. The concern of experienced teachers is often political. Comparisons should focus on relevant characteristics of students and learning needs.

Given these contextual issues, how does one choose a teacher research topic? The next step is to identify a direction for teacher research, a direction we label as a research focus.

Identifying a Research Focus

We define a **research focus** as a statement that identifies a specific direction to an initial topic idea. A research focus refines the view of the topic so issues of students, teaching and assessment, and context can be discussed in a substantive manner. A research focus should be based on two factors: (1) student learning needs and (2) teacher interests. New teachers frequently pick research topics that involve creative activities or innovative teaching techniques. However, new teachers should be observing students as well as talking with their coordinating teachers on student behavior and performance.

When we talk with new teachers, we discuss what learning challenges their students face. We talk about why these challenges should be considered as the focus for teacher research. Learning challenges can be related to behavior, content knowledge, understanding, skills development, as well as the development of affective improvements in motivating, valuing, and internalizing change. Out of this discussion can emerge a focus for teacher research. Commonly, these discussions involve a back-and-forth consideration of student learning outcomes and teaching strategies as displayed in the chapter-opening vignette. Here, we refer to **learning outcomes** as an overarching term that may include broad learning goals or specific objectives. Meanwhile, **teaching strategies** refer to those instructional decisions that teachers make on how to assist students in their learning. Teaching strategies can include research-based teaching models (e.g., cooperative learning, direct instruction) to content-specific strategies (e.g., Readers Theatre, word walls), and general strategies (e.g., review, learning stations).To identify priorities for teacher research, we

1. List several high-priority student-learning challenges

2. Organize by type (i.e., content area, themes, topics)

3. Prioritize the top three student-learning challenges.

Once three options have been identified for teacher research, we think through the following three questions that constitute a research focus:

1. Who are the students to benefit from the study?

2. What are the learning outcomes?

3. What are the teaching strategies to achieve these learning outcomes?

These components can be visualized as interconnected decisions (Figure 3.1). We use these decisions to develop a research focus statement. Typically, the initial statement is too broad, but it serves as a pointer to developing specific research questions from which **data sources** can be identified, sources that serve to answer each research question.

FIGURE 3.1
Research Focus Organizer

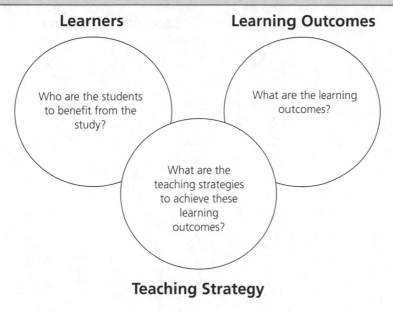

As an example, consider the dreaded word problems that students face in mathematics. A broad research question could be formulated that asks the following: How might a problem-oriented learning approach help sixth graders in X-school learn to solve word problems? An initial choice for the teaching might have been more practice or contextually related practice. A discussion with other teachers and reading of the mathematics literature might prompt consideration of problem-oriented learning (Bransford, Franks, Vye, & Sherwood, 1989). Students tend to rely on facts, formulae, clues, or words that reveal which operation to use. Rather than providing a traditional word problem in which these clues are embedded, Bransford and colleagues recommend providing students with a problem-solving context for students to negotiate. Over time, students become involved in real situations of increasing complexity and authenticity. This problem-oriented context provides an anchor for future learning (anchored instruction). A revised definition of the problem might record the decisions as seen in Figure 3.2.

The general form of a teacher research focus question that centers on student learning typically has the following structure: How does X-strategy help Y-students learn Z-content? Some examples include the following:

- How does a blend of <u>direct instruction and cooperative work groups</u> (strategy) help <u>fifth-grade students</u> (students) learn <u>algebra concepts</u> (content)?

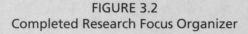

FIGURE 3.2
Completed Research Focus Organizer

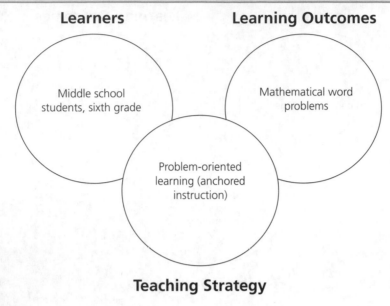

Learners

Middle school students, sixth grade

Learning Outcomes

Mathematical word problems

Problem-oriented learning (anchored instruction)

Teaching Strategy

- In what ways do graphic organizers (strategy) help 10th-grade students (students) represent their understanding of ecological principles (content)?

Teacher research can take a broad inquiry into teaching. The learners can involve both students and the teacher. For example, consider the following research focus questions:

- How will my experiences in a special-education internship influence my identity as a teacher?

- How do the different teacher strategies used in the county's middle schools help eighth graders understand the uses of mathematics in job settings?

The challenge of identifying a research focus requires that one first know the challenges students are facing in their courses and then identify a teaching strategy. The choice of this research focus should be something that is in the teacher's scope of influence and control.

New teachers may find it difficult to self-assess problems of practice and barriers to student learning because of their inexperience. For experienced teachers, the improvement may be broader than specific learning outcomes. For example, experienced teachers may be looking at a curriculum change, external mandate, peer collaboration, or professional development.

How Do You Frame a Research Study?

Framing the study is the process by which a teacher researcher identifies students' learning challenges and potential teaching options. Several issues should be considered to help frame or bound the study. One framing issue is that the choice of a focus for teacher research should be based on what students need, usually identified and prioritized from experiences with teaching content area topics, concepts, and skills. The inquiry should not be driven by a choice of an innovative teaching strategy that appears interesting. This is a solution looking for a problem. Frequently, the choice of a new approach is based on an understanding of student needs, but a discussion of student challenges is not clearly articulated. The choice of a teaching strategy should not be the focus here, although experienced teachers frequently begin a study selection process by saying they want to learn more about X-strategy. The discussion should return to student learning and how this teaching strategy assists learners.

A second framing issue is thinking that the inquiry is about proving the new strategy better than the old, or setting one strategy against another. One could attribute student performance to that strategy; however, such a claim is difficult given the complexity of learning settings, student characteristics, and limited teaching time. Teacher research may identify approaches that help particular learners while another strategy assists others. New teachers are often motivated by new innovations that supplant traditional strategies. However, be wary of setting up an adversarial study in which the teaching of one teacher is set up against a new strategy. With a vested interest by both teachers, negotiation may yield to trying out the new strategy or possibly blending one or more strategies, as daily teaching always taps multiple strategies. The research focus may be worded to reflect this, such as this example: How does a mix of role play and direct instruction help eighth-grade social studies students appreciate and understand how a state government works?

How Do You Identify Research Questions?

A research focus question that considers students, learning outcomes, and a teaching strategy provides a direction to identifying one or more research questions. A research question identifies a specific aspect of the research focus to be studied. An adequately worded research question, as suggested earlier, specifies students, learning outcomes, and teaching strategy. Initial questions may be adequately worded to point to data sources, which are used to answer the questions. Sometimes it helps to determine one or more specific subquestions. These questions may be broken down by skill or concepts or different teaching strategies. For example, consider the following research focus: How does a blend of Direct Instruction (DI) and Cooperative Work Groups (CWG) help fifth-grade students learn algebra skills? Specific questions that look at two algebra skills might include the following:

- How does DI and CWG help fifth-grade students solve linear equations?
- How does DI and CWG help fifth-grade students graph data?

Given that cooperative work groups are part of the teaching strategy, a second set of research questions could be considered that address higher levels of learning, such as problem solving and working together.

- How do CWG help fifth-grade students solve problems in teams?
- How do CWG develop team-building skills in fifth-grade students?

Such questions prompt the teacher to develop activities that help students achieve these outcomes. Studying outside sources can also expand the choice of teaching strategy beyond your immediate experience.

Part of whether a question is researchable involves being able to collect information that will answer the question. Once the study is framed, we can identify the specific data sources. New teachers frequently attempt to identify data sources before they have framed their study. Experienced teachers, meanwhile, are more flexible and less uneasy about modifying their studies as the realities of practice unfold. The research focus question frequently points a teacher researcher to identify specific research questions, which, in turn, suggest possible data sources (see, for example, Figure 3.3). The data sources are selected based on their potential to answer each of the research questions. In many cases, data sources, such as a reflective journal, may contain notes that answer one or more questions.

The Visualizing Key Decisions in Framing Your Study Chart in Figure 3.3 summarizes the flow of thinking that leads a teacher researcher from a research focus to specific research questions. (A reproducible version of this chart appears in Appendix B.) Specific data sources can be identified that enable the teacher researcher to answer each question. These data sources are likely existing activities already used by the teacher to assess student learning. However, at this stage the teacher researcher may realize that existing data provide insufficient evidence to answer one or more questions. Student work may need to be collected or a summary of students' needs assessments may need to be recorded. These additional research procedures actually provide you with information about where students are in their learning and where you need to be as a teacher.

Synthesis and Concluding Thoughts

Teacher research is a fascinating process to observe in others as well as for those who take the risks of experiencing becoming a teacher researcher. This chapter

FIGURE 3.3
Sample Visualizing Key Decisions in Framing Your Study Chart

Research Focus

In what ways do graphic organizers and concept maps help 10th-grade students represent their understanding of ecological principles?

Research Question(s)	Data Sources
Q1-How do students represent ecological principles?	Lesson plans, reflective journal, student journals
Q2-What conceptual challenges do students have?	Reflective journal, student journals
Q3-How do students transfer their understanding of ecological principles to solve ecological problems?	Ecological project

Description of Data Sources

Lesson plans: record teaching
Reflective journal: records implementation and reflection or revision, action steps
Student journals: record students' visual organizers and concept maps
Ecological project: records student performance

presents some interesting dilemmas that reinforce this notion of teacher research as fascinating and rewarding.

The first dilemma is that we recommend a prescriptive approach to generating a research focus, to provide direction—one that is focused on student learning—then to formulate a set of research questions that provide further direction for the study. In particular, identifying students, learning outcomes, and teaching strategies provide a means to "unpacking" an initial idea. The actual implementation of the research necessitates that a new set of research procedures (e.g., ongoing data collection, analysis, action steps) be incorporated into teaching procedures. Research activity thus becomes embedded into teaching activity. The implementation details of teacher research will vary to adjust for changing classroom conditions. The research questions themselves may change as a result. Some questions may be deleted while others are broken out into their own research questions. Although we suggest a prescriptive approach to frame the study, we do so to keep student learning in the forefront and to help the teacher researcher understand the purposes of the research and provide direction for the study. An emergent frame of mind, however, is necessary to account for the realities of the classroom and subsequent adjustments in the research.

A second dilemma revisits our discussion about "what counts" as teacher research (Paul & Marfo, 2001). The wording, "what counts," acts as a metaphor for this dilemma. "What counts" is frequently thought of in terms of numbers. The numbers cannot fully characterize or explain what occurs in the classroom. All results from teacher research, no matter how they are expressed as words or categories, must be qualified by the context of the school setting. As teacher research is not conducted in a laboratory but in a classroom, the principles governing laboratory research do not apply fully to the wonderfully rich settings of schools and classrooms, and students and educators.

A third dilemma addresses how teacher research can be added to the knowledge base of the individual teacher and the collective wisdom of the school. Although "best practices" is the term used to denote this knowledge, how best practices are actually used in the context of specific classrooms still remains in the teacher's head. Specific results of teacher research cannot be "counted" upon to transfer to other settings, as the conditions of one third-grade classroom differ substantially from other third-grade classrooms. What does transfer is the benefit of educators in examining issues of student learning and systematically discovering what works, what doesn't, and why. Teacher research helps to illuminate the complexities of teaching that go beyond what works. Much of teacher knowledge is archived in the heads of individual teachers; as such, unique experiences have eluded efforts to record this knowledge so that others might benefit from it. However, localized forms of knowledge, such as those that can be found in individual schools, can become shared and distributed among educators (Salomon, 1993), in the school and with educators in other schools. Teachers, principals, and state officials who manage to find a way to coordinate their mutual priorities serve the needs of students in the long run. Chapters 12 and 13 provide information that encourages you to share your teacher research findings with others through publication and presentation.

PROBLEM-SOLVING VIGNETTE FOR DISCUSSION

Following is a discussion that took place among a team of fourth-grade teachers. How would you use the process described in this chapter to determine what questions the teachers should consider to frame their research?

Sarah: You know, I think having our students use all the technology skills we've worked on so far to put together multimedia presentations in all of our classes is a great way for them to demonstrate those skills. We know the students love using technology, but are we sure it is worth the investment of time and energy?

Amy: I agree. I still believe that technology is just a set of tools—beyond teaching students to use particular pieces of hardware or software, what's the meaningful learning? Maybe we should think about how using the technology and tapping into students' engagement with it can create other learning opportunities.

Rob: You know, we've been focusing on integrating reading comprehension and process writing because those are still areas of weakness for a large number of our students, and we know students have to use those literacy skills to create their presentations. I'm wondering if we should look beyond just checking off the technology skills and start to assess the impact of creating the presentations on their use of reading and process writing.

Sarah: That's a great idea! If we can make sure the assignment requires them to use those literacy skills and we can figure out a way to assess how the students use them and what effect that has, it would help us think about how to strengthen all our technology assignments.

Amy: Yes, then we can really focus on how using technology can be an opportunity for improving the reading and writing skills of our fourth graders!

TIPS FOR TEACHER RESEARCHERS

The following guidelines and caveats are provided for each of the three questions that organize this chapter.

Question 1: What is researchable and what is not researchable?

Determine the following:

▪ What student or teacher learning is to be studied?

▪ What inquiry is in the teacher's control?

▪ Does the teacher work alone or with others?

Question 2: How do you frame a research study?

Consider the following:

▪ Student need takes priority over teaching strategy.

▪ Avoid trying to prove that one strategy is better than another. Instead, consider how a blend of teaching strategies produces performance improvements.

Question 3: How do you identify research questions from a research focus?

■ Research questions may differ by skill, concepts, or teaching strategies.

■ Research questions may be developed that look at incidental learning, such as social learning, and which may not have originally been an explicit learning outcome.

■ Teaching choices can be informed by personal experience and what research or practice has been conducted using this strategy.

■ Specific research questions usually point to data sources.

QUESTIONS FOR REFLECTION

■ What are some of the teacher research topics that will help your students?

■ What are some of the ethical issues that might arise as you frame your research question?

■ What are some of your concerns in actually implementing your study?

■ How can you make this research useful to educators outside of your classroom?

Acknowledgments

We would like to acknowledge the many experienced teachers who have mentored the teacher research projects conducted in our professional development schools by students in the Benedum Collaborative Five-Year Teacher Education Program at West Virginia University. We would also like to thank these new teachers who completed the research requirement and have gone on to become exemplary teachers.

REFERENCES

Bransford, J.D., Franks, J.J., Vye, N.J., & Sherwood, R.D. (1989). New approaches to instruction: Because wisdom can't be told. In S. Vosniadou & A. Ortony (Eds.), *Similarity and analogical reasoning* (pp. 470–497). New York: Cambridge University Press.

Clark, C., & Peterson, P. (1986). Teachers' thought processes. In M.C. Wittrock (Ed.), *Handbook of research on teaching* (pp. 255–296). New York: Macmillan.

Cochran-Smith, M., & Lytle, S. (1999). Relationships of knowledge and practice: Teacher learning in communities. In A. Iran-Nejad & P.D. Pearson (Eds.), *Review of research in education* (Vol. 24, pp. 249–305). Washington, DC: American Educational Research Association.

Hitchcock, G., & Hughes, D. (1989). *Research and the teacher: A qualitative introduction to school-based research.* New York: Routledge.

Kemmis, S., & McTaggert, R. (1988). *The teacher research planner* (3rd ed.). Geelong, VIC, Australia: Deakin University Press.

Magliaro, S., & Shambaugh, N. (2005). Teachers' personal models of instructional design. In J. Brophy & S. Pinnegar (Eds.), *Learning from research on teaching: Perspective, methodology, and representation: Advances in research on teaching series* (Vol. 11, pp. 101–134). New York: Elsevier.

McCutcheon, G., & Jung, B. (1990). Alternative perspectives on action research. *Theory Into Practice, 29*(3), 144–151.

Mills, G.E. (2007). *Action research: A guide for the teacher researcher* (3rd ed.). Upper Saddle River, NJ: Prentice Hall.

Munby, H., Russell, T., & Martin, A.K. (2001). Teachers' knowledge and how it develops. In V. Richardson (Ed.), *Handbook of research on teaching* (4th ed., pp. 877–904). Washington, DC: American Educational Research Association.

Paul, J.L., & Marfo, K. (2001). Preparation of educational researchers in philosophical foundations of inquiry. *Review of Educational Research, 71,* 525–547.

Salomon, G. (Ed.). (1993). *Distributed cognition: Psychological and educational considerations.* New York: Cambridge University Press.

Shambaugh, N., & Webb-Dempsey, J. (2003, January). *What counts as teacher research?* Presentation at the American Association for Colleges of Teacher Education (AACTE), New Orleans, LA.

Shulman, L. (1988). The dangers of dichotomous thinking in education. In P. Grimmett & G. Erickson (Eds.), *Reflection in teacher education* (pp. 31–38). New York: Teachers College Press.

CHAPTER 4

Types of Research Methods

Kim T. Shea, Anthony J. Onwuegbuzie

KEY TERMS

Mixed methods

Qualitative research methods

Quantitative research methods

Research method

BEFORE-READING QUESTIONS

■ What is a research method?

■ What research method options are available to you?

■ How do you decide which research method to use?

M rs. Coleman is a 10-year veteran educator. She has a master's degree in Reading/Language Arts Instruction, and she aspires to pursue a doctoral degree someday. She has been the reading specialist at Morrison Elementary School (pseudonym) since the beginning of the school year. As she visits classroom teachers, Mrs. Coleman is concerned that the 22 teachers at this low-income school do not understand how to tailor adequate literacy instruction to meet the needs of the diverse students who attend the school. She has just visited a second-grade classroom where she did not see any plans for literacy centers, reading groups, or individualized instruction. In fact, each time she has visited Ms. Thomas's classroom, Mrs. Coleman has witnessed whole-group, basal-reader instruction with accompanying worksheets.

Mrs. Coleman wonders why Ms. Thomas teaches literacy the way she does and whether other teachers at the school might have similar or contrasting views on literacy instruction. Mrs. Coleman remembers that she may be able to conduct teacher research to inform her practices as a reading specialist, but she does not know which type of research method might work best for her inquiry.

Introduction

As former classroom teachers, we understand that the very idea of conducting research may invoke feelings of stress. We think that knowledge of research method options may reduce those feelings and provide a sense of clarity, focus, and ability. As you gain knowledge and an understanding of research methods and how

Teachers Taking Action: A Comprehensive Guide to Teacher Research, edited by Cynthia A. Lassonde and Susan E. Israel.
© 2008 by the International Reading Association.

to put a study together, teacher research can become *your* way of being, as discussed in chapter 1.

In the opening vignette, we empathize with Mrs. Coleman. We understand her desire to use teacher research as a way to improve literacy instruction in her school. How will she go about looking at the situation systematically to reveal relevant facts or principles? Her first step is to review the options for which type of research method to use. A **research method** is "any of several general types of systematic inquiry into a subject or problem in order to discover, verify, or revise relevant facts or principles having to do with that subject or problem" (Harris & Hodges, 1995, p. 219).

This chapter is designed to assist the teacher researcher who wants to use research methods appropriately to answer questions that may provide practical information for the delivery of instruction. In this chapter, we outline research method options available to teacher researchers. We introduce research method terminology typically used in teacher research and provide examples to illustrate each type of method.

A Broad Picture of Research Methods

In the broadest sense, research methods may be categorized as quantitative, qualitative, or mixed methods. **Quantitative research methods** generally address questions that necessitate the collection, analysis, and interpretation of numeric data (i.e., numbers), whereas **qualitative research methods** use methodological approaches to study people, events, programs, problems, and the like in their natural settings (Creswell, 1994, 1998, 2003, 2007; Denzin & Lincoln, 2005). **Mixed methods** involve some combination of quantitative and qualitative research methods and approaches (Johnson & Onwuegbuzie, 2004). Researchers select a research method based on the research questions to be answered.

For quantitative research methods, qualitative research methods, and mixed methods, we will present our "5-5-5" or "triple-five" typology, in which we outline the five most common quantitative research methods, the five most common qualitative research methods, and the five most common mixed methods. Table 4.1 outlines these methods. We discuss the broad areas of quantitative, qualitative, and mixed methods research and the five suggested methods for each in the following sections. For each type of quantitative, qualitative, and mixed methods research, we will provide an example with which teacher researchers may be familiar. It is our intention that this chapter inform you of your options by broadly describing multiple methods. As you read on, think about whether or not each of the quantitative research methods, the qualitative research methods, and the mixed methods is appropriate for Mrs. Coleman's dilemma. We realize that to implement fully any of them, you will need to undertake further reading and study. You may find the references at the end of this chapter helpful for that purpose.

TABLE 4.1
Overview of the Triple-Five Typology

Quantitative Research Methods

Historical	Examination of past events; used to explain current events or predict events
Descriptive	Examination of a situation in its current state
Correlational	Examination of the relationship between two or more quantifiable variables
Quasi-experimental	Analysis of relationships; explanation of why certain events occurred
Experimental	Examination of causality through manipulation of one or more independent variables

Qualitative Research Methods

Phenomenological	Study undertaken to understand how participants describe, understand, and attach meaning to an experience
Ethnographic	Description and interpretation of a cultural group or social system in its natural setting
Case study	A bounded system limited by time, activity, and space
Grounded theory	Development of a theory from data collected in multiple stages
Biography	Study undertaken to understand an individual's life experiences

Mixed Methods

Quantitative-dominant concurrent	Quantitative component has highest priority; quantitative and qualitative data collected at the same time; use qualitative approaches to offset weaknesses of quantitative approaches
Qualitative-dominant concurrent	Qualitative component has highest priority; qualitative and quantitative data collected at the same time
Quantitative-dominant sequential	Quantitative phase tends to come first; qualitative phase explains, expands, clarifies, or develops the quantitative findings
Qualitative-dominant sequential	Qualitative component has highest priority; qualitative phase tends to come first
Multiple-wave	Qualitative and quantitative data collection and data analysis phases occur in different orders for different sets of participants

Quantitative Research Methods

Researchers who engage in quantitative research seek to

- Describe (i.e., delineate the nature and characteristics of a phenomenon)
- Explore (i.e., utilize inductive methods to investigate a concept, construct, phenomenon, or situation with the goal of developing tentative hypotheses or generalizations)
- Explain (i.e., develop a theory with the intent of clarifying the relationships among phenomena and determining reasons for occurrence of events)

- Predict (i.e., use previously acquired information to determine what will occur at a later point in time)

- Influence a phenomenon (i.e., manipulate a variable in an attempt to produce a desired outcome; [Gay & Airasian, 2003; Johnson & Christensen, 2004])

Teacher researchers may choose among five distinct types of quantitative research methods: historical, descriptive, correlational, quasi-experimental, and experimental. Each of these methods typically is used to address questions of who, when, where, how much, how many, and/or what is the relationship among specific variables (Adler, 1996). Each of these methods is discussed in the following sections.

Historical Research

When a teacher researcher uses the historical research method, he or she examines past events—usually events in the remote past. The researcher who conducts historical research seeks to understand how past events may explain current events and predict future events. Numerical data are obtained from records, artifacts, or verbal reports, typically to test hypotheses about relationships or differences. Historical data can be classified as representing either primary (e.g., eyewitness reports, original documents) or secondary (e.g., secondhand information) sources. Of the five quantitative research methods presented in this chapter, teacher researchers appear to use historical research methods the least (Onwuegbuzie, Jiao, & Bostick, 2004).

High-stakes testing is now commonplace in most school districts in the United States. A teacher researcher may want to predict how well his students might perform on this year's reading comprehension section of the state's high-stakes test. To answer his research question, the teacher researcher might consider historical research—for example, using past reading comprehension high-stakes test scores to predict reading comprehension scores for the current high-stakes testing cycle.

Descriptive Research

When a teacher researcher uses descriptive research, he or she examines a situation in its current state. These studies are a way of discovering new meanings, describing what exists, determining the frequency with which a phenomenon occurs, or categorizing information. However, results of a descriptive research study are not generalized beyond the sample. Teacher researchers usually use questionnaires, surveys, interviews, or observations as instruments for descriptive research. Often, the instruments are designed for a particular study and should be field-tested (i.e., piloted) and revised until they yield scores that are both reliable and valid. The teacher researcher uses descriptive statistics (e.g., means, totals, proportions, percentages, standard deviation) to organize and summarize data obtained from questionnaires, surveys, interviews, or observations.

Descriptive studies typically involve self-report or observation. Self-report studies include

- Survey research (i.e., collecting information from individuals or groups at one point in time, known as cross-sectional—or over time, known as longitudinal)

- Developmental research (i.e., describing behaviors that differentiate children at different levels of age, growth, or maturation with respect to various factors such as intellectual, emotional, physical, or social development)

- Follow-up research (i.e., monitoring an individual or group of interest after some period of time)

- Sociometric studies (i.e., assessing and analyzing interpersonal relationships within a group of individuals)

- Questionnaire studies (i.e., involving the use of questionnaires comprising exclusively or predominantly closed-ended items)

- Formal and informal interviews

Might Mrs. Coleman develop a questionnaire or interview questions or even collect observational data to determine the literacy beliefs and practices of the teachers with whom she works?

Correlational Research

In correlational research, the teacher researcher is concerned with the relationship between two or more quantifiable variables. If the relationship exists, the teacher researcher determines whether the relationship is positive (e.g., as level of self-esteem increases, academic performance increases) or negative (e.g., as level of anxiety increases, academic performance decreases), as well as the degree or strength of the relationships (i.e., effect size). When using the correlational research method, the teacher researcher does not seek to determine cause and effect. However, correlational studies often provide a basis for generating hypotheses that guide future intervention studies (e.g., experimental studies), which do focus on cause-and-effect relationships (Gay & Airasian, 2003). Also, correlational research can be used to make predictions. For example, a teacher researcher may want to understand the relationship between grade point average and reading level among fifth-grade students based on results of the informal reading inventory that has been mandated by the local school district. Correlational research would be most appropriate for this type of research question.

Quasi-Experimental Research

The quasi-experimental research method, sometimes referred to as causal-comparative research, is used to analyze relationships or to identify differences among groups that are naturally formed. The quasi-experimental research method can begin with an outcome and tries to identify possible antecedents. This approach is called retrospective research. Alternatively, the quasi-experimental research method can begin with the identification of two or more groups that are different in some way (e.g., male vs. female; first-grade students vs. second-grade students; school that received a new literacy curriculum vs. school that did not receive the new literacy curriculum) and then compare these groups with respect to one or more outcomes. This approach is called prospective research. In any case, the quasi-experimental research method does not involve manipulation of people, conditions, or events; rather, this method uses groups that are formed already. Quasi-experimental research methods allow investigation of a number of variables that cannot be studied experimentally, such as ability variables, personality variables, family-related variables, and school-related variables (Gay & Airasian, 2003). For example, if a teacher researcher is interested in comparing male and female students with respect to levels of reading achievement in a particular grade level at a certain point in time, use of a quasi-experimental research method would be very appropriate, as would be the case if the teacher researcher wanted to compare two or more different grade levels on any quantitative variable(s).

Experimental Research

Many experts consider experimental research to be the most powerful quantitative research method. This belief is based on the fact that in experimental research, there is rigorous control of variables. The overall objective of experimental research is to examine causality. In experimental research, the alleged cause (independent variable) is manipulated. Simply put, unlike with quasi-experimental research wherein groups that are formed naturally are compared, experimental research involves comparing groups that are formed randomly. For example, students might be randomly grouped into either the intervention group or groups (e.g., group in which a new literacy curriculum is taught) or the control group or groups (e.g., a group in which the traditional method of teaching reading is followed). By randomizing participants to groups, the chances are maximized that the groups do not differ significantly on any important variables except for the intervention. Thus, if better outcomes are observed for the intervention group(s) than for the control group(s), then the teacher researcher can conclude with confidence that the intervention caused this result.

We now turn our attention to the second component of our triple-five typology, namely, the five most common qualitative research methods.

Qualitative Research Methods

In contrast to quantitative research methods, qualitative research methods typically follow an inductive way of knowing, moving from the specific to the general. In this section, we will discuss five types of qualitative research methods: phenomenological, ethnographic, case study, grounded theory, and biographical. Each of these methods typically is used for answering why and how questions (Adler, 1996).

Phenomenological Research

When a researcher engages in phenomenological research, he or she seeks to understand how participants describe, understand, and attach meaning to an experience (Creswell, 2007; Holstein & Gubrium, 2005; Johnson & Christensen, 2004). This method involves studying a small number of participants to develop patterns and relationships of meaning (Lincoln & Guba, 1985). To understand the participants' experiences, the researcher engages in lengthy interviews to understand the experience from the perspective of numerous participants.

A teacher researcher may select a minimum of five participants for a phenomenological study or may conduct a phenomenological study with an entire classroom of students. For elementary students who are experiencing their first encounter with high-stakes testing, a teacher researcher may choose to conduct a phenomenological inquiry to understand the meaning students attach to the experiences of preparing for and taking a standardized high-stakes test.

Ethnographic Research

In ethnographic research, the researcher describes and interprets a cultural group or social system that is studied in its natural setting (Creswell, 2007; Gay & Airasian, 2003; Johnson & Christensen, 2004). To do so, the researcher becomes immersed in the cultural group or social system by becoming part of the group. As such, ethnographic research involves extended time in the field collecting observational data. In ethnographic research, the researcher describes the cultural group or social system, analyzes the group dynamics for themes or perspectives, and interprets the themes or perspectives for larger meanings (Creswell, 2007; Johnson & Christensen, 2004).

In the field of literacy, a teacher researcher may want to understand how literacy coaches interact with one another, with school district administrators, and with classroom teachers. To do so, the teacher researcher may become a literacy coach and examine this group to understand better their roles in literacy education.

Case Study Research

Stake (2005) and Creswell (2007) describe a case study as a bounded system, meaning that it has specific parameters in relation to time, activity, and space. For example, a teacher researcher may want to learn more about Samantha, one of her kindergarten students, or about how Samantha's literate life at home is related to her literate life at school.

Sometimes, to investigate a phenomenon fully, a researcher may use the multiple case study method. In this method, the researcher jointly studies more than one participant to understand a general condition. For example, a teacher researcher might consider a multiple case study in which all 18 of her first-grade students are participants. The teacher researcher may seek to understand the phenomenon of the Accelerated Reader program (i.e., a computer-based reading management system that includes a database of thousands of books ranging in reading levels from 1 to 12, in which students earn points that are redeemed for prizes or other incentives as they read books and pass a comprehension test on each book) from the students' points of view. So, the students provide insights on the general phenomenon of the Accelerated Reader program, and their responses are studied jointly as part of one multiple case study.

Grounded Theory Research

Grounded theory research, developed by Glaser and Strauss (1967), involves the development of a theory from data collected in multiple stages during a research study. A theory explains why and how something functions (Johnson & Christensen, 2004). Grounded theory research seeks to use participants' experiences to generate a theory about the phenomenon being studied (Creswell, 1998, 2003, 2007). Grounded theory research optimally involves extensive interviews with 20 to 30 participants (Creswell, 2007) to ensure the researcher has reached the point where findings in the data begin to repeat and no new conclusions can be reached (Onwuegbuzie & Leech, 2007). For example, if a teacher researcher is interested in studying coping strategies used by struggling readers, he or she may interview students, teachers, literacy coaches, principals, and so forth. Based on these sources of data, the teacher researcher could develop a theory of coping among this group of students.

Biographical Research

When a researcher seeks to understand an individual's life experiences, he or she may conduct a biographical study that results in a biography of the individual's life. In a biography, the researcher recounts an individual's lived experiences as told by the individual directly to the researcher or as gathered from historical documents, others' accounts of the individual's life, or archival material. Other types of biography methods include

- Autobiography, in which a researcher reports his or her life experiences

- Autoethnography, in which a researcher writes reflexive, personal narratives he or she has experienced (Hayano, 1979)

- Oral histories, in which the researcher seeks to understand a person's life as the person recalls events and provides personal reflections of the causes and effects of those events (Plummer, 1983)

For example, if a teacher researcher does not understand why Kevin, a fourth-grade student, struggles with reading and has such a negative affinity to school in general and reading in particular the teacher researcher might ask Kevin to write a literacy autobiography that describes his lived literacy experiences. Or the teacher researcher may gather information from Kevin, from his former teachers, from his family, and from direct observations of his literacy behaviors. The teacher researcher could then compile the information into a biography. Another option might be for the teacher researcher to tape record Kevin's account of his literacy experiences and his beliefs about how those experiences shaped his attitude toward school and reading for an oral history of Kevin's literacy life.

We now turn our attention to the third and final component of our triple-five typology, namely, five common mixed methods research approaches.

Mixed Methods

Johnson and Onwuegbuzie (2004) define mixed methods research as the type of investigation wherein the researcher mixes or combines quantitative and qualitative research techniques within the same study. Teacher researchers should use mixed methods research when the research question suggests that combining quantitative and qualitative approaches is likely to provide more comprehensive and coherent research findings and outcomes. In this section, we will discuss five common mixed methods research approaches: (1) quantitative-dominant concurrent method, (2) qualitative-dominant concurrent method, (3) quantitative-dominant sequential method, (4) qualitative-dominant sequential method, and (5) multiple-wave method. For each type of mixed methods research approach, we will provide an example with which teacher researchers may be familiar.

Quantitative-Dominant Concurrent Method

The quantitative-dominant concurrent method is used as a means to use qualitative approaches to offset the weaknesses of quantitative approaches. Here, the quantitative component (e.g., studying the effect of a new literacy program on reading performance) is given higher priority than is the qualitative component (e.g., examining students' perceptions about the new literacy program). The quantitative data collection and qualitative data collection occur at the same time (i.e., the data collection phases are independent of one another), and then the results are integrated during the data interpretation phase. When using this method, teacher researchers can mix the quantitative and qualitative findings during the data analysis phase. For instance, in conducting an action research study involving the whole class, a teacher researcher could count the number of students who express negative perceptions about reading during an interview (i.e., qualitative phase; less dominant) and compare this figure with the number of students who are reading below grade level (i.e., quantitative phase; dominant). The teacher researcher can mix the quantitative and qualitative data to an even greater extent by examining whether students who express negative perceptions about reading during an interview (i.e., qualitative phase; less dominant) also tend to be those who are reading below grade level (i.e., quantitative phase; dominant). This is known as correlating the quantitative and qualitative data (Onwuegbuzie & Teddlie, 2003).

Qualitative-Dominant Concurrent Method

In the qualitative-dominant concurrent method, the qualitative component (e.g., studying the experiences of select students in a new literacy program) is given higher priority than is the quantitative component (e.g., examining the number of hours students in a class spend reading for leisure at home). For example, in studying the role that peer pressure plays in the formation of perceptions about reading among struggling readers (qualitative phase; dominant), the teacher researcher also might examine the reading performance of the struggling readers' friends (quantitative phase; less dominant).

Quantitative-Dominant Sequential Method

In the quantitative-dominant sequential method, the quantitative phase tends to come first, with the qualitative phase being used to explain, expand, clarify, or develop the quantitative findings. For instance, in the quantitative phase of an action-research study, a teacher researcher could determine both the reading performance scores and levels of reading attitudes (e.g., using a quantitative measure of overall reading attitudes such as the Elementary Reading Attitude Survey [McKenna & Kear, 1990]) of a class of third-grade students. Based on these scores, the teacher researcher could classify each student into one of the following four groups: (1) high reading performance/positive reading attitudes, (2) high reading performance/negative reading attitudes, (3) low reading performance/positive reading attitudes, and (4) low reading performance/negative reading attitudes. In the qualitative phase, the teacher researcher could compare all students in these four groups with respect to subsequent qualitative data such as their reflections about the reading process. In the quantitative-dominant sequential method, rather than examining all students who were selected for the quantitative phase in the example, in the qualitative phase the teacher researcher could study only two or three students from each of the groups.

Qualitative-Dominant Sequential Method

In the qualitative-dominant sequential method, the qualitative component is given higher priority than the quantitative component. Although either phase could occur first, the qualitative phase tends to come first, with the quantitative phase being used to explain, expand, clarify, or develop the qualitative findings. For instance, in conducting a case study of the reading experiences of a fourth-grade student with attention deficit hyperactivity disorder (qualitative phase; dominant), a teacher researcher could count the number of times the child leaves his or her seat during a specific period of time (quantitative phase; less dominant).

Multiple-Wave Method

In the multiple-wave method, the qualitative and quantitative data collection and data analysis phases occur in different orders for different sets of participants (Li, Marquart, & Zercher, 2000). For instance, a teacher researcher might be interested in conducting a longitudinal action research study of how literacy develops during elementary school. This could involve a teacher researcher collecting quantitative and qualitative data in multiple phases over a five-year period. Because this method is more complex than are the other four mixed methods discussed previously, it is likely that a team of teacher researchers would have to implement it.

Synthesis and Concluding Thoughts

In this chapter, we introduced our triple-five typology of research methods. Select one of the five quantitative research methods when your goal is to describe, explore, explain, predict, or influence a specific variable. Of the five quantitative methods presented, use the descriptive method to describe characteristics or attributes; use the correlational method to explore relationships among variables; use the quasi-experimental method to explain relationships among variables or differences between groups or subgroups; use the historical method to explain the past; or use the experimental method to influence a specific variable or to study the causal effect of an intervention.

On the other hand, if your goal is to tell how or why through words or observations, select one of the five qualitative research methods. Conduct a phenomenological study to understand a group's lived experiences, or conduct an ethnographical inquiry to study a culture-sharing group. You may wish to study an individual or a group as a case study to understand better the individual or group (intrinsic case study) or to understand the phenomena in which the individual or group is involved (instrumental case study). If your goal is to develop a theory, engage in grounded theory research. Finally, if you seek to tell a person's life story, engage in a biographical study.

If you are interested in combining both quantitative and qualitative research methods, engage in mixed methods research. Your mixed methods research may be dominated by either quantitative or qualitative data approaches. You may collect the data either concurrently or sequentially. When you use mixed methods, you may use one type of approach to complement, elaborate, enhance, illustrate, clarify, triangulate, converge, corroborate, cross-validate, confirm, expand, contradict, or develop the other approach.

PROBLEM-SOLVING VIGNETTE FOR DISCUSSION

Mrs. Kimball is a first-grade teacher at Washington Elementary School. She is dedicated to teaching all of her students to read. It is the middle of the school year, and she has succeeded with all of her students except one. Miranda, who is repeating first grade, continues to struggle to learn to read. Mrs. Kimball has access to Miranda's standardized test scores from last year. She also has developed a successful working relationship with Miranda's parents. Mrs. Kimball wants to understand why Miranda continues to struggle with reading whereas the rest of her classmates read near or above grade level.

What would you suggest as Mrs. Kimball's research questions? Based on the research questions you think Mrs. Kimball should address, which of the triple-five research methods should she use? Why?

TIPS FOR TEACHER RESEARCHERS

The following tips may be helpful as you make research methodology decisions and search for additional sources of information.

■ Match the research questions to the research method.

■ Consult with a mentor researcher about which research method to use to match your research objectives.

■ Remember the triple-five typology.

■ Be flexible and do not limit yourself to a particular research method.

■ Be able to justify your research method selection.

QUESTIONS FOR REFLECTION

■ As you think about the triple-five typology, weigh the strengths and challenges of the broad areas of quantitative research, qualitative research, and mixed methods research.

■ Within each broad category, consider the five specific research methods. What are the strengths and challenges of each?

REFERENCES

Adler, L. (1996). Qualitative research of legal issues. In D. Schimmel (Ed.), *Research that makes a difference: Complementary methods for examining legal issues in education* (pp. 3–31). Topeka, KS: National Organization on Legal Problems of Education.

Creswell, J.W. (1994). *Research design: Qualitative & quantitative approaches*. Thousand Oaks, CA: Sage.

Creswell, J.W. (1998). *Qualitative inquiry and research design: Choosing among five traditions*. Thousand Oaks, CA: Sage.

Creswell, J.W. (2003). *Research design: Qualitative, quantitative, and mixed methods approaches*. Thousand Oaks, CA: Sage.

Creswell, J.W. (2007). *Qualitative inquiry and research design: Choosing among five approaches* (2nd ed.). Thousand Oaks, CA: Sage.

Denzin, N.K., & Lincoln, Y.S. (2005). Introduction: The discipline and practice of qualitative research. In N.K. Denzin & Y.S. Lincoln (Eds.), *The Sage handbook of qualitative research* (3rd ed., pp. 1–32). Thousand Oaks, CA: Sage.

Gay, L.R., & Airasian, P.W. (2003). *Educational research: Competencies for analysis and application* (7th ed.). Upper Saddle River, NJ: Pearson Education.

Glaser, B.G., & Strauss, A.L. (1967). *The discovery of grounded theory: Strategies for qualitative research*. Chicago: Aldine.

Harris, T.L., & Hodges, R.E. (Eds.). (1995). *The literacy dictionary: The vocabulary of reading and writing*. Newark, DE: International Reading Association.

Hayano, D.M. (1979). Auto-ethnography: Paradigms, problems, and prospects. *Human Organization, 38,* 113–120.

Holstein, J.A., & Gubrium, J.F. (2005). Interpretive practice and social action. In N.K. Denzin & Y.S. Lincoln (Eds.), *The Sage handbook of qualitative research* (pp. 483–505). Thousand Oaks, CA: Sage.

Johnson, B., & Christensen, L. (2004). *Educational research: Quantitative, qualitative, and mixed approaches*. Boston: Allyn & Bacon.

Johnson, R.B., & Onwuegbuzie, A.J. (2004). Mixed methods research: A research paradigm whose time has come. *Educational Researcher, 33*(7), 14–26.

Li, S., Marquart, J.M., & Zercher, C. (2000). Conceptual issues and analytical strategies in mixed-method studies of preschool inclusion. *Journal of Early Intervention, 23*(2), 116–132.

Lincoln, Y.S., & Guba, E.G. (1985). *Naturalistic inquiry*. Thousand Oaks, CA: Sage.

McKenna, M.C., & Kear, D.J. (1990). Measuring attitude toward reading: A new tool for teachers. *The Reading Teacher, 43,* 626–639.

Onwuegbuzie, A.J., Jiao, Q.G., & Bostick, S.L. (2004). *Library anxiety: Theory, research, and applications*. Lanham, MD: Scarecrow Press.

Onwuegbuzie, A.J., & Leech, N.L. (2007). A call for qualitative power analyses. *Quality & Quantity: International Journal of Methodology, 41,* 105–121.

Onwuegbuzie, A.J., & Teddlie, C. (2003). A framework for analyzing data in mixed methods research. In A. Tashakkori & C. Teddlie (Eds.), *Handbook of mixed methods in social & behavioral research* (pp. 351–383). Thousand Oaks, CA: Sage.

Plummer, K. (1983). *Documents of life: An introduction to the problems and literature of a humanistic method*. Sydney, NSW, Australia: Allen & Unwin.

Stake, R.E. (2005). Qualitative case studies. In N.K. Denzin & Y.S. Lincoln (Eds.), *The Sage handbook of qualitative research* (pp. 443–466). Thousand Oaks, CA: Sage.

CHAPTER 5

Examining the Possibilities: Planning Your Research Project

Amy D. Broemmel, Elizabeth A. Swaggerty

BEFORE-READING QUESTIONS

▪ How can you plan research that is doable and a part of everyday teaching, yet rigorous and credible?

▪ What role does theory play in teacher research?

▪ What processes are associated with planning teacher research?

After finally determining her question, What are the effects of Sustained Silent Reading (SSR) on students' attitudes toward reading and their perceptions of themselves as readers? Amy, a third-grade teacher, is faced with the daunting task of planning the details of her project.

It seems logical to do a pre- and posttest, so she decides to find the assessments that will give her the data she needs. Amy knows she needs to search for attitude and motivation assessments that are age- and grade-level appropriate, but she doesn't want anything that is too long or monotonous. So she goes to the literature to find the assessments she thinks will work best. Then, she decides exactly how to carry out her plan. Amy knows that the more data she can collect, the more patterns and evidence she can uncover. She decides to take the next grading period, a full six weeks, to collect her data, administering the assessments before, at the midpoint, and after the intervention, and carefully observing throughout.

Amy admits that it is overwhelming collecting data using two different assessments for each of her 19 students, but, she finds it is all worth it in the end. She is not only able to relate what she finds to the established professional literature but, more important, learn more about her students and their reading attitudes, interests, strengths, and weaknesses.

Teachers Taking Action: A Comprehensive Guide to Teacher Research, edited by Cynthia A. Lassonde and Susan E. Israel.
© 2008 by the International Reading Association.

Introduction

In *The Courage to Teach: Exploring the Inner Landscape of a Teacher's Life*, Palmer (1998) indicates that the separation of theory and practice results in "theories that have little to do with life and practice that is uninformed by understanding" (p. 66). The limited research on teachers' attitudes toward research indicates that teachers do indeed find educational research to be either inaccessible or irrelevant and reflects the truth in Palmer's statement (Gitlin, Barlow, Burbank, Kauchak, & Stevens, 1999). McBee (2004) hypothesizes that one of the reasons teachers struggle to apply research to their daily lives has to do with the fact that little published research is conducted by teachers; they view research as something that others do for teachers, not something in which they are actively involved. We might add that teachers are often intimidated by the language and formality of educational research because it does not reflect the often hectic nature of their daily lives. However, as chapter 1 established, this does not have to be the case.

In the chapter-opening vignette, Amy, like many beginning teachers, often found herself overwhelmed by the day-to-day responsibilities of a being a teacher. Unlike most beginning teachers, Amy was pursuing her master's degree for which she was required to engage in teacher research as a part of her program of study. Amy's structured approach worked for her; a longer time frame with more anecdotal observation may have worked for someone else. Teacher research looks just as varied as the teachers who are researching. Regardless of what form it takes, there are key points to consider when planning a project. This chapter is intended to serve as a means of helping teachers realize that teacher research does not have to be complicated or elaborate to be rigorous and effective; to provide a vision of how this type of research can become a part of everyday teaching; and to empower teachers to step into the role of researcher, understanding the role of theory in research and further informing both the knowledge base and the practice of the profession.

Conceptualizing Your Research

The very nature of this type of inquiry-based research is diverse, somewhat messy, and often unpredictable despite careful planning. When teachers begin to conceptualize their research projects, there are three theoretical issues we deem especially important for consideration: (1) situating the study, (2) considering the primary approaches to research, and (3) establishing credibility.

Situating the study generally includes paying conscious attention to how the research question relates to the teacher's personal experiences and to how the research question fits or does not fit into past and current research on the topic. In teacher research, questions develop out of teachers' own personal interests, wonderings, confusions, or frustrations. As such, it is logical to thoughtfully examine how these personal experiences could potentially affect the processes and, ultimately, the outcomes of the research. However, examining how the question fits into the larger body of research is not quite so straightforward; there is some debate about the importance of grounding teacher research in the context of the established knowledge base.

Conducting a **literature review**—that is, examining the available professional literature on a topic, is generally accepted as a valuable activity, despite the widely accepted fact that teachers have so many important tasks to accomplish and so little time in which to do them (Mills, 2003). Hubbard and Power (1993) suggest that teacher researchers, like all researchers, must learn more about the field by examining the "legacy of distant teachers" (p. 100) who have shared similar wonderings. Thomas (2004) agrees, suggesting such reviews are most effective when the research question has been established. It appears that teacher researchers themselves agree, because virtually all published results of teacher research include some sort of literature review and are firmly grounded in theory (Baumann & Duffy, 2001).

A second theoretical issue critical to effectively conceptualizing a research project is consideration of the **research paradigms**, the two primary research methods to research: qualitative and quantitative. Although research methods were introduced in chapter 4, they will be discussed further here as they relate to planning your research. It is, in most cases, the question itself that drives the answer to the question of selecting the most appropriate research paradigm. Qualitative studies are most common in teacher research and allow for exploration of the topic of inquiry (Baumann & Duffy-Hester, 2000; Creswell, 1998). Qualitative research uses systematic observations to develop understanding of a situation, context, or other phenomenon. It results in rich description and can be useful in informing similar situations; however, it is not considered generalizable. **Generalizability** refers to the applicability of the research results to settings and contexts different from the one in which the research was conducted (Mills, 2003).

Quantitative research typically involves some sort of statistical analysis and is sometimes used to supplement qualitative research (Baumann & Duffy-Hester, 2000). This type of research is typically considered generalizable and can be thought of as asking how or why, with the intent of establishing relationships (Creswell, 1998). Each approach is associated with specific types of data, which can be observations, measurements, and other information collected and recorded by the researcher. However, it is especially important to note that the purpose of teacher research is for teachers to systematically examine their practice. So, even when quantitative methods are used, it is typically for the purpose of describing a situation, of providing a picture of what's happening, rather than to attempt to prove or disprove the effects of an instructional strategy, assessment, or other variable.

Finally, researchers at all levels must concern themselves with establishing credibility within the context of their study. Validity and reliability are often seen as the keys to such credibility. **Reliability** refers to consistency in results over time. Although this is highly valued, especially in quantitative studies, it is sometimes viewed in slightly different terms when discussed in relation to qualitative research, where description of a particular situation is the focus. Johnson (2005) suggests that in those cases, and often in teacher research, reliability must be about noticing recurring themes or patterns in the data. **Validity**, which refers to whether the data actually reflect what they claim to reflect, however, is critical for all research. Interestingly, there are a number of accepted aspects of validity described in the professional literature on qualitative research, including accurate representation of multiple perspectives, successful resolution of the research problem, and competency and dependability in carrying out the process (Anderson, Herr, & Nihlen, 1994; Guba, 1981; Maxwell, 1992). Regardless of these specific definitions, it is well established that teacher researchers must be diligent in selecting methodological approaches and data collection strategies that are in clear alignment with the questions they are intended to inform.

Getting Down to Business: Understanding Research Processes

Teacher research has emerged as a powerful tool for supporting the professional growth of teachers in their classrooms. It is a way that teachers can systematically investigate what goes on in their classrooms in an attempt to improve both student learning and their teaching abilities and efficacy. To effectively engage in this type of endeavor, teachers need to consider three main processes: (1) consulting the literature, (2) selecting appropriate methods and data collection strategies, and (3) developing a suitable timeline.

Consulting the Literature

The literature review is an important component in any research project. Spending some time with the relevant literature provides pertinent background information about the research and theory on the topic of inquiry. It can be used to inform teacher research at any point, before, during, or after the data collection, but can be especially helpful in the planning stages of the project.

Baumann and Duffy (2001) found that most teacher researchers do, in fact, go to the literature to familiarize themselves with existing research and theory on their topic of inquiry. Recognizing that most teachers struggle to find the time to read a novel for pleasure during the school year, it is important for teachers to take the time to read the relevant literature to get a sense of what others have done, to "stand on the shoulders of those who came before" (Falk & Blumenreich, 2005,

p. 41). At this point in the process, it is helpful to search for research pieces that will inform your study, not just how-to articles or books that list strategies. Most original research is published as direct reports in peer-reviewed journals, which simply indicates the articles have been read by other experts in the field who offer their expertise to verify the accuracy of the article. Common examples include *The Reading Teacher, Language Arts, Reading Research Quarterly,* and *Journal of Adolescent & Adult Literacy.* (See more about publication in chapter 12 in this volume.)

It is important to note that focusing on pieces from peer-reviewed journals does not mean that information from other, non–peer-reviewed sources doesn't have value. They do, however, warrant further examination. Websites, popular magazines, and newspapers might contain interesting information, but it is wise to be wary of anything that is undocumented. If indeed some sort of citation or reference is included, a general guideline is to always consult the original source to verify the information within its intended context. It is also wise to be wary of research written or supported by a specific program's originator or publisher. Unbiased representation of information is critical for the credibility of all research.

There is something to be said about spending time within the walls of a college or university library, with your hands on actual books, anthologies, and journals. However, the Internet can serve as an effective medium for searches of professional literature. There are a number of search engines that will search for documents available on the Internet. Google Scholar, a search engine, and the Education Resources Information Center, a Web-based resource center, provide access to research abstracts and some full-text articles. In any case, by using key terms with connecting words, such as *and, or,* or *not,* topic-specific information can be located. For example, in Amy's vignette, she may have searched using the key terms *reading motivation, Sustained Silent Reading (SSR), independent reading,* and *reader self-perception.*

Once at least three to five key articles have been located, it is time to read and record. Using a matrix like the sample in Figure 5.1 can help provide an organizational structure that helps identify patterns and trends in the body of available research (see Appendix B for a reproducible version of this form). It can be especially helpful to scan the reference lists in relevant books and articles for other references that might be on-target with your topic. As you read, examine how others have approached your question and think about how you might design your study.

Once the matrix is complete, it becomes the teacher researcher's task to look for patterns and varying perspectives that may help to provide a full picture, informing the research question at hand. As you examine the research available on your topic, there are a number of things you need to consider. First, note the research design. What kind of research has been done on your topic of inquiry: qualitative, quantitative, or mixed methods? More specifically, are the studies

FIGURE 5.1
Sample Literature Review Matrix

	Overview	Context	Methods	Findings	Other Notes
Study #1 Yoon, 2002	Meta-analysis of effects of SSR on attitudes toward reading	Participants in the selected studies ranged from second-grade students to college-age students	Analysis of seven research studies	When kids choose own books, intrinsic motivation is enhanced, resulting in increased comprehension and positive attitude toward reading	Fantastic reference list on pp.193–195
Study #2 Lee-Daniels & Murray, 2000	Description of a teacher's use of DEAR program	Participants were second-grade students in a regular, self-contained classroom	DEAR: reading pairs, discussion, interviews/ student "informants" bookworm bulletin board activity	Teacher observed negative affects of DEAR and modified the program to work for her students	Find: Moore, Jones, & Miller (1980): What we know from a decade of sustained silent reading. *The Reading Teacher*
Study #3 (Name, Date)					
Study #4 (Name, Date)					

ethnographic, case studies, experimental studies, or descriptive studies? (See chapter 4 for a detailed discussion of the research methods and types of research.) Do they compare specific strategies or approaches or do they describe instruction? Once you've identified the research design, note the context for each study. Think about where the research took place, the age level and number of participants, and the duration of the study. Take a closer look at any definitions pertinent to your topic of inquiry. Do the definitions vary or are they consistent? Finally, note the findings as they relate to your research question. How do they compare to one another? How do they differ? Is there evidence that specific strategies work better than others? Once these questions are answered, you can think about how they relate to what you want to accomplish, finalize your research question, and move into planning your methodology and data collection strategies.

Selecting Appropriate Methods and Data Collection Strategies

Typically, teacher research either describes or measures changes in academic performance, behavior, or attitudes depending on the research method best suited to the research question. For example, Bill, a first-year teacher working to complete his master's degree, wanted to investigate how using guided-writing groups to teach revision affected his first-grade writers. This led him down a path of research that included deep layers of description through copious anecdotal records and analysis of student writing over time. Although this type of qualitative research is not broadly generalizable, it results in a rich description that helps to understand particular situations and can be useful in informing similar situations. This type of research results in development of a theory so that the researcher gains understanding of a particular situation. Common methods include observations, interviews, and document collection.

Quantitative research, on the other hand, can be used to describe, explore, explain, predict, or influence a specific variable. For example, Kristi and Ellie, experienced first-grade teachers, wanted to investigate the effects of reading time on fluency. They asked, "What happens to the oral reading abilities of first graders when they are given 30 minutes of individual reading time with materials at their independent levels?" This method typically involves some sort of statistical analysis and is sometimes used to supplement qualitative research (Baumann & Duffy-Hester, 2000). In conducting quantitative research, you might attempt to test the impact of a variable to gather information about trends. Quantitative methods include collecting and analyzing test scores, data sets, or surveys. Ellie and Kristi decided to use a pre- and posttest model to identify changes in the speed and accuracy rates of their students. It is especially important to note that the purpose of teacher research is for teachers to systematically examine their practice, so even when quantitative methods are used, it is typically for the purpose of describing a situation or providing a picture of what's happening, rather than to attempt to prove or disprove a hypothesis. Ellie and Kristi used a quantitative approach appropriately to provide a picture of what was going on as a result of their instructional changes.

Like all researchers, teacher researchers must select data sources that best equip them with the information necessary to answer the research question. Teachers most commonly use classroom observation, interviews, videotaping, audiotaping, student documents, and other documents to gain insight on their research questions. Data typically falls into one of three categories: (1) observational data, (2) inquiry data, and (3) document data (Wolcott, 1992). The three columns in the Data Collection Checklist in Figure 5.2 correlate easily to the action that goes along with each type of data:

- To collect observational data, you observe.
- To collect inquiry data, you ask or reflect.
- To collect document data, you examine.

FIGURE 5.2
Sample Data Collection Checklist

Observing (observational data)	Asking/Reflecting (inquiry data)	Examining (document data)
X Field notes	**X** Informal interviews	__ Student work samples
X Anecdotal records	__ Formal interviews	__ Student tests
__ Log, diary, journal	__ Questionnaires and surveys	__ Student self-assessments
X Checklists	__ Attitude scales	__ Portfolios
X Videotapes and audiotapes	__ Sociograms	**X** Standardized test scores
__ Photographs	__ Focus group interviews	__ Lesson plans
__ Behavior scales	__ Conferences	__ Peer reviews
	__ Reflective journal	__ School records

Adapted from Arhar, Holly, & Kasten. (2001). *Action research for teachers: Traveling the yellow brick road.* Upper Saddle River, NJ: Prentice Hall. p. 137.

A blank form corresponding to Figure 5.2 has been included in Appendix B for you to reproduce and use as you consider which data collection methods will best lead to more insight on your question.

Rigor is defined as "the strength of inference made possible by the given research study" (Staw, 1985). It is a desirable quality in research of any sort. To add rigor to the study, teacher researchers must think about ways to collect multiple data sources. In any research, this type of triangulation of data is especially important. In simplest terms, **triangulation** means that there are multiple (usually three) sources of data collected for analysis in an attempt to corroborate evidence from varied perspectives. Triangulating data helps teacher researchers establish credibility and validity within their research study. However, when selecting data sources, teacher researchers are wise to consider what will provide the necessary information without negatively affecting their ability to provide effective instruction for their students. In the opening vignette, Amy scoured the related literature for attitude and motivation assessments that were relatively easy to administer in a group setting because she wanted to get feedback from all of her students. Certainly, if she had chosen to do pre- and postinterviews with each of her third graders, she would have increased the potential of gaining much deeper insight on the subtle changes in her students' attitudes and motivation. However, conducting 38 such interviews would have undoubtedly cut into either her planning or her instructional time.

Developing a Suitable Timeline

Establishing a timeline is a useful tool for planning and completing a research project. Research projects will inevitably be affected by things outside of the teacher researcher's control, including student absences, fire drills, school holidays, testing, and so on. It is important to be mindful of these challenges and plan for them, as much as possible, in advance.

Amy, the teacher from the chapter-opening vignette, used the timeline shown in Figure 5.3 as a guide in pacing her entire research project on examining the effects of SSR on student attitudes and perceptions. As shown on the bottom half of the timeline, she found it helpful to focus the timeline even further, scrutinizing the data collection period specifically.

It is important to realize that things unavoidably take longer than initially conceptualized. It is critical to keep an open mind, stay focused, and continue plodding along, even if the study takes a few more weeks than planned.

Pulling Together a Plan

Consider the following questions as you formalize your research plan:

- What are you trying to accomplish?
- Who are your subjects?
- What type of study are you planning to conduct?
- What are you going to do? (What is your intervention?)
- What do you intend to measure?

FIGURE 5.3
Sample Timeline

September	Develop research questions
October	Create research plan; conduct an initial literature review; obtain any necessary permissions
Mid-October/ November	Collect data; return to the literature
December/January	Continue collecting data; begin reviewing, coding, and analyzing once a week
February/March	Analyze data for findings and conclusions
March/April	Revisit the literature; begin writing for publication

Week 1	Administer reading attitude survey
Weeks 2–8	Implement daily SSR periods; observe and document student behavior
Week 9	Administer reading attitude survey

- What data will you collect as evidence?
- When will you be completing this research?

It is important to recognize that it is essential to begin a research project with a detailed plan, but it is also important to be mindful of the responsive nature of methodological choices (Baumann & Duffy, 2001). In other words, methodological decisions are likely to evolve as research progresses. For example, once the process of collecting data begins, the researcher might find that the selected method isn't producing information adequate for answering the research question. As a result, revisiting the professional literature may stimulate alternative ways to collect data. Teacher researchers may also find that more data is necessary to adequately investigate the question. It may be that six weeks' worth of student journal entries are not adequate for providing the necessary insight, so the decision is made to continue to collect journal entries for a few more weeks, or until there is enough data to explore the question. Teacher researchers have a responsibility to make any modifications necessary for answering their research questions in the most fulfilling way possible.

Synthesis and Concluding Thoughts

Inevitably, teacher research varies depending on the teacher, the classroom, and the students. The same research question has the potential to look completely different, depending on the choices the researcher makes. However, the most effective teacher research is well planned, typically addressing key points such as situating the study in terms of personal experience and relevant literature, considering the appropriate methodological approaches, and choosing appropriate data-collection methods before actually implementing the research, thus establishing the credibility of teacher researchers.

In their overview of the history of teacher research, McFarland and Stansell (1993) ominously caution that

> powerful groups in many nations are now at work on various educational reforms, including national curricula and national tests, which presume no need for further inquiry among teachers and which cast them as mere technicians who will have no role in building curricula from their research in the classroom. Quite possibly, teacher researchers will face serious challenges in the 1990s, challenges that will severely test their commitment as well as the theory, curricula, and teaching practices they have developed. (p. 17)

Scarcely more than a decade later, we, as educators, find ourselves in just such a situation. How can we overcome the prevalent view of teachers as passive receivers of pedagogical knowledge and dictated curricula? We must reestablish ourselves as professionals by engaging in teacher research. By sharing the systematic reflection, inquiry, and action we do in our classrooms, we can help others come to see us as "the heirs to a professional and intellectual tradition that has very deep roots and has persisted in spite of many challenges in the past" (McFarland & Stansell, 1993, p. 17).

PROBLEM-SOLVING VIGNETTE FOR DISCUSSION

Paige, a first-grade teacher, wasn't sure where to start. She knew that she really wanted to figure out how to help her struggling readers become more fluent, but she didn't really have any idea of how to get moving in the right direction. Paige describes her approach toward working through her struggle with planning her research: "I wanted to find out how to improve the fluency of my struggling readers—not just the speed or accuracy at which they read, but how to make them really fluent. So, I went to the research. I found many references to teaching fluency in a purposeful and natural way, using meaningful passages, and allowing students multiple reading and rereading opportunities. Based on the information I found in the research, I decided to use Readers Theatre as an instructional tool with my struggling first graders, and my question immediately became more focused: Does Readers Theatre improve the overall fluency of struggling first-grade readers?"

Although Paige's question is more focused, she still isn't sure what kinds of data will give her the information she needs. What kinds of collection strategies would be both manageable and meaningful? There are no easy and right answers to this question. Revisit the checklist shown in Figure 5.2 (see p. 64), and examine Paige's choices.

Is it realistic to use all of the selected data sources? Would some provide more information than others? If this were your project, what data sources would you choose?

TIPS FOR TEACHER RESEARCHERS

Adequately planning your research project can be critical for its overall success, because it is so easy to get lost in the details. We suggest keeping the following ideas in mind as you progress through each stage of the process:

■ Find a way to access the professional literature related to your topic. Spend some time in a university library if you can. Otherwise, use Internet search engines like Google Scholar, which are specifically designed to find this kind of information.

■ As you read the research, think about what other researchers have done and how it can inform your research design.

■ Remember to look at the reference lists of especially informative articles to find even more potential sources of information.

- Stay focused on your research question; make sure the data you plan to collect will help you answer your questions in meaningful ways.

- Be as specific as you can when developing your timeline, then use it to help guide your project.

In general, your big tasks during the planning stage of your research project are to specifically identify the type of research study you will conduct, who will participate in your study, the data you will collect, and your timeline for implementation.

QUESTIONS FOR REFLECTION

- What do you see as your biggest challenges as you move forward in planning your research? How might you overcome these challenges?

- Who could you call on for professional support as you engage in your research?

REFERENCES

Anderson, G.L., Herr, K., & Nihlen, A.S. (1994). *Studying your own school: An educator's guide to qualitative practitioner research.* Thousand Oaks, CA: Corwin Press.

Arhar, J.M., Holly, M.L., & Kasten, W.C. (2001). *Action research for teachers: Traveling the yellow brick road.* Upper Saddle River, NJ: Prentice Hall.

Baumann, J.F., & Duffy, A.M. (2001). Teacher-researcher methodology: Themes, variations, and possibilities. *The Reading Teacher, 54,* 608–615.

Baumann, J.F., & Duffy-Hester, A.M. (2000). Making sense of classroom worlds: Methodology in teacher research. In M.L. Kamil, P. Mosenthal, P.D. Pearson, & R. Barr (Eds.), *Handbook of reading research* (Vol. 3, pp 77–98). Mahwah, NJ: Erlbaum.

Creswell, J.W. (1998). *Qualitative inquiry and research design: Choosing among five traditions.* Thousand Oaks, CA: Sage.

Falk, B., & Blumenreich, M. (2005). *The power of questions: A guide to teacher and student research.* Portsmouth, NH: Heinemann.

Gitlin, A., Barlow, L., Burbank, M.D., Kauchak, D., & Stevens, T. (1999). Pre-service teachers' thinking on research: Implications for inquiry oriented teacher education. *Teaching and Teacher Education, 15,* 753–769.

Guba, E.G. (1981). Criteria for assessing the trustworthiness of naturalistic inquiries. *Educational Communication and Technology, 29*(2), 75–91.

Hubbard, R.S., & Power, B.M. (1993). *The art of classroom inquiry: A handbook for teacher-researchers.* Portsmouth, NH: Heinemann.

Johnson, A.P. (2005). *A short guide to action research.* Boston: Allyn & Bacon.

Maxwell, J.A. (1992). Understanding and validity in qualitative research. *Harvard Educational Review, 62,* 279–300.

McBee, M.T. (2004). The classroom as laboratory: An exploration of teacher research. *Roeper Review, 27*(1), 52–58.

McFarland, K.P., & Stansell, J.C. (1993). Historical perspectives. In L. Patterson, C.M. Santa, K. Short, & K. Smith (Eds.), *Teachers are researchers: Reflection and action* (pp. 12–17). Newark, DE: International Reading Association.

Mills, G.E. (2003). *Action research: A guide for the teacher researcher* (2nd ed.). Upper Saddle River, NJ: Prentice Hall.

Palmer, P. (1998). *The courage to teach: Exploring the inner landscape of a teacher's life.* San Francisco: Jossey-Bass.

Staw, B.M. (1985). Reports on the road to relevance and rigor: Some unexplored issues in publishing organizational research. In L.L. Cummings & P.J. Frost (Eds.), *Publishing in the organizational sciences* (pp. 96–107). Homewood, IL: Richard D. Irwin.

Thomas, R.M. (2004). *Teachers doing research: An introductory guidebook.* Boston: Allyn & Bacon.

Wolcott, H.F. (1992). Posturing in qualitative research. In M.D. LeCompte, W.L. Millroy, & J. Preissle (Eds.), *Handbook of qualitative research in education* (pp. 3–52). San Diego, CA: Academic Press.

PART III

Engaging in Teacher Research Projects

Part Opener: Engaging Novice Teachers in Classroom Inquiry
Barbara H. Davis

Working with a small group of students at the guided reading table, Jill Touchstone, wearing a Hawaiian lei as a do-not-disturb signal to the children, glances up to scan her kindergarten classroom. She smiles as she sees the rest of the class purposefully engaged in literacy centers. In the library center, two girls rest comfortably on big, fluffy pillows and buddy-read small books, which they read previously in their guided reading group. Two students manipulate magnetic letters to create words from the word wall in the ABC center. They write the words on their ABC word list and then practice reading them to each other. After putting the letters away, they select an ABC puzzle from the center.

A timer beeps. Jill watches from the guided reading area as small groups of students, wearing differently colored sentence-strip headbands, quickly and quietly move to their next center location. In less than one minute, the orange-headband group settles into the Big Book center while the green-headband group moves to the ABC center. In a similar fashion, the yellow-, pink-, and blue-headband groups rotate to their respective literacy centers. As children choose from various activities at the centers, Jill calls three students to join her at the guided-reading table. She works with them uninterrupted for the next 20 minutes.

This description of Jill's kindergarten classroom, drawn from the videotape records of literacy center time during the spring semester of the school year, contrasts sharply with the videotaped scene from the fall semester of the same year. What happened from the fall to spring semester? How did center time change from being a chaotic three-ring circus in the fall to a smoothly running performance in the spring? What strategies did Jill implement to help her students learn how to make an effective transition during center rotations? How did students learn to work independently and cooperatively while she conducted guided reading groups? The case study of Jill's teacher research project addresses these questions. (To read the complete case study, go to this book's link on the IRA website at www.reading.org and click on Case Study #3: Engaging Novice Teachers in Classroom Inquiry.)

Moreover, this case study illustrates principles from chapter 6 of how a novice teacher organized, analyzed, and summarized the findings from her study. It shows how various collaborations, as outlined in chapter 7, can assist teachers in sustaining their projects.

Organizing and Analyzing Qualitative Data

Leanne M. Avery, Daniel Z. Meyer

BEFORE-READING QUESTIONS

- What are codes and how are they formed?
- How can claims be supported and affirmed?
- How can multiple data sources be coordinated?

During her study on curriculum development and teacher practice, Leanne collects multiple sources of data. Although she is unsure about what and how much data to collect, she makes numerous classroom observations, collects curricular artifacts from teachers, and conducts interviews with the teachers. As the study progresses, she begins to see insights surface—a picture of each teacher's practice begins to emerge. Although the insights are exciting, she knows she has to use her multitude of data to support these insights. She finds herself asking, How do I go from piles of data to claims? How do I find a way to analyze all of this data in a manageable and systematic way?

Dan's study, on the other hand, has only one data source—audio recordings of graduate students working together in groups on a curriculum development project. Although Dan does not have a variety of data sources to organize and analyze, he does have many hours of audio recordings to analyze. His question becomes, How do I employ a coding system that not only allows me to code the data but also allows me to track patterns over time?

Introduction

Researchers can start with a lot of data and know intuitively it's interesting—but how do you organize it? This chapter provides a systematic way and a set of research tools to do just that.

Teachers Taking Action: A Comprehensive Guide to Teacher Research, edited by Cynthia A. Lassonde and Susan E. Israel.
© 2008 by the International Reading Association.

There are four themes that form the core message of this chapter. First, qualitative data analysis is very much an iterative, trial-and-error process. Uncertainty about how to proceed is a very natural and inevitable part of the process. Often it is only through seeing how an initial approach is insufficient that the better approach becomes clear. In this chapter we will show examples of reflecting on and modifying initial approaches.

Second, both qualitative and quantitative analyses begin with more data than is possible to view at once. But quantitative analysis overcomes this by filtering out irrelevant or aberrant information and summarizing the data in a form that is viewable (e.g., a mean). With qualitative analysis, it is often those connections that are removed in such a distillation that researchers are precisely interested in. Qualitative analysis can be characterized as a tracking problem—being able to connect two or more bits of data across the span of the totality of data.

Third, qualitative analysis is about storytelling—accurately representing the research subjects and their work. This is often accomplished through a case study approach (Yin, 1994). Here, a subject is studied in detail in a specific context where specific questions about some phenomenon are explored. The job of the researcher is to collect enough data to paint a portrait of the subject.

Fourth, while data analysis is not a straightforward, linear process, having a systematic framework is essential. This is true at both the methodological and theoretical levels. A methodological framework will keep your data organized, allow you to keep a paper trail of the details, and provide you with a systematic routine for analyzing your data. Also integral to analyzing data is having a theoretical framework to use as a foundation or lens through which to view the data. Such a body of existing work will guide your work and help you decide what is and is not important. There are many theoretical frameworks from which to choose. In this chapter, we focus on using perspectives from Science and Technology Studies (S&TS), which are defined later in the chapter. One of the primary reasons for both methodological and theoretical frameworks is simply to provide forward momentum—better solutions often only reveal themselves after you try something else.

To illustrate the themes and the points mentioned here, we use examples from two of our own qualitative research projects (Avery, 2003; Meyer, 2003). One (Dan's) is a study of preservice teachers in a curriculum class collaborating on a long-term, curriculum design project. The data collected in this study consisted of audio recordings of the groupwork sessions. The second study (Leanne's) involved two groups of inservice teachers—more experienced curriculum designers and less experienced curriculum users involved in a university educator and scientist collaboration. In this study, multiple data sources were collected including interviews; classroom observations; audio recordings; and notes from project meetings, group meetings, conferences, and curricular **artifacts** (materials such as lesson plans, activities, handouts, and so on).

In addition to devising a systematic way to organize your data, there are a variety of tips to pay attention to. We share the tips that we learned along the way—the easy and the hard ways—and offer suggestions for using these in your research.

Concepts

In this section, we briefly discuss the methodological and theoretical frameworks we apply to our research cases. The role we want to emphasize is that these frameworks provide a lens through which to view the phenomena being researched and a direction in which to proceed. We have found significant utility in the frameworks we describe here. However, the main point is not that you adopt these particular frameworks but rather that you choose frameworks to drive your work.

Constant Comparative Analysis

Constant comparative analysis (CCA) is a popular approach to qualitative research analysis. The broad conceptual nature of CCA is that coding and analyzing occur simultaneously in an iterative process when, while coding the data, the researcher is constantly assessing the patterns that emerge and adjusting the scheme accordingly. **Codes** are labels applied to units of data to track similar occurrences. At its most detailed level, the mechanics of CCA can be summed up as follows:

> The analyst starts by coding each incident in his data in as many categories of analysis as possible. To this procedure I add the basic defining rule for the constant comparative method: *while coding an incident for a category, compare it with the previous incidents coded in the same category.* For example, as the analyst codes an incident in which a nurse responds to the potential "social loss"—loss to family and occupation—of a dying patient, he compares this incident with others previously coded in the same category before further coding. (Glaser, 1969, pp. 220–221, italics in the original)

Hence, CCA begins by asking of each codeable unit, How is this incident the same as, related to, or different from previous incidents? Codes can, therefore, develop in this iterative manner.

The aim of CCA is not merely to develop a set of codes and a body of coded data. In fact, the key characteristic of CCA is the notion of simultaneously carrying out coding and analysis. As the researcher progresses, reviewing the data repeatedly in this systematic manner will naturally lead to patterns emerging. "[A]s the coding continues the constant comparative unit changes *from* comparison of incident with incident *to* incident with properties of the category [that] resulted from initial comparison of incidents" (Glaser, 1969, p. 221). In other words, one begins comparing the trees and naturally shifts to comparing trees with the forest. In this manner, what begins as a seemingly overwhelming mountain of data becomes manageable. As more progress is made, a focusing feature will set in. It will become clearer what the researcher does and does not care about. Often the focus will narrow and the range of codes will diminish.

Case Study Methodology

As teacher researchers, we often are involved in qualitative studies that require prolonged, in-depth contact with our subjects. The nature of such studies is that they are often both exploratory and theory generating, and have interest in detail and depth rather than in broad generalization. In addition, it is very common for a qualitative researcher to collect multiple sources of data for each subject. A case study approach (Yin, 1994) is one method for handling a large variety of data. Case studies were initially introduced in chapter 4, but here we will provide further in-depth information on them.

According to Yin (1994), "Case studies are the preferred strategy when how or why questions are being posed, when the investigator has little control over events, and when the focus is on a contemporary phenomenon within some real-life context" (p. 1). He also goes on to say that as a method,

> it copes with technically distinctive situations in which there will be many more variables of interest than data points, and as one result, relies on multiple sources of data needing to converge in a triangulating fashion, and benefits from the prior development of theoretical propositions to guide data collection and analysis. (p. 1)

According to Grossman (1990),

> To call something "case study research," however, says more about the nature of the unit of analysis than about any particular strategies of data collection. Each individual case becomes the first unit of analysis, as the researcher identifies patterns and themes within the individual case that can be useful in the cross-case analysis. Case study research can draw on a wide variety of data collection strategies; the common thread of case study research is the identification, conceptualization, elaboration of an individual case, while setting the particular case writing a larger theoretical and naturalistic context. (p. 150)

The basic aim of case study research, therefore, is to coordinate data sources to paint a picture of the case as a whole.

Science and Technology Studies

Both of our research case studies are attempts to adapt perspectives from **science and technology studies (S&TS)** to the field of education, specifically teacher practice. S&TS seeks to study the development of science and technology as historical, cultural, or sociological phenomena. As previously mentioned, our purpose for presenting this perspective is to demonstrate the role of a conceptual framework of guiding data analysis. S&TS seeks to provide a full sociological account to the formation of scientific knowledge (for two comprehensive literature reviews see Collins, 1983, and Shapin, 1995). A central principle is that scientific knowledge is underdetermined by empirical evidence, which is data collected based on or characterized by observation and experiment (Latour, 1987; Pinch, 1986). Significant instances occur where multiple interpretations of data arise and no external authority exists to guide the formation of a single obvious conclusion (Collins, 1981a, 1981b; Pinch & Bijker, 1987). Formation of facts thus depend on social interaction over various claims (Latour & Woolgar, 1986). These interactions include formal procedures such as peer review. Informal interactions are also significant. Any new use of an idea, procedure, framework, or conclusion validates the previous use.

Context is a crucial element in the social formation of knowledge. The stability of a particular interpretation of data or conception of technological design depends on its location in a social network of actors, artifacts, data, concepts, routines, and beliefs (Bijker, Hughes, & Pinch, 1999). Various actors can have different perspectives that affect the ways in which they interact with data and artifacts. Problems in data can be seen in one manner by one set of scientists and in another by a different set (Pinch, 1981). Technological artifacts can be modified by later users for purposes other than the ones their designers intended (Kline & Pinch, 1996).

Exemplar Research Cases

As we discuss our two research cases to illustrate the concepts we have discussed thus far, note that we do not intend to put forth one best way to analyze research data. Rather, we intend to model what is an inherently messy process. Part of our reason for presenting two cases is to illustrate the range of possibilities—in terms of problems and solutions. The first case focuses primarily on transcript data and the use of CCA. The second case focuses primarily on coordinating multiple data types and case study methodology.

Curriculum Design Case

The first case comes from a study of teachers engaged in collaborative curriculum design. The subjects were preservice teachers enrolled in a curriculum design course, as part of a certification program. The data consist of audio recordings of their groupwork sessions. The aims of the study included demonstrating the application of concepts from S&TS to the formation of educational practice. That is, the teachers would be viewed as designers and their curriculum as a designed artifact.

First-Pass Constant Comparative Analysis. Figure 6.1 shows a sample of the transcript dialogue very early in a group's work on an inquiry-based curriculum about sewage treatment. (Although the coding is shown here, think of the data as uncoded as I describe how I applied coding strategies.) This process began in a very standard CCA manner of considering how each unit of analysis was similar or different from what had come before. Almost immediately, I realized that two

FIGURE 6.1
Sample Transcript Dialogue

Line	Speaker	Talk	Note	speech action	speech content1	speech content2	speech content3	speech content4	artifact action	Issue1	Issue2	logistic	pedag	content	concept
0074	Darrin	Well it seems like- having kids play with chlorine, and microbes are not gonna really, isn't gonna really be realistic.		judgen					chal	11		n			
0075	Megan	mm		acknow						11					
0076	Darrin	So we may have to have them kind of, design only on paper.		suggest	content	activ			add	11		p			
0077	Darrin	Or in a system like, Stella for example, or,		sugalt	content	activ			add	11		p			
0078	Megan	mmm, yeah		agree					sup	11					
0079	Darrin	Like Stella might be a really good way to, model this.		judgep	activ				sup	11		p			
0080	Darrin	that adds a whole nother completely serious element to it.		support	content				sup	11		p			
0081	Megan	yeah		agree					sup	11					
0082	Darrin	we'll stick with the,		metacurdes						11					
0083	Darrin	the basics first.		contd						11					
0084	Kevin	So, are we gonna I guess, thinking that we want to do a design challenge	OL	question	goal					11		x	x		
0085	Megan	Can I see the- wastewater treatment thing?	OL	request	exismat								x		
0086	Darrin	What's that?		question											
0087	Kevin	Do we want to do a design challenge?		question	goal	activ			quest	11		x	x		
0088	Darrin	I think the cool part about a design challenge, is that you can give them, um,		judge	content	activ				11	33				
0089	Darrin	what you can give them as parameters, essentially.		refer	content	concept	pedog	activ	sup	11	33	x	p	x	x
0090	Darrin	you can tell them, we can do a whole day on, how much, waste is generated, kind of thing.		suggest	content	struct								x	
0091	Darrin	We can do kinda this whole i- whole notion of like, what the quality of the stuff is, like "what's in there?" first of all "what's in the sewage?",		suggest	content	concept	struct		add	37					x
0092	Darrin	it's gonna be everything from your shampoo that you wash your hair with, to, um, obviously human waste, to, like- stuff that gets flushed down the toilet, you know, solid stuff, condoms,		refer	content				intro	37				x	
0093	Darrin	I mean all this stuff has to get filtered out.		refer	content	concept				37				x	x
0094	Darrin	So, these are the kinds-													
0095	Darrin	we can do a day where we introduce- what's there,		suggest	content	struct			add	13		x		x	

independent categories of coding should be made. *Speech action* would describe the nature of the utterance and *speech content* would describe the content of the utterance. As shown in Figure 6.1, each utterance would have one exclusive speech-action code while it could have multiple speech-content codes.

The transcript sample shows the application of CCA and its generation and use of coding. The speech-action and speech-content cells that are grayed show the first instance of that particular code. So the following may have been my rationale behind the coding of the first few lines:

74: I've already coded previous cells as positive and neutral judgments, so a negative judgment code is a natural addition.

75: This is an acknowledgement, like previously seen (before this segment).

76: This is a suggestion, like previously seen (before this segment).

77: This is also a suggestion, but made as an explicit alternative to what has come before, so I'll make a new code.

78: This is not just an acknowledgement, as before, but agreement.

79: This is a positive judgment, as previously seen (before this segment).

80: This is different—it is not making a suggestion or judgment but rather a supportive statement.

81: This is another agreement.

Significantly, these codes are not made by considering the data in a vacuum. They reflect my interest in studying how the group forms their curriculum design. In other words, they entail judgments about what I care about.

Too Much Detail. This process yielded a robust corpus of codes for describing the subjects' discussions (specifically, 36 speech-action codes and 24 speech-content codes). Although I felt that these were accurate in that they correctly reflected the data, I also felt there was a difficulty in discerning any pattern. For example, lines 78, 79, and 80 are different types of statements, as reflected in their different coding. But they are also all referring in a supportive manner to the idea of using Stella (a computer modeling program). Which is more important here—the differences or the similarities? My ultimate conclusion was that the similarities were more important—the current scheme provided too much separation.

Adjusting. An adjustment was needed. Reconsidering our conceptual framework provides a solution. The codes I have described look at the participants and ask what they are doing. But this is an investigation of the formation of curriculum as a designed technology. So the better question to ask is what each utterance is doing to the group's project. Aided by that question and the range of speech-action codes, I formed a much more limited set of artifact-action codes:

- *add*—the addition of an element to the curriculum design
- *intro*—the introduction of information or concept to the group discourse, but not an addition to the design
- *sup*—statement meant to support a claim, action, or component of the design
- *summ*—a statement summarizing work
- *chal*—a challenge to a position
- *quest*—a question intended to get information (rather than a challenge or support made in the form of a question)
- *mod*—a statement that only modifies a previous suggestion (rather than makes an addition as well)
- *clar*—a clarification meant to better state a previous suggestion

A similar collapse was made connected to the speech-content codes. A pattern that emerged is that participants assessed potential parts of the project from different perspectives. Again using the initial speech-content codes, I developed a narrower set reflecting those perspectives—what I termed *curricular contexts*, mirroring *evidential contexts*. Therefore, the participants could assess their ideas based on logistics, pedagogy, content, and concepts. When coding the data, I determined not only which of these curricular contexts were being used, but also whether based on that context a positive, neutral, or negative judgment was being made.

Supporting Conclusions. A key concept in CCA is that the process of developing and implementing coding schemes such as those described allows patterns to emerge. As noted, one of these patterns was how participants could make judgments on their ideas using what I called different curricular contexts. Now with the coding in place, those patterns can be more formally verified and supported. Line 80 shows one of many instances where ideas or components that could be supported through multiple contexts would gain considerably in their acceptability.

Professional Development Case

The second case comes from a study on the impact of teachers' participation in a curriculum development project on their science teaching practice. The subjects of this study were two groups of inservice teachers: "Makers," who were involved in the design, writing, and implementation of an innovative science curriculum, and "Users," who were involved only in the implementation phase of the curriculum development project.

Multiple sources of data were collected. Significantly, these included sources originally in electronic form or easily put into electronic form (e.g., interviews, focus groups, e-mails, curriculum artifacts) and sources in hard-copy form (e.g., questionnaires, classroom observation notes, classroom work, project update notes).

The aims of the study included demonstrating the application of concepts from S&TS to teacher practice. That is, the curriculum would be viewed as a technology and teachers as makers and users of this technology. I was particularly interested in how teachers' identities as makers and users influenced their practice and how their roles in the curriculum development project community influenced their proclivity for creating communities of practice in their science classrooms. Consequently, I needed not only to look at individual teachers and their practices, I also had to make comparisons within and across teachers and data types. Therefore, I needed to find a system that would not only allow me to organize my data but also display my data so that I could see connections within and across data types and teachers.

Housing Data. My data were housed in one of two ways—electronically in Microsoft Excel Workbooks or as hard copies in file folders. The audiotaped data were transcribed and put in Workbooks so that I had a Workbook (i.e., file) for each teacher and a Worksheet within the Workbook for each individual data source such as interviews, project updates, classroom observations, and focus group conversations. I had a large file folder for each teacher that included all data in hard-copy form. The data were put in chronological order in both the Workbook and the file folders. I made this decision for organizational purposes and so that I would be able to see change over time.

Immersive Process. To make meaning of my numerous types of data sources, I had to engage in the iterative, immersive process on multiple levels from individual data sources (like one classroom observation) to each larger pool of data (all the classroom observations for one teacher). For example, I listened to my audiotaped data literally dozens of times before transcribing my data and again when coding my data. I did this for several reasons. First, to get an overall sense of the topography of the data I just simply listened to the conversations and listened to my data. Second, to become more familiar with the conversations, I listened again. Third, I listened to take summaries about what I was hearing to begin to synthesize the data. Fourth, I transcribed the audiotapes (typed out the verbatim interview conversation). At this point, I was very familiar with the audiotapes so transcribing didn't involve "hearing" the tapes for the first time and, consequently, it was easy and fast to transcribe and code the data.

Coding. Once I had my audiotaped data transcribed and housed in Workbooks, it was time to begin coding the data. There are three common sources of coding, all of which were used in this study: (1) codes based on theoretical frameworks, (2) codes from previous empirical studies, and (3) codes that emerged from the new data. I used the CCA process for coding all of my data types.

Figure 6.2 is an example of interview data that includes headers that display the organizational format I used: a note to myself to use the quote, a summary of the interviewee talk, analytical codes, and an adaptation column (used to record any changes in coding). *GOAL* ended up being one code that I used as I ana-lyzed Andy's comments about getting students ready for the work place. This **emergent code** refers to a skill (or content) that the teacher wants to impart to students that is not specifically science-based (e.g., how to write, how to think, self-confidence, workplace skills). The emergent code was used in this interview data as well as in other data sources.

Hard-Copy Data. I followed a similar process in reading through my hard-copy data sources from the file folders. For example, in reading over my classroom-observation notes, I made sure to tag interesting quotes from teachers or incidents in the classroom so I could refer to them later. When I found an interesting quote or incident that I thought represented aspects of a teacher's classroom practice or com-munity, I circled the quote with a pen or marker, put an asterisk or star by the cir-cle, and made a note to myself about the quote. I then put a sticky note on the right border of the page, so I had an additional flag that stuck out in my pile of notes. Then I could go directly to this interesting data point easily. I did this so these salient comments made by my teachers were not lost in the process of the overall data analysis. I also applied this process to comments teachers made to me about nonobservation days and other conversations that arose outside of the classroom. Figure 6.3 shows an instance of this involving classroom observation notes.

When I was ready to synthesize a data source, such as a classroom observa-tion for one teacher, I read over my hard-copy data sources again. On a separate sheet of paper I created a bulleted summary outline so I could obtain a sense of the overall points made during the observation. This outline basically amounted to several words or a phrase that represented a synthesis of a key idea, occurrence, or theme. I also copied the tagged quotes from the classroom observation and put them on this summary outline and followed the same process of circling the quote. Each summary outline is now a condensed version of the classroom observation with significant quotes. Figure 6.4 shows one of my summary outlines for one classroom observation. This bulleted outline also has codes in column form on the left side of my outline. I coded these outlines in the same manner I coded the interview data. Note that the code *GOAL* appears again in this data source along with other codes. As a result of this process, each hard-copy data source now had a summary outline

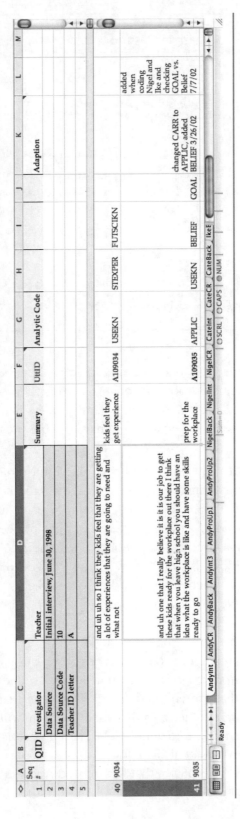

FIGURE 6.2
Sample Interview Data

FIGURE 6.3
Sample Classroom Observation Notes

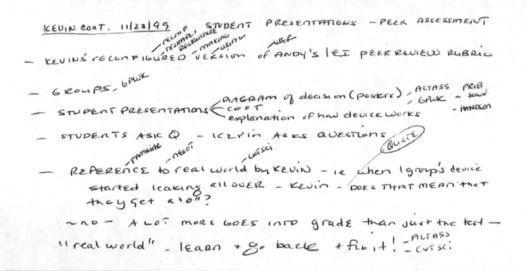

(about a half to one page in length) that includes key themes that emerged, significant instances in the classroom or conversation, tagged quotes, and codes. In addition, note that the tagging and summarizing process is also similar across different data sources like the interview and summary outline presented here.

Triangulating Data. By now I had organized and analyzed my individual data sources by creating summary outlines, flagging salient quotes, and coding interviews and artifacts. I had complete data sets for each subject in my study. At this point, it is likely that researchers, like me, might notice some interesting themes emerge from the data and could possibly see some potential assertions or conclusions unfold. But how do you "know"? How do you make connections between the data sources for each subject and across subjects? Is there a story to tell? In my study, I was able to show the impact of a curriculum development project on my teachers' practices both within and across maker and user groups. I was able to see connections emerge during my analysis.

By triangulating multiple data sources (observations, interviews, ongoing conversations, focus groups, classroom artifacts), I was able to identify several behaviors or evidences that I interpreted as links between teachers' project experiences and their classroom practices. In this case, a common thread of focusing on the workplace and teaming in teachers' classroom practices began to emerge (see Table 6.1). For instance, if you look at the two columns "Workplace" and "Teaming" in Table 6.1, you see that Kevin used Andy's PowerPoint presentation in one of his classroom lessons. This was taken from the classroom observation notes

FIGURE 6.4
Sample Summary Outline

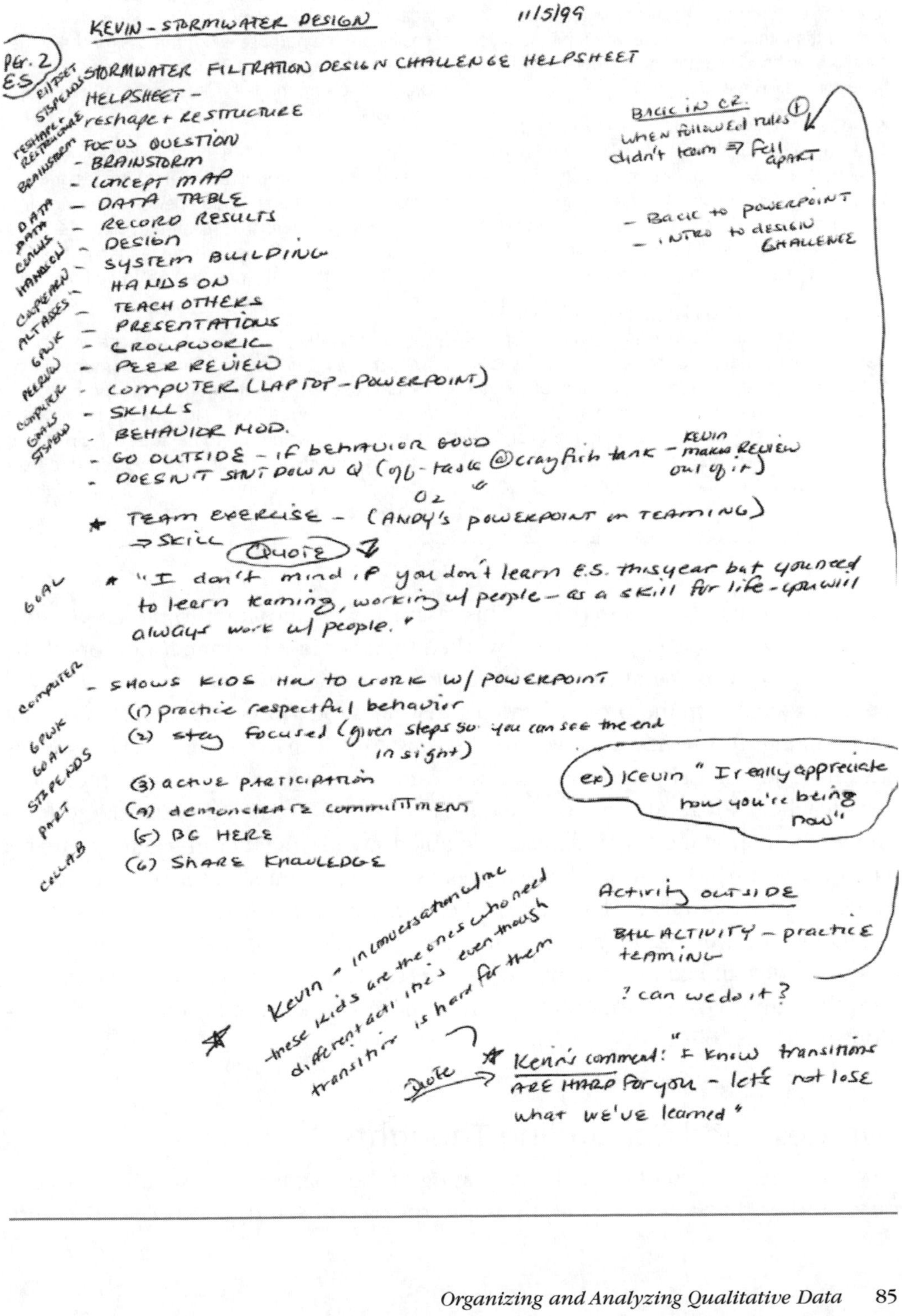

TABLE 6.1
Themes Resulting From Triangulating Multiple Data Sources

Workplace	*Teaming*
Andy: [A.M. Int. 6/98]: "I really believe it is our job to get these kids ready for the workplace out there. I think that when you leave high school you should have an idea what the workplace is like and have some skills ready to go."	Andy's [A.M. Int. 6/99]: "And that comes back again to the philosophy. Like to me, the design challenge, the purpose is not the design challenge, the purpose is getting kids to work in groups, problem solving models. Like they're gonna have throughout life."
Kevin's Basic Environmental Science class [K.U. CrO. 11/00]: After showing Andy's PowerPoint presentation on teaming, Kevin states to his students, "I don't mind if you don't learn environmental science this year, but you do need to learn teaming, working with people is a skill for life. You will always work with people."	Kevin's [K.U. CrO. 11/00]: Kevin talking to his E.S. class during the Stormwater Retention design projects, "When one group's device is leaking all over the place, does that mean they get a "0"? No, a lot more goes into the grade than just the test, it's like the real world, learn and go back and fix it."
Ike [I.U.Int. 4/00]: "You know when they get out and get a job some day there's gonna be people stabbing them in the back constantly and trying not to do as much work as possible and blaming it all on them. You know, that's the way it works—that's human behavior. So deal with it now and see if you can come up with some strategies to get people to work and they don't mind."	Ike [I.U.Int. 4/00]: "This is really how we are being evaluated. I'll get them in a lot more groups and start looking at each other and being more responsible about things.... If someone is blowing something off it's not up to me to say this person's blowing something off—it's up to you. You're the group of four and if you want them to get away with not doing anything...then fine."

depicted in Figure 6.3 (see p. 84). This instance was important to notice because Kevin (a user) and Andy (a maker) worked together in the summer portion of the curriculum development program. Andy ran some of the sessions for user teachers that focused on the project curricula that he wrote. Kevin got this PowerPoint on "teaming" from Andy. I viewed Kevin using Andy's materials in his classroom as one instance that showed the influence a maker teacher had as a mentor on a user teacher, Kevin. Also, if you look at the quote from Andy and the quote from Kevin, the importance of students being able to work together in groups or teams like they will need to in real life emerges as an important skill for both Andy and Kevin to convey in their classrooms. Likewise, you can also see the same sorts of similarities between Andy and Ike, another user teacher who worked with Andy. These quotes all had the common code: *GOAL*. This workplace theme was a pattern that can be traced not only to both of these subjects but also to their interactions with each other.

Synthesis and Concluding Thoughts

The four themes described at the beginning of the chapter were significant to our case studies. Each case entailed multiple reviews of the data sources. The very occurrence of multiple, immersive review was as important as the way in which that review was carried out. Each subsequent review was informed by its precursors. The success of each methodology was, to a large extent, reflected in the degree to which they allowed the tracking of concepts and themes across the wide range and volume of data. Success was also indicated by the picture that the analyzed data could make of the cases. Last, having both a methodological and theoretical framework was crucial. These frameworks allowed us to jump-start the iterative process and simply get started, even if this initial direction was soon changed. They provided guidance as to what was important and aided in overcoming roadblocks. All these combined to move along what was naturally an involved and nonlinear process.

PROBLEM-SOLVING VIGNETTE FOR DISCUSSION

Now, several years after the research studies described in this chapter, we are involved in a new but similar study. Like the curriculum design case, this involves teachers working in small teams to design inquiry-based instructional plans. But, in addition, they are also involved in group discussions to review and critique videos of one another's teaching.

How can analysis of this project use the analysis of the previous project? It would seem that the curriculum design portion can be identical, but is the critiquing portion similar enough? Are there elements of this case that are not captured by the analysis schema created in the context of the design case? And how are the answers to these questions affected by the fact that comparing the design and critiquing portions is a central research question?

TIPS FOR TEACHER RESEARCHERS

Here are a few additional points to keep in mind:

- Don't reinvent the wheel. Use previous research—studies covering similar topics and, perhaps more importantly, studies using a similar methodology.
- Get to know Microsoft Word and Microsoft Excel. These programs have a number of features (e.g., Find and Replace, Tables, Conditional Formatting, Shading) that are often overlooked and have great utility for research.
- Have a system for backing up everything.
- Start your system of organization early so you are not stuck trying to organize, systematize, or format at the end.
- Be patient. When you aren't sure how to proceed, try anything. Play with the data. Seeing how a method fails often gives you clues as to what will work.

QUESTIONS FOR REFLECTION

- Are you representing your subjects accurately?
- When do you stop collecting and analyzing data? How do you know enough is enough?
- What research questions cannot be answered?

REFERENCES

Avery, L.M. (2003). *Knowledge, identity, and teachers' communities of practice.* Unpublished doctoral dissertation, Cornell University, Ithaca.

Bijker, W.E., Hughes, T.P., & Pinch, T. (Eds.). (1999). *The social construction technological systems: New directions in the sociology and history of technology.* Cambridge, MA: MIT Press.

Collins, H.M. (1981a). Son of seven sexes: The social destruction of a physical phenomenon. *Social Studies of Science, 11,* 33–62.

Collins, H.M. (1981b). Stages in the empirical programme of relativism. *Social Studies of Science, 11,* 3–10.

Collins, H.M. (1983). The sociology of scientific knowledge: Studies of contemporary science. *Annual Review of Sociology, 9,* 265–285.

Glaser, B.G. (1969). The constant comparative method of qualitative analysis. In G.L. McCall & J.L. Simmons (Eds.), *Issues in participant observation: A text and reader* (pp. 216–227). Reading, MA: Addison-Wesley.

Grossman, P.L. (1990). *The making of a teacher: Teacher knowledge and teacher education.* New York: Teachers College Press.

Kline, R., & Pinch, T. (1996). Users as agents of technological change: The social construction of the automobile in the rural United States. *Technology and Culture, 37,* 763–795.

Latour, B. (1987). *Science in action: How to follow scientists and engineers through society.* Cambridge, MA: Harvard University Press.

Latour, B., & Woolgar, S. (1986). *Laboratory life: The construction of scientific facts.* Princeton, NJ: Princeton University Press.

Meyer, D.Z. (2003). *Social engagement in curriculum design.* Unpublished doctoral dissertation, Cornell University, Ithaca.

Pinch, T.J. (1981). The sun-set: The presentation of certainty in scientific life. *Social Studies of Science, 11,* 131–158.

Pinch, T.J. (1986). *Confronting nature: The sociology of solar-neutrino detection.* Dordrecht, Holland: D. Reidel.

Pinch, T.J., & Bijker, W.E. (1987). The social construction of facts and artifacts: Or how the sociology of science and the sociology of technology might benefit each other. In W.E. Bijker, T.P. Hughes, & T.J. Pinch (Eds.), *The social construction of technological systems: New directions in the sociology and history of technology* (pp. 17–50). Cambridge, MA: MIT Press.

Shapin, S. (1995). Here and everywhere: Sociology of scientific knowledge. *Annual Review of Sociology, 21,* 289–321.

Yin, R. (1994). *Case study research: Design and methods* (2nd ed., Applied Social Research Methods Series, Vol. 5). Thousand Oaks, CA: Sage.

CHAPTER 7

Collaboration in Teacher Research: Complicated Cooperation

Donna Ware, Christine A. Mallozzi,
Elizabeth Carr Edwards, James F. Baumann

BEFORE-READING QUESTIONS

■ What is collaborative teacher research?

■ How does it work?

O n a Friday afternoon, the students scramble out of Donna's door for a long
weekend break. Donna, a full-time teacher and teacher researcher, rushes around
the classroom as she prepares for her scheduled meeting with Jim and Elizabeth,
coresearchers from the university. Donna gathers her research notebook, calendar, and
reflective journal and piles them on a student desk. Donna has just enough time to race to
the bathroom, grab a bottle of water, and begin setting the room straight for the meeting.
Jim and Elizabeth arrive, and they all settle into the designated tasks of reviewing where
the instructional program they are researching is going and how they might improve it....

[Another time, another project] Donna, Jim, and Christine, also a university researcher,
meet at Jim's house for a data analysis meeting. They prepare for their marathon session by
setting out snacks and settling into their usual places around the coffee table, which is
laden with computers, student work samples, researchers' notes, and several cups of
strong coffee. Christine gets the group going: "All right, does anyone have a suggestion
for how to go about this? There are multiple ways of analyzing all the data."

Introduction

We are all teachers. We are all researchers. We all have worked together on teacher
research projects. As the chapter-opening vignette demonstrates, however, there

Teachers Taking Action: A Comprehensive Guide to Teacher Research, edited by Cynthia A. Lassonde and Susan E. Israel.
© 2008 by the International Reading Association.

are challenges when groups of researchers work together. As Lytle (2000) notes, "There is little disagreement that teacher researchers have complicated relationships to their teaching and research" (p. 696). In this chapter, we examine the complex nature of **collaborative teacher research**, that is, pragmatic inquiries conducted by teachers and others seeking to understand teaching and everyday classroom life (Arhar, Holly, & Kasten, 2001).

Collaboration in teacher research is common. Results of an analysis of the methodologies employed in 34 published teacher research studies (Baumann & Duffy-Hester, 2000) revealed that a significant majority (91%) of them involved collaboration of some kind. Collaborations included groups of teachers working together, teachers and families participating in the research, teachers and students serving as coresearchers, and cooperative studies involving school district and university personnel. This diversity of collaborative models led the reviewers to conclude that the "data affirm the prevalence and power of teachers collaborating with students and others in the teacher-research process" (Baumann & Duffy-Hester, 2000, p. 89).

Although tallying the different types of teacher research collaborations is informative, it says little about the nature or character of various teacher research associations. In the following stories, we each describe our teacher research experiences in different collaborations and our perceptions of the possibilities and complexities of working with others on research projects. We consider a variety of issues that complicate classroom inquiries in ways that lead to sometimes uncomfortable but always productive enterprises.

Our Stories and Perspectives

Donna's Story

Teaching and Teacher Research Experience. I have been an elementary teacher in Athens, Georgia, for more than 30 years, teaching third and fifth grades in schools serving children from low-income families in diverse neighborhoods. I presently work as a literacy coach. My experience with researching began many years ago, asking questions and reading books. I kept a journal and I began filling it up with more questions than answers. In 1995, I chronicled my teaching and my third-grade students' literacy learning in a reflective teacher journal, for which I received the 1995 International Reading Association's (IRA) Regie Routman Teacher Recognition Award ("IRA Salutes Award Winners," 1995).

As a classroom researcher working alone for many years, I kept a reflective journal in which I noted things about my teaching and my students, and I filled pages with questions. I spent many hours reading professional books to find answers. But I was reading about other people's students, other people's problems, other people's answers. In 2002, Jim Baumann contacted me about participating in a research project that would be conducted in my own classroom; I excitedly agreed. I saw this opportunity as a chance to study my practice closely and for my students to enter into meaningful conversations with others. As my four-year-old granddaughter aptly stated as she climbed into my lap, "I need some conversation!" Those exact words are the reason I became a collaborative researcher: I needed some conversations.

Jim and I were awarded an IRA Elva Knight Research Grant to explore a year-long vocabulary instruction program in my fifth-grade classroom. Elizabeth, then a doctoral student at The University of Georgia, joined the project, which we have recently brought to fruition (Baumann, Ware, & Edwards, 2007). The following year, Christine joined Jim and me on a follow-up project, in which we explored the impact of vocabulary instruction on fifth-grade students' word choice, or diction, during writing workshop (Mallozzi, Ware, & Baumann, 2006).

Reflections on Collaborative Teacher Research. My first experience with research was done on my own through my reflective journal in which I constantly questioned my practice. I waded through issues making inferences and trying new things in my classroom. There were few professional conversations with knowledgeable others. I could only assume the changes I made in my teaching led toward more effective teaching...or didn't.

Collaborative research offered a second pair of eyes to really see what was going on in my classroom while I was immersed in teaching, a second pair of ears to listen to my issues and brainstorm alternatives and suggestions, and a second mind to help me understand what I did not understand before. There were drawbacks—the first and foremost being I had to be open to letting others enter my classroom and brave enough to let others really examine what was happening. In *Quantum Teaching: Orchestrating Student Success*, DePorter, Reardon, and Singer-Nourie (1999) state, "Everything from your classroom environment to your body language, from the handouts you distribute to the design of your lesson: everything is sending a message about learning" (p. 7). I knew this and knew that everything I did and wrote would be open to analysis. This was scary. I was lucky to work with three very supportive and nonthreatening cohorts. Jim, Elizabeth, and Christine all spent time in my room observing and teaching. They earned my respect with their willingness to come into my room and teach a group of rowdy fifth graders, and that made me feel more comfortable when they came in to observe me.

I entered the first project with no reservations, excited to be a part of authentic, meaningful research and ready to tackle all the ins and outs of whatever I was asked to do. I soon realized I wasn't going to be asked to do anything. As a member of a collaborative team, I was on equal footing with Jim, Elizabeth, and Christine, and they looked to me for insights and contributions on our research. I admit this was a struggle for me. I had to come around to the realization that what I thought and believed was a relevant part of the research. Still, my comfort zone and knowledge level centered on teaching reading and writing to fifth graders, and the language and process of the research were intimidating. Being part of a collaborative research team allowed me, a busy classroom teacher, to learn so much about my students and my teaching in a way that I could not have done on my own.

Elizabeth's Story

Teaching and Teacher Research Experience. During my first few years of teaching, I taught at several different grade levels. Although my teaching positions changed, every year my students were similar in that they came from low-income, minority backgrounds. What defined me as a teacher was my ability to cross cultural boundaries to make personal connections (Delpit, 1995), causing my students to view me as a caring teacher. This view increased my effectiveness: Because my students knew I cared, they accepted what I was teaching (Dillon, 1989).

Entering the world of research was intimidating. I knew that the only way to overcome such fears was to throw myself wholeheartedly into it. Therefore, my collaborative research began early in graduate school when I worked with a fifth-grade teacher studying narrative writing (Edwards & Perry, 1999). Just when I began to feel comfortable as a researcher, the study ended. I needed more. Like Donna, I needed conversations. Fortunately, Jim asked me to be a part of the Elva Knight study in Donna's classroom (Baumann et al., 2007). I anticipated that a yearlong project would allow me to work with an accomplished researcher, and I knew that Donna was an award-winning teacher from whom I would learn.

Reflections on Collaborative Teacher Research. As I had anticipated, Jim provided apprenticeship support, but at the same time, he treated me as a colleague. With each step and task of the project, his and Donna's reactions to my work reassured me that I had met challenges. What I did not realize at the beginning of the project was that my knowledge and confidence as a researcher would grow not only because of Jim, but also because of Donna. I quickly learned that we all were to take on different roles, and when we gathered for meetings I was impressed by Donna's insights. Although I knew that she was an exceptional teacher, I came to see her in another light. She was also an extraordinary researcher, and every time I entered her room I would note something about her teaching to share later with my preservice teachers. Donna kept me current by demonstrating teaching at its finest.

Although there were many positive aspects that came with collaborative research, there was also one negative aspect. When I embarked on my first project, I returned not only to the school where I had spent four years teaching but also to the exact classroom. As I entered the school for the first meeting, I was excited. There were a few minutes left before dismissal, so I listened and watched as Mr. Perry, the classroom teacher, interacted with his students. Immediately, I could sense the closeness between them, and it was enjoyable to watch. Then I was overcome by an emotion that I had not anticipated—emptiness. I recognized its root. I knew that no matter how long the research project lasted, no matter how much effort I put into making connections with students, those connections would never be on the same level as when I was the classroom teacher. Sure, these students would like me, and they would open their lives to me as I spent time there. Still, the experience would be different. My role had changed. I was no longer the teacher. I was a guest teacher. Perhaps it was naïve of me to expect anything different; it was just something I had to accept.

Christine's Story

Teaching and Teacher Research Experience. I taught fifth and sixth grade for five years in a small school district near Cincinnati, Ohio. As a teacher, I used classroom inquiry, whereby students investigated published texts and examples of writing to determine the characteristics of a certain genre or the qualities of strong writing.

I quickly realized that this highly intuitive process was time-consuming but valuable. Unfortunately, because of the constraints of teaching duties, I found that using inquiry to explore my own teaching while teaching was more than I could handle. When the opportunity came to work with Donna as she investigated her teaching practices, I found myself very interested to be a part of this challenge. During the study exploring diction in students' writing (Mallozzi, Baumann, & Ware, 2007; Mallozzi et al., 2006), I was a participant observer, getting to know the students, conducting student interviews and gathering data, and exploring three focal case study students. This study offered a hopeful connection between my former life as an elementary school teacher and my new life as a doctoral student and researcher.

Reflections on Collaborative Teacher Research. Part of the challenges I faced as a new doctoral student came from my volition to challenge myself to get involved with research and whether I felt ready. Hoping that I might establish myself as an academic "go-getter," I expressed my interest to Jim, who was my advisor at the time. When he offered the possibility of working with Donna and him on a collaborative teacher research project, I was intrigued. This project seemed like an apropos way to stay connected to classroom teaching and to have a chance to inch into the research world—perhaps I missed being with students or perhaps research in classrooms seemed less "ivory tower." This challenge held promise, but I could not anticipate all I would learn.

Collaborative communities of teacher research and teacher learning (Cochran-Smith & Lytle, 1993) may not look the same as they have been described in the past. Traditionally, in collaborative teacher research projects the **campus-based re-searchers**, who serve as university faculty researchers, and the **classroom-based teacher researchers**, who serve as classroom teachers studying their practices, were called to bridge the divide between the university and school sites. My experiences in this project taught me that it is difficult to determine when Donna, Jim, or I were acting as teachers and when we were acting as researchers. Aren't there elements of each constantly active in any teacher research collaborative project? Further, con-crete aspects of the collaborative research sites tend to bleed. For our project, this played out as we combined classroom visits, face-to-face meetings in Jim's home, and Web-based sharing. In a constantly changing, globalized world, components of collaborative learning among educators are being opened up and shared not only across university and classroom sites but across hemispheres, cultures, and languages (Laferrière, Lamon, & Chan, 2006). From engaging in this project, the body of work that counts as collaborative teacher research projects may be more complicated than I initially thought.

My initial assumptions about collaboration were confronted in productive ways. I assumed everyone in a collaborative effort has the same theoretical outlook and goals. The deeper we proceeded into the project—namely, when we began to write up the research for an article submission—I realized that we had never dis-cussed theories (Crotty, 2003). We guessed that our counterparts saw the world in the same way, but in naming an ad hoc theory for our research it was clear that dif-ferent paradigms were at work. Our successful collaborative endeavor served as evidence that a completely unified viewpoint was not necessary. After all, several people with the same views add nothing to collaboration except confirmatory "preaching to the choir." Surprisingly, I was convinced of the value in periodic the-oretical conversations during the process to discuss the relationship of theory and data over a decision made at the beginning or end of the project.

I realized collaboration was not a steady course but was marked by ebb and flow. Our collaboration did not look like every person pitching in 100% of the time with a shared and gentle leadership. In actuality, at different stages of the process and with different tasks, one or more of us held the reigns on the project. This occurred for several reasons, such as a loosening of one person's schedule, en-thusiasm, expertise for a certain portion of the project, or a necessity to reach a cer-tain deadline. Sometimes no one really wanted to lead the group, but someone always volunteered for the good of the research. This fluidity allowed each per-son's strengths to lend power to the project.

I was particularly worried about leaving the "teacher" out of the teacher re-search, and we often asked Donna how she felt when schedules and deadlines necessitated us moving on despite her packed teaching schedule. Donna often re-iterated that teaching needed her concentration. Frankly, this was just what I would have wanted a talented professional teacher to say, but I tried to remain sensitive that many a teacher research project has been taken over by university researchers

(Goldstein, 2000). Still, I trusted in Donna and the working relationship that we had built. I believed that our rapport continually rested on our being respectful and trustworthy to one another, and I had faith that neither the others nor I would put that relationship at risk. The changes in attention and leadership given to this project did not mean that we were more or less successful than any romanticized version of collaboration that I had imagined (Cochran-Smith & Lytle, 1993). I had realized there was no ideal type of collaboration—only what worked for us.

Jim's Story

Teaching and Teacher Research Experience. In the 1990s, I became involved with classroom inquiry through the National Reading Research Center's School Research Consortium, a teacher research community (Allen, Shockley, & Baumann, 1995). A **teacher research community** is a network "of individuals who enter with other teachers into a collaborative search for definition and satisfaction in their work lives as teachers and who regard research as part of larger efforts to transform teaching, learning, and schooling" (Cochran-Smith & Lytle, 1992, p. 298). The work Donna, Elizabeth, Christine, and I engaged in involved small-scale teacher research communities.

An early foray into teacher research was in my second-grade classroom, in which Gay Ivey, then a doctoral student and participant observer, and I investigated my strategy/literature-based program (Baumann & Ivey, 1997). In another study, I worked with two fifth-grade teachers, Helene and Pat, on a yearlong study of comprehension instruction in a trade book–based reading program (Baumann, Hooten, & White, 1999). Subsequently, Elizabeth, Christine, and I, as they have noted, have had the pleasure of conducting research on vocabulary as guests in Donna's fifth-grade classroom.

Reflections on Collaborative Teacher Research. What have I learned about collaboration in teacher research? First, the research questions and impetus for a study can come from different persons and sources. For example, in the second-grade study, I asked how a program integrating reading strategies with literature would unfold. Gay was comfortable with this question, and she subsequently joined me in the study. In contrast, in the reading comprehension/trade book study, Helene and Pat wanted to move away from traditional basal instruction, and I wondered about teaching comprehension in a literature-based framework. Thus, we co-constructed a research question that addressed our collective musings. In our first vocabulary study, Donna was intrigued by how some students demonstrated vocabulary growth in writing. Thus, she proposed a follow-up study exploring vocabulary instruction and composition more explicitly, with Christine and I embracing Donna's question. Teacher research questions can come from different sources

(Baumann, Allen, & Shockley, 1994), so one lesson I have learned is to be aware of, listen for, and construct research questions with all collaborators.

Second, there are potential tensions related to the roles researchers may assume in collaborative studies. For instance, the role of the classroom teacher researcher and the role of the guest or visiting researcher in a classroom study differ. Whereas Elizabeth, Christine, and I had the opportunity to come and go from Donna's classroom with time to analyze data and reflect on the study back at our offices, Donna had no such luxury. She was there day in and day out preparing to teach and teaching. Her responsibility was for the academic and social welfare of her students, and sometimes the research had to be subordinate to her teaching.

I have some appreciation for this tension. Early in my second-grade study it was difficult for me to provide sufficient attention to data collection and analysis, given that my primary role as the children's teacher had to take precedence over the research (Baumann, 1996). The collaboration with Gay eased this tension and enabled me to continue to teach with full verve while Gay assumed more of the data-gathering responsibilities. Some teacher researchers report that teaching and researching are fully integrated or "organic" (Allen & Shockley, 1996) while others do not. Although teaching and researching in my classroom were very rewarding, they never quite attained an organic level of complementarity.

Third, the multiple viewpoints we brought to the research were important features of our collaborations. Having multiple sets of eyes to examine classroom interactions, multiple ears to listen to the audiotapes, and multiple perspectives for examining data brought insights that would have not emerged without one another. There were times when Christine, Elizabeth, or I would point out student interactions that Donna could not observe during her teaching. There were times when Donna set us straight about the background for an instructional action on her part that we had missed. There were times that Gay told me that my interpretation of a lesson was all wrong given my myopic view. Although not always efficient and comfortable, our candid discussions brought greater depth to our analyses and interpretations than had we drawn conclusions only from a single perspective.

The Complexity of Teacher Research Collaborations

What do our individual stories mean? Is there any commonality in their diversity? One clear theme we see is the complexity of collaborations. Lytle (2000) argues that in teacher research "teaching issues and research issues…become complexly entangled with each other" (p. 697). Evidence of this entanglement comes from the occasional ambiguity of our roles. Sometimes we taught; sometimes we observed; sometimes we did both. Sometimes we were not sure which role or roles we were assuming. In a professor–classroom teacher collaboration, Edelsky and Boyd

(1993) talked about their "interesting intermingling of roles" in which they would "switch back and forth as we each became a student or an expert" (p. 12).

It is our experience that such role switching can be both productive and disconcerting. Role switching enabled us to see and feel the inquiry from multiple stances, enhancing insight on the implementation and analysis phases of our studies. But there also was disconcertment, often because of vulnerabilities we felt. Whether it was Christine's, Elizabeth's, or Jim's discomfort with exposing their "rusty" teaching skills to Donna's gaze, or Donna's uneasiness with opening her private classroom world to the critical eyes of her university guests, we all experienced disquietude at times. Hubbard and Power (1999) note how "teacher researchers challenge the identity of university researchers" (p. 245), and Lytle (2000) acknowledges how "teacher researchers open their teaching *practice* up to...examination, critique, and evaluation" (p. 697). Such is the intrigue of revealing ourselves to one another as teachers and researchers in collaborations.

Another complexity involves attribution for collaborative projects. We considered our work to be egalitarian, so it was never an issue of whether we all were coresearchers and hence coauthors on research products. But determining whose name went first, second, and so forth was not so clear. Should it be the person who wrote the grant, the one who did most of the teaching, the person who wrote more of the words on the report, or the researcher who provided the most conceptual work? What were the "rules" of collaborative authorship (Fine & Kurdek, 1993)? Academia can often privilege the research reporting over the process of the research, negating the important work that has steered the project to an endpoint. Attending to the matter of authorship in a collaborative teacher research project is something that we continually spoke of but never mastered. We wish we had clear-cut guidelines to offer, but the best we can suggest is for teams to have frank conversations about authorship and to revisit them as a project unfolds. As a case in point, the authorship of this chapter changed from an initial default alphabetical listing of names to its final reverse alphabetical listing, which we believe reflected Donna's prominence as the source for this writing (although Donna protested right up to the final revision, writing in an e-mail, "I liked the ABC listing of contributing authors you had first").

In conclusion, we hope that our exploration of the complicated cooperation of teacher research provides insight on how classroom inquiry can be enriching and productive when various professionals work together on studies meaningful to all involved. In a description of a study involving several teacher and university communities, teacher researcher Zoe Donoahue (1996) noted that "teacher research often begins with one teacher working alone with his or her students, but its full power and influence is not felt until the community is extended beyond the classroom walls" (p. 102). The subsequent "complex entanglement" (Lytle, 2000) endemic to collaborative teacher research studies that go beyond the confines of a single classroom can result in greater depth and richness, as Donoahue

(1996) reported: "Collaboration, communication, and community were central to the effectiveness of our inquiry" (p. 106). This also was true for us, so we encourage others interested in examining classroom questions to work together in the messy, complicated, and enriching world of collaborative teacher research.

Synthesis and Concluding Thoughts

Collaborative teacher inquiry may not be for every literacy researcher. If you are uncomfortable with sharing decision making, living with a degree of uncertainty, and navigating the inevitable questions and problems inherent in teacher research, a collaborative effort is probably not for you. If, however, you have a research question that is amenable to a classroom inquiry, know colleagues or other professionals who share your passion for action-oriented research, and are willing to enter the complex world of classrooms and schools, we urge you to engage in teacher research. Doing so will be a fulfilling, productive, and beneficial experience for you, your coresearchers, and your research participants.

PROBLEM-SOLVING VIGNETTE FOR DISCUSSION

Imagine that you and a colleague are both fourth-grade teachers and have decided to study alternative assessments that will better inform your reading and writing instruction. You have several decisions to make before engaging in your study. One is to decide whether to invite a university professor to join the project. The professor is well informed about literacy assessments, but you do not know her well and wonder if she understands classroom issues. How do you determine whether and how to expand your research team to three people?

Another issue involves how to negotiate with your principal to use some of the time normally dedicated for test preparation for the district's high-stakes assessment for implementing various performance assessments. How will you approach your principal about this? What rationale will you use to argue that your plans for alternative assessments will not impede the students' performance on the standardized test?

TIPS FOR TEACHER RESEARCHERS

From our experiences in collaborative teacher research, we suggest that prospective teams consider the following:

- Identify coresearchers you know and trust and with whom you have common interests.

- Construct and refine research questions that address the interests of all researchers.

- Determine goals for division of labor up front, knowing that these may need to be revised. Talk about who will provide the instruction, gather data, analyze data, and draft reports.

- Discuss authorship order and how it may rotate across papers and presentations.

- Communicate often and candidly regarding the planning and implementation of the study.

QUESTIONS FOR REFLECTION

- Think about a potential joint research effort. In what ways does this project lend itself to working with fellow teachers or other literacy professionals?

- How do you envision the project promoting student learning and your teaching ability?

- How might you negotiate with others about the planning and implementation of the study?

REFERENCES

Allen, J., & Shockley, B. (1996). Composing a research dialogue: University and school research communities encountering a cultural shift. *Reading Research Quarterly, 31*, 220–228.

Allen, J., Shockley, B.B., & Baumann, J.F. (1995). Gathering 'round the kitchen table: Teacher inquiry in the NRRC school research consortium. *The Reading Teacher, 48*, 526–529.

Arhar, J.M., Holly, M.L., & Kasten, W.C. (2001). *Action research for teachers: Traveling the yellow brick road*. Upper Saddle River, NJ: Prentice Hall.

Baumann, J.F. (1996). Conflict or compatibility in classroom inquiry? One teacher's struggle to balance teaching and research. *Educational Researcher, 25*(7), 29–36.

Baumann, J.F., Allen, J., & Shockley, B. (1994). Questions teachers ask: A report from the National Reading Research Center School Research Consortium. In C.K. Kinzer & D.J. Leu (Eds.), *Multidimensional aspects of literacy research, theory, and practice* (43rd yearbook of the National Reading Conference, pp. 474–484). Chicago: National Reading Conference.

Baumann, J.F., & Duffy-Hester, A.M. (2000). Making sense of classroom worlds: Methodology in teacher research. In M.L. Kamil, P.B. Mosenthal, P.D. Pearson, & R. Barr (Eds.), *Handbook of reading research* (Vol. 3, pp. 77–98) Mahwah, NJ: Erlbaum.

Baumann, J.F., Hooten, H., & White, P. (1999). Teaching comprehension through literature: A teacher-research project to develop fifth graders' reading strategies and motivation. *The Reading Teacher, 53*, 38–51.

Baumann, J.F., & Ivey, G. (1997). Delicate balances: Striving for curricular and instructional equilibrium in a second-grade, literature/strategy-based classroom. *Reading Research Quarterly, 32*, 244–275.

Baumann, J.F., Ware, D., & Edwards, E.C. (2007). "Bumping into spicy, tasty words that catch your tongue": A formative experiment on vocabulary instruction. *The Reading Teacher, 61*, 108–122.

Cochran-Smith, M., & Lytle, S.L. (1992). Communities for teacher research: Fringe or forefront? *American Journal of Education, 100*, 298–324.

Cochran-Smith, M., & Lytle, S.L. (Eds.). (1993). *Inside/outside: Teacher research and knowledge*. New York: Teachers College Press.

Crotty, M. (2003). *The foundations of social research: Meaning and perspective in the research process.* Thousand Oaks, CA: Sage.

Delpit, L. (1995). *Other people's children: Cultural conflict in the classroom.* New York: New Press.

DePorter, B., Reardon, M., & Singer-Nourie, S. (1999). *Quantum teaching: Orchestrating student success.* Boston: Allyn & Bacon.

Dillon, D.R. (1989). Showing them that I want them to learn and that I care about who they are: A microethnography of the social organization of a secondary low-track English-reading classroom. *American Educational Research Journal, 26,* 227–259.

Donoahue, Z. (1996). Collaboration, community, and communication: Modes of discourse for teacher research. In Z. Donoahue, M.A. Van Tassell, & L. Patterson (Eds.), *Research in the classroom: Talk, texts, and inquiry* (pp. 91–107). Newark, DE: International Reading Association.

Edelsky, C., & Boyd, C. (1993). Collaborative research: More questions than answers. In S.J. Hudelson & J.W. Lindfors (Eds.), *Delicate balances: Collaborative research in language education* (pp. 4–20). Urbana, IL: National Council of Teachers of English.

Edwards, E.C., & Perry, D.P. (1999). Instructing low-achieving, fifth-grade students in story structure: Effects on narrative writing. In J.F. Baumann (Chair), *Academic diversity: Theory, issues, and studies.* Symposium conducted at the annual meeting of the National Reading Conference, Orlando, FL.

Fine, M.A., & Kurdek, L.A. (1993). Reflections on determining authorship credit and authorship order on faculty-student collaborations. *American Psychologist, 48,* 1141–1147.

Goldstein, L.S. (2000). Ethical dilemmas in designing collaborative research: Lessons learned the hard way. *International Journal of Qualitative Studies in Education, 13,* 517–530.

Hubbard, R.S., & Power, B.M. (1999). *Living the questions: A guide for teacher-researchers.* York, ME: Stenhouse.

IRA salutes award winners. (1995, June/July). *Reading Today, 12,* 34–35.

Laferrière, T., Lamon, M., & Chan, C.K.K. (2006). Emerging e-trends and models in teacher education and professional development. *Teaching Education, 17,* 75–90.

Lytle, S.L. (2000). Teacher research in the contact zone. In M.L. Kamil, P.B. Mosenthal, P.D. Pearson, & R. Barr (Eds.), *Handbook of reading research* (Vol. 3, pp. 691–718). Mahwah, NJ: Erlbaum.

Mallozzi, C.A., Baumann, J.F., & Ware, D.B. (2007, April). *"Sounds right," "Makes sense": A case study of vocabulary and writing composition in a fifth-grade reading-writing classroom.* Paper presented at the annual meeting of the American Educational Research Association, Chicago, IL.

Mallozzi, C.A., Ware, D., & Baumann, J.F. (2006, December). *Finding the "just-right" word: A case study of diction development in a fifth-grade reading-writing classroom.* Paper presented at the 56th annual meeting of the National Reading Conference, Los Angeles, CA.

PART IV

Supportive Strategies and Funding

Part Opener: Facing Research Issues and Perceived Stumbling Blocks
Mark A. Hogan

Elaine, the literacy coach at Elison Primary Elementary School (pseudonym), faces a dilemma: Does she listen to her colleagues' concerns about the new Reading First model, or does she ignore the concerns and follow the district's direction? For Elaine, it is not an easy decision. She knows that reading comprehension scores indicate second-grade students are not progressing as well as they should. Two specific populations, Title I and English-language learners, are showing very little growth. Her former colleagues, the second-grade team, blame the decline on the school district's decision to move to a highly structured reading program. The principal just wants the problem to be solved.

Taking a proactive stance, Elaine solicits approval from the principal for the second-grade team to become teacher researchers. Throughout the process, Elaine encounters potential stumbling blocks and critical research issues that might derail the research study. Elaine takes time to instruct her colleagues about these stumbling blocks: the desire to use studies to prove biased beliefs, the extra time required to participate, the distrust of research that can be used to create agenda-laden policy, and the fear that engaging in classroom research will negatively influence student growth.

Ultimately, the greatest growth that Elaine and the second-grade team discover is finding a voice for their practice. By becoming informed teachers—that is, after having read related research, conducted in-class research on their practice, and analyzed data to support their claims—they are able to speak to concerns about a curriculum. (To read the complete case study, go to this book's link on the IRA website at www.reading.org and click on Case Study #4: Facing Research Issues and Perceived Stumbling Blocks.)

By employing techniques similar to those presented in chapters 8 through 10, Elaine helps to move the research design forward. As you continue to read part IV, you will gain valuable information and learn strategies for preventing and managing stumbling blocks and critical issues that challenge the integrity of your research. You will also learn several strategies teachers can use for securing funds.

CHAPTER 8

Coping With the Stumbling Blocks in Teacher Research

Deborah Eldridge, Michelle Stein, Alyson Wasko, Alexandra Peña

BEFORE-READING QUESTIONS

■ What is the difference between a stumbling block and a barrier to teacher research?

■ What are some of the stumbling blocks that relate to teacher research?

■ What strategies or processes can you use to overcome these stumbling blocks?

Alyson, Michelle or "Shelly," and Alexandra, three teacher researchers, begin their individual studies with enthusiasm. Alyson wants to know more about the impact of family contact in her high school, Shelly wants to learn how teacher perceptions of students influence student learning, and Alexandra wants to know how to help an unmotivated and reluctant but gifted student in her class. And at first they each think that finding the answers to their questions seems so easy to do! Then, the stumbling blocks begin to appear. Alyson is told she can't survey the teachers in her school, Shelly finds that not many teachers share her enthusiasm, and Alexandra finds that time itself is against her.

Consequently, they each discover ways to adapt, adjust, and overcome the stumbling blocks to their research. Alyson limits herself to her classroom records (self-study), Shelly provides incentives (schoolwide survey), and Alexandra cuts back on the volume of activities and interviews that she originally intended to conduct (case study).

Introduction

The reality is that any teacher research project, no matter how meticulously planned, will encounter stumbling blocks that must be overcome for the project

Teachers Taking Action: A Comprehensive Guide to Teacher Research, edited by Cynthia A. Lassonde and Susan E. Israel.
© 2008 by the International Reading Association.

to proceed. Stumbling blocks are different from barriers. **Stumbling blocks** are actual events or circumstances that precipitate a change in a teacher's research plan. **Barriers**, on the other hand, are potential or actual internal or external conflicts that inhibit or prevent engagement in teacher research. A stumbling block, in other words, is a bump in the road, or even a detour. A barrier is a trip cancellation or postponement.

This chapter explores the reality of conducting teacher research once the research question is formed, the research design is described, and the data collection is about to begin or is in progress. The three teacher researchers who report on their research projects in this chapter each encountered stumbling blocks to their original research plans. Their stumbling blocks are unique because each teacher's research project was personal, based on each individual's concern, interest, or issue with school policy, the individual's practice, or a student in the classroom. This variability in focus, circumstances, and context make stumbling blocks, unlike barriers, difficult to anticipate or even to characterize. Therefore, this chapter presents the stumbling blocks in relation to each unique project rather than as an artificially typical set or class of impediment to teacher research.

The strategies for overcoming stumbling blocks are, necessarily, as unique as the circumstances and settings in which they occur. As each teacher describes her intended research plan and the stumbling blocks that caused her to adjust her plan, it becomes apparent that the strategies for overcoming stumbling blocks are situational and best characterized as decision-making endeavors. In other words, given a unique set of circumstances surrounding an individual research project, the most appropriate strategy for overcoming a stumbling block is apparently a process, rather than a strategy, of identifying alternatives and deciding which one offers the best way to proceed.

A Brief Overview of Barriers to Teacher Research

Throughout the 1990s while teachers were becoming involved in classroom-based research, educators' concerns about the existence of barriers to teacher research began to arise for two reasons: (1) Some barriers were preventing or inhibiting teachers in conducting research (Fischer et al., 2000; Nixon, 1987) and (2) teacher research was not widely accepted within the education community (Cochran-Smith & Lytle, 1990, 1999). These two reasons for concern contextualized a long list of barriers that were internal to a teacher's efficacy as a researcher and external to a teacher's classroom while the teacher struggles for a voice within the research community that existed outside a teacher's research.

Barriers that affect a teacher's efficacy as a researcher include being overwhelmed with the two roles of being a teacher and a researcher (Fischer et al., 2000). Teachers have expressed discomfort with open-ended questions, with finding there are no easy beginnings, and with discovering there is no straightforward process for getting the research completed (Nixon, 1987). Other barriers include finding time to write and encountering a dilemma in doing research because it takes a teacher away from the students (Fischer et al., 2000). In addition, there is some concern about teachers having a basic contempt for research that prevents them from engaging with it (Cochran-Smith & Lytle, 1992).

Barriers to teacher research having a voice and a place in the research community stemmed from teachers not having a community to share a common language for their process and findings (Cochran-Smith & Lytle, 1992). There has been a huge debate amongst researchers in higher education over the validity of the methodology of teacher research (Cochran-Smith & Lytle, 1990; Nixon, 1987) as well as a growing criticism of teacher research in general amongst academic researchers (Cochran-Smith & Lytle, 1999). In addition, there is concern that the culture of schools is against teachers asking questions about their practice and positioning teachers in roles that are knowledge based, but not knowledge generating (Cochran-Smith & Lytle, 1992). Any and all of these barriers could result in a teacher's decision to dismiss teacher research as a legitimate professional endeavor, to abandon research as a way to learn, or to discontinue or postpone a research project when support for it is minimal or nonexistent.

There are other impediments to teacher research that have less to do with the larger questions of the legitimacy of teacher research or teachers' perceptions of themselves as researchers. There are stumbling blocks that a teacher researcher may encounter while engaged in research that are simply the occupational hazard of asking a question and gathering data as a way to answer it. Stumbling blocks are day-to-day, mostly unanticipated, circumstances or events that cause a teacher to adjust a research plan.

Navigating the Stumbling Blocks in Teacher Research

If teacher research is to gain respectability with teachers and acceptability with researchers, there needs to be a common acceptance and discussion of the hazards of doing research. Every one of us experiences delays and stumbling blocks as we engage with research. Barriers and stumbling blocks shouldn't be confused. Researchers, including teacher researchers, need to engage in a dialogue about the degrees of flexibility in research plans, about what constitutes unacceptable alternatives, and about the boundaries that, when overstepped, compromise the integrity of a project. Teachers, particularly, need to understand that research is a messy and ever-changing endeavor and to learn to distinguish stumbling blocks from barriers. In learning to tell them apart, teachers learn to cope with them.

The following three stories of navigating around the stumbling blocks in teacher research highlight the unanticipated events or circumstances that will occur in teacher research. Each of the three teachers responded to their unique stumbling blocks by making adjustments in their research plans as needed and by learning what to do and not to do in the future. The Tips for Teacher Researchers feature at the end of this chapter synthesizes these teachers' experiences into five "nuggets" for anticipating or preventing the kinds of stumbling blocks they encountered. It is important to remember, however, that stumbling blocks will happen to you, too. The key is to make a decision about how to navigate them, just as these teacher researchers did, without giving up all together.

Alyson's Story: A Schoolwide Study That Became a Self-Study

As a high school science teacher in a diverse setting in the Northeast, I started out wanting to investigate how family involvement affects student behavior. My original idea was to collect as much data as possible from teachers about how they involve families, and then analyze the results in terms of the impact on student behavior. I wanted to devise a list of interventions used with students from both the school and home, such as calls home from school and family-student signed contracts. Unfortunately, I was thwarted by a stumbling block that threatened to undermine my entire project—my district does not allow the surveying of staff or students without previous written consent from central administration, and then only after a formal written request has been submitted and reviewed by district personnel. As this was a final project for a master's course and it was already June, I had only three weeks left. The district proposal process usually took at least a month. Therefore, I couldn't investigate the school's approach to family involvement. Although I wanted a larger data pool to help me understand the impact of what we were doing as a whole school, I had to limit my vision. Instead, I decided to engage in a **self-study**, or an exploration of my experience, to understand the issue of family involvement and its impact on student behavior. For the self-study, I used family communication and school intervention from my experience during the current year to see how student behavior was affected. It was probably easier to limit my study to my experiences, but I had to sacrifice the more extensive information I would have gathered in a schoolwide study.

Instead of creating a survey to ask my colleagues about the frequency and type of interventions they used with their students, I looked more closely at the tools I used for organization of family communications. I had created a form in September to keep a record of all verbal family communications. The **Family Call Log Sheet**, a teacher-created record of family contacts and outcomes, included the student's name, time of call, outcome of call (conversation or message), and a section for a brief overview of the communication. (See Appendix B for a reproducible version of the log.) This log provided documentation that could be referenced later by an administrator or myself as needed. I could also use it simply to document how many attempts were made to leave messages. These forms, instead of the survey I had constructed, served as my data on family involvement. I could analyze why I had contacted the family members, what they had said, and whether the contact had been successful in reaching the family member and having a discussion.

In addition, I had access to schoolwide **student referral forms**, a school-specific disciplinary referral form of behavioral infractions and interventions. (See Appendix B for a reproducible form.) These forms were useful to track the effect of family communications on student behavior. By matching the forms to the dates of family communication, I could determine whether family involvement or a disciplinary intervention had been successful. Having effective and useful tools made it easier to identify a data source and to assemble all of the paperwork when it came time for data analysis, organization, and reflection.

Navigating the stumbling blocks taught me three important lessons. The first lesson is to make sure that you invite as many people as you can to give you feedback on your research plan well in advance of beginning the research. I had very knowledgeable staff in my school to let me know what the procedure for surveys was, but I should have asked much earlier. Everything has a procedure and a policy; you just have to investigate properly. Of course, having an alternative plan is essential. That is my second lesson. My third and final lesson is to give yourself enough time to adjust your project, if necessary. Although I budgeted my time, I needed much more time when it came down to actually doing the research.

Shelly's Story: Conducting Surveys

As a novice teacher, I often look to my colleagues for guidance and support. Therefore, polling my colleagues seemed like a natural approach to answering my research question: Does a teacher's interest in the personal lives of his or her students have an impact on classroom management? I adopted a **schoolwide survey methodology** to collect information by asking a set of structured questions to colleagues who were representative of a defined population (in this case, high school teachers). I prepared myself as best I knew how: My questions were clear, the spreadsheet was complete, and the letter to my colleagues explaining the purpose along with other useful information about my research was ready to be distributed. Deadlines were set to allow sufficient time to compile my data and complete my analysis. I sent out a preliminary e-mail to my colleagues explaining the packet of information they would soon be receiving. Then, I photocopied everything and placed it in each mailbox.

When conducting a schoolwide survey, it is important to remember that you can never be too prepared. Plan as meticulously as you can, but always leave room for unexpected changes. First and foremost, you must make sure that you are not violating any school policy in polling your colleagues. Although this was not a problem in my district, many of my peers who teach in other districts, such as

Alyson's, were unable to poll their colleagues when looking for opinions on a specific study. In my case, getting approval to proceed was the easiest part. As it turned out, my stumbling block was getting the surveys back from my colleagues in a timely manner.

Once you are given the permission, you can begin the polling process. I planned to make the process as easy as possible, not only for my colleagues but also for myself. For those reasons, I printed a hard copy and placed it in each mailbox, in addition to sending an electronic copy through e-mail. I did not hear any complaints from colleagues about receiving duplicate copies and determined that it catered to both those who are electronically inclined and those who are not. In addition, both methods allowed me to compile my data and analyze the results quickly and efficiently. You may choose one method, both, or another of your choice; in any case identify a few critical friends to give you ideas and feedback during your research.

No matter which method you choose, remember that timing is everything. Before you even begin your survey, you need to know the length of time you have to complete your research. I recommend working backward from your deadline by estimating the time for revising, compiling data, distributing the survey, draft writing, and other important components to your work. From this estimate, you can set a deadline for the distribution and return of the surveys, making sure to allow colleagues a reasonable amount of time to contribute. Remember that your colleagues are teachers, mothers, fathers, and graduate students who also have responsibilities to attend to beyond the walls of the school. If at all possible, try to distribute your survey at a time in the year that is less busy than others. Holiday seasons, examination periods, the end of grading terms, or the last few weeks of school may be a poor time to poll your colleagues.

Although I did not have 100% participation, I believe my study was successful. However, as I mentioned previously, even though I thought I was prepared, I faced a stumbling block that I hadn't anticipated—that is, getting back the surveys in a timely manner. Based on this experience, the next time I use a survey to collect data, I plan to poll more people than I really need to ensure I have the numbers I want, and I plan to follow up with people—and more often. In this case, I did send e-mail reminders to my colleagues, but I could have done so more often. I also plan to make the surveys easier to complete, as I found that lengthy surveys that ask a lot of information might be a turn-off. Of course now I know that another alternative is to look into administering the surveys by computer, using a survey site such as SurveyMonkey.com. Sites such as this one offer templates for designing surveys, which can save a lot of time. They typically offer free memberships but may restrict you from asking certain questions important to your research.

Alexandra's Story: Case Study Research

When I started my research I wanted to know why, despite having strong potential for excellence, one of my fifth-grade students appeared unmotivated and disinterested in learning. I planned a case study, a research design most appropriate to answer my questions about why (he was so disinterested) and how (I could engage him more fully). But I ran out of time. It was the end of the school year when I had the yearly testing schedule to complete. In addition to intense test-preparation stress, my lunch and preparation periods disappeared because of meetings and other demands on my time. Instead of the month-long period over which I planned to interview and observe my student, I had a little more than a week to complete the project.

The stumbling block of pressing commitments was compounded by the stumbling block of the student being absent from my class for almost five days. Amidst the chaos of year-end activities and demands, the student was missing on the days that I thought I had time to meet or work with him. What if, as disengaged in schooling as he was, he simply "dropped out" for the last two or three weeks? What would I have done then? Or what if he had not agreed to work with me? I should have made alternative plans (more than one of them) for what could have gone wrong.

Another stumbling block of sorts was deciding to take notes rather than audiotape my interviews with the student. I thought that the tape recorder would distract and intimidate him. But when it came time to share my results, I found I wanted to record his exact words, categorize the comments, and do more analysis of the actual interview. I didn't have the data that I needed.

Overcoming the stumbling blocks was simple for me. I had to make do with the time and the data that I had. Although I had planned more extensive interviews and discussions with the student, I cut them short and observed him fewer times and interviewed him for shorter periods and on fewer occasions. Although I was able to tentatively answer my research question with the information and notes I had on hand, I found that I wanted more direct and exact data than I had collected. Furthermore, if you plan to work with one student over a period of time, think about what can happen. As teachers, we all know we have to be flexible, make up for student absences when we have an important lesson, and have back-up plans when unexpected events occur, such as fire drills or interruptions. The same kinds of interruptions and situations will happen in research. Always have a back-up plan, just as you do in teaching.

Synthesis and Concluding Thoughts

Stumbling blocks to teacher research are often unpredictable but need not be fatal. The three teacher researchers who reported their work in this chapter acknowledged the regulations, differential enthusiasm, and lack of time that caused them to adjust their research plans while in the process of collecting data. All of the stumbling blocks were unique to the projects these teachers envisioned and to the contexts in which they researched and taught. However, overcoming or coping with stumbling blocks is an easy process of thinking through the alternatives and adjusting the research plan in a way that allows the project to proceed.

PROBLEM-SOLVING VIGNETTE FOR DISCUSSION

Imagine that you are concerned about the performance of the English-language learners (ELLs) in your class. You believe they could be doing better than they are, and every year your class seems to have one or two more ELLs than the previous year. It is a growing challenge to your teaching. You have designed a research project to determine which 2 instructional strategies, out of the 10 you routinely use, lead to the greatest improvement in the performance of ELLs in your class. Then the following happens:

■ Your literature review reveals there are two or three strategies you had never tried that might be better for ELLs than the ones you are currently researching. Is this a stumbling block or a barrier? What do you decide to do?

■ Although you sent out permission slips to the ELLs in their home languages, not one single student brought it back on the due date. Is this a stumbling block or a barrier? What do you do?

■ No one in your school understands your project or even seems to care about the results. The results clearly show that two strategies, one you use and one you had never used prior to the project, result in a significant increase in ELLs' performance in literacy and math. Is this a stumbling block or a barrier? What do you do?

TIPS FOR TEACHER RESEARCHERS

The following tips may help you avoid the stumbling blocks Alyson, Shelly, and Alexandra experienced.

■ Design a research proposal carefully. Then invite families, administrators, and school or district personnel to provide feedback as early as possible before you settle on a plan.

■ Budget your time wisely, but add a few extra weeks or months to get the job done.

■ Plan meticulously, but remain flexible to allow for variations and alternatives within your plan.

■ Rely on your resources and intuitions first and foremost, but recruit a few critical friends who can serve as your cheerleaders and confidantes when the going gets tough.

■ Always have an alternate Plan B and C, and maybe even D.

QUESTIONS FOR REFLECTION

■ How can you prepare to give a preview of your research plan with colleagues, administrators, families, and other stakeholders to provide you with feedback before you begin?

■ When does encouraging colleagues to participate (e.g., to complete a survey) become undue coercion?

■ What are some common reasons for being flexible in your teaching that you can apply to help you anticipate stumbling blocks in your research?

REFERENCES

Cochran-Smith, M., & Lytle, S.L. (1990). Research on teaching and teacher research: The issues that divide. *Educational Researcher, 19*(2), 2–10.

Cochran-Smith, M., & Lytle, S.L. (1992). Communities for teacher research: Fringe or forefront? *American Journal of Education, 100*(3), 298–324.

Cochran-Smith, M., & Lytle, S.L. (1999). The teacher research movement: A decade later. *Educational Researcher, 28*(7), 15–25.

Fischer, D., Mercado, M., Morgan, V., Robb, L., Sheehan-Carr, J., & Torres, M.N. (2000). The curtain rises: Teachers unveil their processes of transformation in doing classroom inquiry. *Networks: An On-line Journal for Teacher Research, 3*(1). Retrieved July 31, 2007, from people.ucsc.edu/~gwells/networks/journal/Vol%203(1).2000april/Article1.html

Nixon, J. (1987). The teacher as researcher: Contradictions and continuities. *Peabody Journal of Education, 64*(2), 20–32.

CHAPTER 9

Strategies for Dealing With Other Research Issues

Moira A. Fallon, Dixie D. Massey

KEY TERMS

Bias

Confidentiality

Ethics

Informed consent

Internal or institutional review board (IRB)

Pilot study

Sampling

Spheres of influence

Statistical techniques

BEFORE-READING QUESTIONS

■ What common critical issues might teacher researchers face?

■ What are effective ways of minimizing or overcoming these critical issues?

■ How do you ethically balance the sometimes competing roles of teacher and researcher?

Joe, a third-grade teacher, hurries into his school. He is engaged in conversation with his friend, Sally, who teaches fourth grade next door.

"Slow down, I can hardly keep up," Sally complains.

Joe continues on as if Sally hasn't said a thing, "I feel great that I can apply the expertise I got while completing my graduate degree in literacy directly to my classroom. There are so many ways I can use our district curriculum and still positively influence the writing skills of these students." Joe has just returned from a workshop in creative writing. He is thrilled with the techniques he has learned for teaching and motivating his students' written work. He can't wait to begin to apply the suggestions.

"You know these kids, Sally. None of them has much of a background in reading at all because of their early home experiences," Joe says earnestly. "I really want the opportunity to help them improve their creative writing skills, as well as their overall appreciation for lots of different kinds of literature."

"How are you going to do that?" Sally asks.

Joe explains, "I have a plan. Over the two days of the workshop, I embedded these creative writing suggestions into the reading and language arts curricular standards. I want to objectively measure the impact they have on the students' writing skills and on their overall appreciation of literature. I just can't wait to get started!" With that, Joe heads off to his classroom with an eager step.

Introduction

Given the desire of a teacher such as Joe from the opening vignette to embrace the role of research in the classroom setting, novice researchers in teacher education will still often encounter critical issues in their research work. For example, although Joe is about to embark on an adventure in research, one that will engage his curiosity and cause frustration, he will face a number of unforeseen issues in his new adventure, including managing his investigation in an ethical manner; negotiating the political climate of his district and of conducting research in his classroom; and coping with biases that will potentially taint his results. Issues such as these can be frustrating and, more importantly, lead to problems in the research design and methodology itself. Because of the nature of working in a classroom setting, several concerns may arise. These concerns include planning appropriately, being aware of others' perceptions about the research itself, obtaining permissions, managing time, maintaining organization, recognizing the demands of the setting, and managing unexpected results. Understanding these issues and managing the potential conflicts is a challenge for every teacher researcher.

Other issues that might affect the results of a teacher research study revolve around the ability and knowledge base of the researcher. Important skills for every teacher researcher include the ability and knowledge of how to critically review the research of others and to exercise a critical eye to evaluate the quality of their research efforts (Leedy & Ormrod, 2005). Novice researchers in teacher education also need to be familiar with research tools, such as electronic planners, and know how to use support services, such as a research advisor or support group. These tools and services can greatly assist researchers like Joe. Novice researchers need to carefully plan their research design and methodology to minimize potential problems. They need concrete examples of classroom research that they can understand and apply to their setting. Also vital to one's effectiveness as a teacher researcher is having and maintaining flexibility, making ethical choices, and having a positive attitude as the research project is carried out. The purpose of this chapter is to understand the potential for these critical issues to occur. Based on our experience, we will offer objective and ethical strategies to suggest how to manage research issues as they arise.

Critical Issues Faced by Teacher Researchers

There are many challenges or critical issues faced by teacher researchers. Such challenges or issues often arise during the research process. However, with careful planning they may be prevented or their impact minimized. The theoretical basis of these challenges is varied but lies primarily in three areas of difficulties for the teacher researcher. The first issue is this newly evolving role of teacher as the facilitator of curriculum and instruction balanced with the need for an objective eye of the researcher. As the pressure rises for teachers to increase student test scores, time for research and reflection is limited. When conducting research, teachers like Joe often focus their attention on immediate needs and not on sustained research. Hubbard and Power (1999) write, "Teachers tend to concentrate on immediate, local needs" (p. 286). This can introduce bias into the research. **Bias** in teacher research usually refers to the teacher looking for a specific outcome of the research (Hubbard & Power, 1999). However, bias can be any influence or condition that distorts data. It is almost impossible to remove bias from teacher research. However, it is important to identify and report bias as part of the research process. The teacher researcher should identify and explicitly communicate personal or political beliefs, values, or assumptions about the research problem. This can be accomplished in the informed consent document, in the research proposal itself, or in the debriefing handout.

The second issue is the increasing use of outcomes-based measures derived solely from empirical measures to direct policy decision making and changes. Specifically, if teachers are to conduct teacher research in areas of high-stakes accountability, they must be fully aware of the current political context and pressures of mandated curricula and high-stakes testing. Competing **spheres of influence**, that is, people or issues that will exert undue pressure, can negatively affect the outcome of the research process (Leedy & Ormrod, 2005). Often, teachers are frustrated with the pressure of mandates and requirements but may not know how to channel that frustration into balanced responses. As an example, Joe might be faced, as many teachers might be, with a scripted curriculum adopted by the district for teaching creative writing. Scripted curricula present another issue, especially if teachers are held accountable for following the curriculum exactly. For example, Joe is interested in studying writing issues and the integration of reading and writing. However, if the adopted reading curricula takes 90-minute blocks and does not integrate writing and reading, Joe may feel he does not have time to add another block of time to integrate reading and writing. Joe's study might provide useful information on the effectiveness of that curriculum to teach his students and possible alternatives to that curriculum. Often decisions about what to teach and how to teach it are being made at district levels, without teacher input. Teacher researchers can bring important empirical evidence to these discussions and the decision-making process.

The third issue is the difficulty that many teachers face in applying research knowledge to the daily practices and routines of the classroom. The teacher researcher must become a critical consumer of research, understanding and blending quantitative and qualitative approaches. Research is everywhere: in the popular media, in library archives, and in the social dynamics of the classroom (Leedy & Ormrod, 2005; Moje, 1999). The application of research to daily classrooms requires thoughtful resolution and critical judgment. Ultimately, as in the case of Joe, this understanding and application can be both exciting and overwhelming. Joe's difficulty is to balance his eagerness to confront the research problem while tempering his eagerness with extensive planning, an objective eye, and understanding the political climate of his school district.

These critical issues in teacher research are important themes to understand as educators seek to use teacher research to increase teacher knowledge (Burnaford, Fisher, & Hobson, 1996; Cochran-Smith & Lytle, 1993; Hubbard & Power, 1999), improve classroom practice (Allington, 2001; Henson, 1996; Strickland, 2001), and bring about educational reform (Cochran-Smith, 2001, Cochran-Smith & Lytle, 1993). Other issues frequently faced by teacher researchers include obtaining support or collaboration, gaining approval through review boards, and facing time constraints (Massey & Duffy, 2003/2004). Solutions to many of these issues may be complex but offer "grist for thinking and problem solving" (Anders, Hoffman, & Duffy, 2000, p. 733). In the following section, we will look at ways to prepare for the effects of critical issues on teacher research.

Managing Critical Issues

There are many strategies that teacher researchers can employ to deal with research issues. Thoughtful preparation can help prevent these issues from occurring or minimize their effects. These strategies generally fall into one of two categories: (1) improved planning of the research procedures or (2) proactive responses to issues or problems as they arise during the implementation of the plan.

The Planning Stage

Teacher researchers cannot overplan. For example, Joe, the teacher in the opening vignette, should develop a written plan of action for every step of his proposed research project, laying out each detail and anticipated procedure. Preparing extensively for the research project will preclude many issues from occurring. Many people believe that research is a solitary activity; however, we recommend that novice teacher researchers should also establish a research support group of critical friends. Such people are trained in scientific methodology, have conducted many research studies or projects, and are familiar with ethical standards. These groups will be invaluable in brainstorming issues, checking procedures, posing questions, and simply being supportive. Some research groups meet on a regular basis to share and discuss inquiry into their classrooms (Patterson, 1991). Members of the group should have varying levels of expertise and often are interdisciplinary in membership. The teacher researcher can use a more expert researcher or advisor in his or her discipline to ask questions about how to start a research project, what are appropriate research questions, what are effective tools for use in conducting research, and a host of other issues. Similarly, a person not familiar with a particular discipline or project may also assist the teacher researcher with issues of clarity and rationale that seem obvious, but may have been overlooked.

Next, teacher researchers should develop a plan for study (Fallon & Brown, 2002). Your plan should be comprehensive. Take a paper-and-pencil approach, or use software such as Inspiration (www.inspiration.com), to assist you in your brainstorming. You may wish to do a preliminary review of the literature to determine what research is available on your topic. It is helpful to have one large document, subdivided into each of these steps of the planning process: the research problem, the review of the literature, data collection, data analysis, and conclusion/debriefing. Use your planning documents to help you consider all aspects of the topic you wish to study and all possible contingencies you might encounter. Once the teacher researcher determines the research design, whether the study will be quantitative, qualitative, or a combination of approaches, a plan for organizing data should be created. For example, researchers who use a more quantitative approach (e.g., Mertens, 1998) suggest that **statistical techniques**, or planned inferential analyses, such as t-tests, ANOVAs, and so forth, could be organized into a database like Microsoft Excel to maintain accurate records of the planned steps.

To help with the planning stage of your project, ask yourself the following 10 questions. Record your answers to each question, and reflect on your written responses.

1. What is the problem you would like to research?
2. Does this research problem have the potential for providing you with necessary information?
3. Is the research problem worthy of your time and effort?
4. What response have you received from other researchers concerning this research problem?
5. What information on this research problem is available in the literature?
6. What are the potential outcomes, positive and negative, of this research problem?
7. What is the depth of the research problem that you plan to achieve?
8. How able are you to organize your results and draw inferences?
9. What procedures will you follow for

   • Reviewing the literature?
   • Data availability?
   • Data collection?

- Data analysis and interpretation?

10. What research tools are available for your use?

The teacher researcher should also gain the support of the school's administration and the families of the students in the classroom for study of the research question. Certain issues may trigger competing spheres of influence and a good researcher will plan appropriately. Sampling is one of those issues. **Sampling** is the way participants are selected to become part of the research. Sampling is the study of a small, representative subset of a larger population (Leedy & Ormrod, 2005). Sampling in teacher research usually means convenience sampling or the use of subjects more readily available, such as the students in Joe's classroom in the opening vignette. Because a teacher is conducting research in his or her classroom, it is accepted that the sample will be one class. Schoolwide teacher research might include a broader sample of certain classrooms. Purposeful sampling (rather than random sampling) is accepted as part of teacher research, but, again, every effort must be made to report how the sample influenced the teacher research outcomes (Mertens, 1998).

The identification of the population to be sampled can sometimes trigger political issues within a school or district. The school principal can be invaluable in suggesting wording, key personnel, and ways to approach potential participants. Discuss the research problem clearly and ask for assistance in developing the research plan. Routman (1996) discusses this topic in *Literacy at the Crossroads*, encouraging teachers to become politically active. She believes that this activism can empower teachers to take charge of their learning, freeing them and their students to pursue interesting and worthwhile goals rather than prescribed programs. Working through these complex issues can simultaneously improve the quality of the research plan.

Once the plan is agreed upon by all concerned, it is time to develop the research proposal. The proposal must be a precise document from beginning to end (Leedy & Ormrod, 2005). Just as an architect's design is a model of the proposed structure, so the research proposal lays out each step of the study and outlines the resources to be used to achieve the desired results. Planning and conducting research requires that the participants' identities be kept either anonymous or confidential. Ensuring **confidentiality** means using anonymous procedures in which names are separated from data, pseudonyms are used when referring to participants, ongoing data collection is not discussed with those who were not identified as being part of the research team, data is kept in locked areas, and data is destroyed after the study is complete (Mertens, 1998). These terms should all be outlined in the research proposal. Once completed, the research proposal must be submitted for approval to all the appropriate personnel or agencies involved. Approval must be gained prior to beginning the research or collecting any data.

The Implementation Stage

As research is implemented, it is critical to take small steps and appropriately manage time. An electronic planner can be very helpful to the researcher in carrying out the steps outlined in the planning stages in a timely fashion. Thus, the teacher researcher should also maintain a research log or writing journal to track all of the research activities and decisions. Figure 9.1 shows a sample of research log entries. A research log may contain a record of the amount of time spent planning, implementing, or writing about the research. It may also contain all necessary tasks and the dates by which they are to be accomplished. The research log can also serve as a written record of the procedures, including conversations with key personnel, such as the school principal. Records should be kept throughout the research process so that no information is lost or missed.

Teacher researchers often are frustrated by problems in tracking references. Many are incorrectly cited or lack all the required information. As you review the literature, it is essential to record complete references. For example, Joe, as the teacher researcher, should keep a record of all the keywords and terms used in reviewing the research literature. Further, as he reviews each article he should attach some basic analytical and bibliographic information about the article, such as all authors' names, professional journal information, type of research, research methodology, and any other relevant information. See Appendix B, Understanding and Applying References Outline, which is a reproducible form that will help you organize and track important research information and also be invaluable in verifying facts. Know and use the other tools available, such as databases, spreadsheets, and brainstorming software, to keep you on task and on time. There is project management software available that can assist in this part of the process to track the entire research project. See Appendix A, Engaging in Teacher Research—Professional Groups, for a list of these resources.

In the United States, every research institution will have an **internal or institutional review board (IRB)** that monitors the use of human subjects in research (Leedy & Ormrod, 2005). Researchers need to check their institution for guide-

---

FIGURE 9.1
Sample of Research Log Entries

Date	Time In/Time Out	Task (Note: A check mark indicates completion)
11/4/06	7:03 p.m.–8:39 p.m	1. Conduct an advanced search of periodicals, using the key words *literacy, creative writing, elementary students.*
11/5/06	6:00 p.m.–9:15 p.m.	2. Read each article to determine relevancy to problem.
11/6/06	9:00 a.m.–10:05 a.m.	3. Complete and attach electronic bibliographic forms to each article.

---

lines and read them carefully. This is particularly important when conducting research on vulnerable populations, such as children who may be at risk for coercion or harm from the research intervention. Prior to developing a research agenda, teacher researchers should be certified in the use of human subjects. Many institutions use www.citiprogram.org as the website for certifying their researchers. Completion of the certification process will give researchers a certificate to conduct research ethically. Check your institution's guidelines for how to become certified. Once certified, every planned research project involving human subjects should be submitted to the IRB for approval.

The teacher researcher should know the standards for teachers conducting research in his or her particular field and should strictly adhere to that discipline's code of ethics. Maintaining **ethics**, the standards for acceptable practice within one's discipline (Leedy & Ormrod, 2005), is of critical importance for the teacher researcher. Most ethical dilemmas fall into one of four categories: (1) informed consent, (2) right to privacy, (3) protection from harm, or (4) honesty with professional colleagues. **Informed consent** involves telling the participants the nature of the study, the fact that participation is voluntary, and that they may withdraw from the study at any time. Informed consent must be in writing and be included as part of the research proposal. School districts require that informed consent procedures be carefully followed with students under the age of 18 years. Generally, researchers will have letters of consent for both the students and their parents or legal guardians. Ethical dilemmas can evolve if researchers lack objectivity and fail to create a solid plan of action for their research. The American Psychological Association (APA) guides researchers in issues of ethical dilemmas (www.apa.org). In the field of literacy, the International Reading Association (IRA) has established standards for professional practice and a Code of Ethics (www.reading.org/association/about/code.html).

If you feel unsure of the extensiveness of the study, consider and discuss with your research support group the use of a pilot study to try out the procedures on a small sample. A **pilot study** is a brief, exploratory study used for the purpose of trying out instruments, procedures, and analysis methods. This is an excellent way for novice teacher researchers such as Joe to determine the feasibility of the proposed project, and it may prevent ethical or political issues from happening once the study is fully implemented.

During implementation, it is also helpful to have a self-evaluation checklist (Fallon & Ackley, 2001). The teacher researcher can use the checklist to evaluate the quality of the research process and to ensure that the study is carried out as planned. It is suggested that the nature of self-evaluation is a personal one. Therefore, the checklist itself should be adapted to the type of research being conducted or to the particular topic being explored. This document can also be helpful to share with the research support group. See Appendix B, Self-Evaluation Checklist, for a sample of this type of document.

It is helpful to maintain a positive attitude during the implementation of research. Good teacher researchers are flexible, optimistic, and persistent. These dispositions will help you manage the issues as they occur and maintain objectivity in your decision making. Continue to consult your research support team whenever needed and keep the best interests of your students and families at heart.

Synthesis and Concluding Thoughts

Teacher researchers face enormous issues in planning and conducting research in the classroom on important issues such as literacy. However, the potential rewards for such efforts are enormous. Schools and districts must have information directly related to important classroom issues (Anderson, Herr, & Nihlen, 1994). There is a critical need in school districts for research focused on literacy issues of students who are taught with effective instructional methods in environments conducive to learning of all students. Teacher researchers are the best choice for understanding and investigating the complexities of curriculum and instruction. They can be agents for change in education and be more effective in their teaching, instructional, and curricular practices (Strickland, 2001). Teachers, families, and school districts need the empirical evidence and objective information that evolve from research to make responsible, data-driven choices that can be translated into classroom practice. Teacher-directed educational research has a great deal to offer about the most appropriate methods of effectively teaching all children. It is critical then that teacher researchers such as Joe learn as much as possible about the research process and that they organize and implement their research in as ethical a manner as possible.

Increasingly, school districts are responding to the demands to meet standards with empirical evidence to support decisions and policy changes. This response requires teacher researchers to read and understand the current research literature. It also means that teacher researchers can employ scientific methods to investigate the complex nature of the classroom and to find answers that benefit the needs of all students and their families. Teachers are then able to match their classroom practices directly with appropriate research-based methods.

PROBLEM-SOLVING VIGNETTE FOR DISCUSSION

"How is the study going?" Sally inquires as she walks in the classroom door. "I had this so carefully planned, but look at this data. I think I must be missing something," Joe replies. He pushes the examples of the students' creative writing toward Sally. "I am measuring the quality and quantity of their writing with this simple checklist. However, it looks like this is not exactly the information I needed. What can I do? I have already started this thing and so much is riding on it!" Sally looks carefully at the instrument. She looks up and meets

Joe's worried eyes. "I don't think this instrument is measuring everything you thought it would, Joe," she softly says. "It looks to me as if the baseline data are inadequate or maybe incomplete based on this instrument you used."

"Actually," says Joe, "I had to make some adjustments to the instrument. Mrs. Whittier, our principal, felt that some of the wording needed to be 'toned down.' She was afraid that parents might be offended by the wording of the questions about the students' and other family members' writing habits at home." "I see," Sally responds thoughtfully. "Perhaps in changing the wording of the questions, you now have an instrument that doesn't completely measure what you want it to measure."

Teacher researchers will commonly face situations that call for careful decision making that balances the political climate and the needs of the study. Often, there are multiple perspectives in educational research that are held by different individuals. Ethically revealing the natures of these multiple perspectives and giving clear, equal weight to each will only improve the overall quality of the project. This may mean revision in planned procedures, instruments, or other documentation. Still, it is worthwhile to fully explore these issues in a direct and honest manner. So how does an ethical teacher researcher balance these multiple perspectives?

TIPS FOR TEACHER RESEARCHERS

Probably the best tip for managing research issues is that the teacher researcher should be flexible and persistent and should maintain a positive attitude. Conducting quality research in the classroom setting is not easy and, invariably, difficulties will arise. There is a great need to take small steps and to work with the support of your administration. You should monitor closely the decisions you make at every step of the process, along with the suggestions of your research support group and the conclusions of researchers working in your area of interest. Such careful operations will help you to maintain your ethical standards and to act in the best interests of your students and their families.

QUESTIONS FOR REFLECTION

■ How does conducting teacher research in today's classroom influence the political, and sometimes volatile, educational climate? If teachers are to continue building their knowledge, conducting teacher research, and ushering in reform, their learning is of utmost importance. Teacher researchers are well positioned to make meaningful and informed decisions that are in the best interests of students and families.

■ What is the effect of carefully constructed ethical teacher research upon students' learning? Advocates of reform believe changing teachers is the most efficient and direct way to influence students' learning. However, ethical dilemmas can easily arise from uninformed or ill-advised procedures and weak methodology.

■ What is the long-term impact of teacher research on policies related to curriculum and instruction? Clearly, there exists today a real need for research-based empirical evidence in classrooms. However, this information must be used by teachers who are savvy consumers of research and not biased advocates for predetermined changes.

REFERENCES

Allington, R.L. (2001). *What really matters for struggling readers: Designing research-based programs.* New York: Longman.

Anders, P.L., Hoffman, J.V., & Duffy, G.G. (2000). Teaching teachers to teach reading: Paradigm shifts, persistent problems, and challenges. In M.L. Kamil, P.B. Mosenthal, P.D. Pearson, & R. Barr (Eds.), *Handbook of reading research* (Vol. 3, pp. 719–742). Mahwah, NJ: Erlbaum.

Anderson, G.L., Herr, K., & Nihlen, A.S. (1994). *Studying your own school: An educator's guide to qualitative practitioner research.* Thousand Oaks, CA: Corwin Press.

Burnaford, G.E., Fischer, J., & Hobson, D. (1996). *Teachers doing research: Practical possibilities.* Mahwah, NJ: Erlbaum.

Cochran-Smith, M. (2001, April). Constructing outcomes in teacher education: Policy, practice, and pitfalls. *Educational Policy Analysis Archives, 9*(11). Retrieved July 31, 2007, from epaa.asu.edu/epaa/v9n11.html

Cochran-Smith, M., & Lytle, S.L. (1993). *Inside/outside: Teacher research and knowledge.* New York: Teachers College Press.

Fallon, M., & Ackley, B. (2001, August). *Admissions decisions and pre-service teachers' classroom performance.* Paper presented at the summer conference of the Association of Teacher Educators, Portland, OR.

Fallon, M.A., & Brown, S.C. (2002, February). *From student teaching into a profession: One model for guiding professional development.* Paper presented at the annual meeting of the American Association of Colleges for Teacher Education, New York, NY.

Henson, K.T. (1996). Teachers as researchers. In J. Sikula, T.J. Buttery, & E. Guyton (Eds.), *Handbook of research on teacher education* (2nd ed., pp. 53–64). New York: Macmillan Library Reference.

Hubbard, R.S., & Power, B.M. (1999). *Living the questions: A guide for teacher-researchers.* York, ME: Stenhouse.

Leedy, P.D., & Ormrod, J.E. (2005). *Practical research: Planning and design* (8th ed.). Upper Saddle River, NJ: Pearson Education.

Massey, D.D., & Duffy, A.M. (2003/2004). The learning and perceptions of teacher researchers and facilitators in a literacy-focused, teacher-research course: A content analysis of system, learner, and spheres of influence. *Journal of Literacy Research, 35,* 1019–1050.

Mertens, D.M. (1998). *Research methods in education and psychology: Integrating diversity with quantitative and qualitative approaches.* Thousand Oaks, CA: Sage.

Moje, E.B. (1999). From expression to dialogue: A study of social action literacy projects in an urban school setting. *Urban Review, 31,* 305–330.

Routman, R. (1996). *Literacy at the crossroads: Crucial talk about reading, writing, and other teaching dilemmas.* Portsmouth, NH: Heinemann.

Strickland, D.S. (2001). The interface of standards, teacher preparation, and research: Improving the quality of teachers. In C.M. Roller (Ed.), *Learning to teach reading: Setting the research agenda* (pp. 20–29). Newark, DE: International Reading Association.

CHAPTER 10

Powerful Grant Writing: Strategies Teachers Can Use for Securing Funds

Susan E. Israel

KEY TERMS

Education Resources Information Center (ERIC)

Grant proposal

Peer-reviewed refereed journals

BEFORE-READING QUESTIONS

- Why should you be motivated to write a grant?
- What types of strategies will help you write an effective grant proposal?
- What positive action can you take so that your grant is funded?

When Susan was in her Masters of Literacy program, she had a professor who inspired her to write a grant for her class project rather than a traditional research paper. When Susan first started thinking about the research project that she wanted to conduct with her fourth-grade students, she decided to integrate her love of picture books with a desire to learn more about reading comprehension and critical thinking development.

Susan had no idea how much she would need to support her research. Once she started to develop the proposal, she realized children's picture books needed to be available to all her students during the research project. Financial resources were not available in her school's budget to purchase the books she needed.

Susan's professor encouraged her to apply for a grant and use the grant application to fund the purchase of picture books. Susan contemplated the following questions: What funding opportunities are available? Besides picture books, what other expenses might be incurred? Does the school provide support for teacher research projects? If so, what are the filing procedures? How far in advance should a grant be submitted? Is it important to show documentation of costs prior to submitting a grant?

Teachers Taking Action: A Comprehensive Guide to Teacher Research, edited by Cynthia A. Lassonde and Susan E. Israel.
© 2008 by the International Reading Association.

Introduction

The primary goal of this chapter is to share effective strategies to motivate teachers to research grant opportunities and feel more confident when writing a grant proposal. A **grant proposal** is a formal outline submitted to a funding organization by the person or organization that will be conducting the study. Typically, a grant proposal might consist of a summary of your proposed research, review of the literature, methodology of the research, timeline of your project, and projected expenses. When writing a grant, it is important to adhere to the proposal guidelines.

As noted in the opening vignette, I (Susan) began my first teacher research project when I wanted to understand how to effectively incorporate picture books into the language arts program while at the same time develop critical thinking strategies to improve reading comprehension. My university professor pointed me in the right direction, and I obtained a teacher researcher grant from the International Reading Association (IRA) to help with the purchase of children's picture books. (More information about the Teacher as Researcher Grant can be obtained from IRA's website: www.reading.org. Also, see Appendix A, Funding Research—Grants, for additional ideas on grant opportunities.) Because I wanted funds to help me conduct my research effectively, I was driven to write a grant. If you are interested in securing funds but writing a proposal seems like a daunting task to you, I recommend the strategies highlighted in this chapter.

Writing a Successful Grant Proposal

Strategy #1: Identify Area of Research

Engaging in teacher research will undoubtedly take time. However, I try to develop research projects that are related to my professional development goals or the instructional needs of my students. Writing a successful grant proposal to secure funds for projects will require effort; therefore, researching an area that you are really passionate about is very important. You will spend a lot of time working on the grant and research. Grantees will appreciate knowing your rationale for doing the research and your passion related to the project. The topic of inquiry could be some type of classroom problem you would like to solve, or it could be a specific topic area such as phonics or reading comprehension. Sometimes teacher research might be conducted on topics that focus on school initiatives and are not necessarily the teacher researcher's area of passion. The key is working around institutional agendas by looking at things from a different perspective. Ask yourself, How can the goal of the school increase achievement in my classroom? For example, if you have to research an area of assessment and you do not like assessment, focus on a specific type of assessment you want to learn more about, such as self-assessments.

Understanding what you are passionate about takes critical reflection. When I started my research project I knew that I was zealous about integrating children's picture books with literacy engagements, exploring multiple sign systems, and developing strategies to increase reading comprehension. Before going on to the next section, write down three topics that you are passionate about and why. Doing this exercise is helpful when writing your grant. One component of the grant proposal form I completed was a section titled "Significance of the Problem." I used my initial thoughts on what I was passionate about and why to generate the text for this section.

Strategy #2: Locate Supporting Research

Once you have identified your topic, you will need to conduct a literature review on the research related to that topic. In a literature review, as defined and discussed in chapter 5 of this volume, the researcher examines and compares primary and secondary sources relevant to the main topic. Research is reviewed from many different sources, such as refereed journals, handbooks, scholarly books, Internet resources, or yearbooks published by professional organizations. **Peer-reviewed refereed journals** are journals that accept only articles that have gone through several rounds of peer reviews and are accepted, usually unanimously, as being of high quality and worthy of being published. (For more about these journals, see chapter 12.) When conducting a literature review for a grant proposal, teachers should avoid using nonrefereed journals. This is an important step when writing a grant proposal. I have found that most grantees pay close attention to the references mentioned in the proposal. It is important for them to know that the person to whom they are going to provide funds is knowledgeable about the area he or she will be researching in the classroom.

I begin my literature reviews by doing an Internet search on the topic using the **Education Resources Information Center (ERIC)**, an online database that houses academic resources in education (www.eric.ed.gov). I also skim through my reading journals to look for topics related to my area of interests. Because I have been subscribing to literacy journals for many years, I usually begin by reviewing the table of contents, looking for topics or articles on my topic that look promising. I also use the *Handbook of Reading Research* (Kamil, Mosenthal, Pearson, & Barr, 2000) or *Theoretical Models and Processes of Reading* (Ruddell, Ruddell, & Singer, 1994) to learn about the major theories and landmark studies on that topic. I typically identify a minimum of three to four landmark studies that have been conducted and use these studies as starting points for my research. I gather all the research and books at the same time before I begin reading the information. While I am reading, I make notes of additional resources that I want to obtain and that I feel will help me learn more about the topic. I also like to ask my colleagues for ideas on primary studies done on the topic. Following some of these suggestions will help you get started on conducting the literature review for your teacher research project as well as refine your area of interest.

Strategy #3: Obtain Grant Funding Sources

Do not be afraid to seek funding when conducting teacher research. The first place to start is by asking others who have done teacher research and have been awarded grant money. Invite them to share their tips with you. Investigate any funds that might be available from your school district or local community. Many businesses and community organizations provide funding to schools for teacher research projects. The Internet is another resource to obtain funding ideas. Investigate professional organizations for grant opportunities. See Appendix A for a list of potential online grant resources. The library is also another resource of which you should take advantage. Most librarians who work in the children's area are aware of many funding opportunities. In addition, your local university will also be able to assist you in locating funding. Funding opportunities are also available through the U.S. Department of Education (www.ed.gov). Once you obtain several funding ideas, make sure to obtain the official applications and proposal guidelines.

Strategy #4: Apply for a Grant Specific to Your Topic

Once you have a topic of interest in mind, it is important for you to begin to narrow the focus, so that the grant supports your research interests. As I mentioned, one of my areas of interest is reading comprehension. Therefore, I needed to apply for a research grant that supported this type of research. In order to write the grant, you will need to clarify your topic, which is easier when thinking critically about your overall research goals. What specific question do you want to answer on this topic? What is the specific age group that you want to focus on—primary or intermediate? What are the goals of your research project? Do you want to focus on motivation, achievement, or attention?

As you begin to narrow your topic, you get closer to better understanding and writing your research question. Your research question needs to clearly state what your research inquiry will investigate. (See chapter 3 in this volume for more on writing effective questions.) One of the problems I encountered after I started my research was the discovery that my question was too wordy. It started to get confusing when I tried to analyze and communicate the results. To help you narrow your topic, ask yourself the following questions:

- What is the main issue I want to study?

- What questions do I have about this issue that I want answered?

- How will researching this issue help me in my teaching?

For example, let's say you want to try to better understand why your students are unable to comprehend during reading tasks. Your main topic is comprehension. Comprehension is a very broad topic with many different areas that can be researched. Under the comprehension umbrella, you could investigate any of the following subtopics:

- Assessment methods
- Informational text strategies
- Effects of vocabulary
- Impact of decoding
- Social and emotional issues
- Language development
- Comprehension theory

Once you decide what your main topic is, you can narrow your focus by age group, student populations, theoretical perspectives, motivation, and many other specifics. For example, what is the age of the students you want to target in your research? Will you focus on specific theories such as social-cognitive or behavioral methods of instruction? Are you looking at motivational aspects of learning or cognitive ones?

At the same time as you are narrowing your focus, you will be starting to conduct your literature review on the topic. Keep in mind that summarizing research is very important and your teacher researcher proposal should summarize significant contributions made in the topic area. The first paragraph of my literature review details the components that are to follow in the remaining section.

When writing the proposal, clearly communicate exactly what you will do and how you will obtain your information. The research design is like a road map for you to follow. Be very specific about any type of assessment instruments you will be using and when you will administer them. If you are using your observations, as I did, as part of the data analysis, you need to be very specific about what you are observing and why.

Strategy #5: Join a Research Support Network

Identifying a research support network is critical to writing a solid proposal. It is desirable to have multiple people in your network and of various backgrounds. I recommend locating someone who is an expert in the area of your research topic and who is available to help you respond to questions and guide the research project as needed to act as your main support person. My support person was a university professor, and she was extremely enthusiastic about my research. This motivated me to continue to write the grant and eventually obtain funding. One of the ways my support person was extremely helpful was in making me think critically about the research design. For example, she asked questions such as the following: What criteria will you use to select your picture books? What type of strategies or skills will you teach? How will the picture books be organized in your classroom? How much time will be allocated during your day for students to be engaged with invitations? When will you administer your assessments? Because of this line of thinking and questioning, I was able to think critically about the grant proposal guidelines, which included the following:

- Grant application

- Literature review and research

- Student samples

- Data analysis, expenses

During the course of the project my support person and I kept in touch. One mistake I made was waiting too long to analyze my data (which I will discuss in more detail later in this chapter), and my support person was no longer available to assist me in this critical stage of my research. I procrastinated on data analysis for quite a while because I was not confident about writing the results.

Strategy #6: Establish a Budget

One area that I always struggle with is how much money I should apply for when writing grants. For example, the Teacher as Researcher Grant that I received provided me with enough money to purchase the picture books I needed to use in my classroom. Unfortunately, I did not allocate enough money for travel expenses related to dissemination of my research and other incidentals such as copying, postage, and supplies that I needed to conduct the research. To help you plan your budget, make a list of your out-of-pocket expenses. Think about the following items and what each one might include in regard to necessary funding to conduct your research:

- Office supplies—binders; folders; labels; printing cartridges; paper clips; markers; envelopes

- Research expenses and materials—library loan; books; copying expenses for research; possible association fees; grant-related expenses; transcription costs; research-assistance costs

- Technology support resources—software; CDs; computer-technology assistance

- Travel expenses—presentation supplies; food; transportation such as air fare, taxi, or shuttle fees; hotel expenses

- Copying and postage—copying expenses; stamps; shipping products as necessary

- Incidentals—publishing expenses; stipends; participant gifts; thank-you notes; unexpected fees for registration at conferences

FIGURE 10.1
Sample Budget Narrative for Literacy Grant

Item	Description	Justification	Amount
Summer research fellowship	Research assistant/stipend	Data collection and analysis	1 Research Assistant: 10–15 hours a week x 10–12 weeks $1,000.00
Grants-in-aid	Project design/research/ analysis/travel as needed to communities	Project management/ research expenses	$3,000.00
Research equipment	Survey construction/ printing/distribution	Quantitative data will be collected using a survey	$1,000.00
		Estimate distribution of surveys to Teacher Service Institutions	$3,000.00 (Estimate)
		Total	**$8,000.00**

Figure 10.1 shows a sample budget that summarizes my expenses for one of my proposed literacy grants.

Staying Motivated to Conduct Research

Because of my experience with writing grants, I want to help you feel confident so that you are motivated to pursue funding opportunities. When talking to other teachers about their research projects, I always inquire about whether they have pursued funding to support their initiative. To my surprise, the answer is usually no. I have learned that teachers are either afraid to write a grant because they lack confidence in the writing task or they are unaware of grants and do not have time to research funding organizations. If you are an administrator reading this book, I highly recommend that you have a community volunteer or staff person assigned to research grant opportunities. I agree that teachers are very busy. I also understand that they do not have a lot of time to spend researching grants. The more support others can give will benefit teachers who are interested in doing teacher research and securing funds.

Readers can benefit from using the strategies I have provided as starting points to boost their confidence about grant writing. It is my goal that you use this information to minimize your frustrations and any waste of time related to the grant writing process. Following my tips will not ensure grant funding. Effort and persistence on your part is equally important.

Synthesis and Concluding Thoughts

The primary goal of this chapter was to provide you with a window into effective strategies for writing an award-winning grant proposal. To help build your confidence, six effective experientially based strategies were discussed. Your grant should reflect your passion for the research you will conduct. This passion will provide motivation and ongoing enthusiasm until the project is complete. Completing your research is important to the grantee or funding source. Once you have determined your topic, focus only on key issues related to that topic and make sure your grant clearly communicates the issues you have raised. Narrowing your focus will help you effectively write your research question, which guides the methods and research design. Organizing your research project in advance will help you clarify the conceptual focus, which will allow you to think through the methodology, data analysis, as well as an expected timeline and budget. The role of peer support is to provide mentorship throughout your project. Consultation with your support peer or support network should be done prior to grant writing and grant application submission. Use your vision to guide your grant proposal and be confident that you can secure funding!

PROBLEM-SOLVING VIGNETTE FOR DISCUSSION

As a first-year teacher attempts to conduct research, she has difficulty understanding research design and analysis. Because this is part of the proposal guidelines, she realizes that this is valuable and important to receiving the grant. Whom should she contact to help her understand the components of research design and analysis?

The teacher then decides to conduct a pilot study prior to submitting the grant proposal to help her understand design and analysis. What important decisions will she have to make before she conducts the pilot study?

TIPS FOR TEACHER RESEARCHERS

Use the following tips to write a successful proposal:

- Be confident and enthusiastic about your research. Your grant proposal should reflect your rationale for wanting to do the research, as well as your ability to conduct the research.

- Collaborate with peers on grant ideas. Share your research idea with other teachers in your building and be willing to listen to new ideas when shared. Invite colleagues with similar interests to join you with your research and grant writing.

- Focus your grant on specific issues that you want your research to address. Identify specific problems you have been having in the classroom that you want to solve.

- Complete a review of the literature. Communicate your knowledge of prior research or landmark studies that guide your research, as well as studies that have yet to be done and how your research fills the gap. Continue researching your topic while you are conducting the research so as to be knowledgeable about new research published.

- Think holistically about your research design prior to writing your proposal. Thinking about your research in advance will help you maintain a strict timetable and reasonable research agenda.

- Conduct your own peer reviews. Share findings with your colleagues to obtain feedback and invite them to offer a critical review of the research.

QUESTIONS FOR REFLECTION

- What issues should you consider prior to beginning a research project in your classroom? Are there guidelines that you should follow in your area of expertise and within your school before you begin the grant proposal?

- After successfully obtaining funding, how much class time will your project consume? Have you thought critically about what time you can set aside to work on your research project? How will you justify that this time will guide you toward increased levels of exemplary teaching without distracting you from your teacher-related obligations?

- Have you thought critically about the analysis phase of your research? What type of assessments or measurements will you use to obtain data on your students? Do you need permission before administering any assessments? Should you be concerned about validity and reliability of the assessments before you begin your research? Does your grant proposal reflect this thinking?

REFERENCES

Kamil, M.L., Mosenthal, P.B., Pearson, P.D., & Barr, R. (Eds.). (2000). *Handbook of reading research* (Vol. 3). Mahwah, NJ: Erlbaum.

Ruddell, R.B., Ruddell, M.R., & Singer, H. (Eds.). (1994). *Theoretical models and processes of reading* (4th ed.). Newark, DE: International Reading Association.

PART V

Writing, Publishing, and Presenting Teacher Research

Part Opener: Sharing What We Learn in Teacher Research
Ilene R. Rutten, Cheryl Dozier

"You brought more chocolate! Excellent, our supply was running low!" It is Thursday, and Ilene and Cheryl (the authors and subjects of this case study) are beginning another day of scheduled writing. They sit in Cheryl's office, side by side at her desk. Here there is plenty of room to spread out their papers. They have a computer screen they both can read and a chocolate stash for when they need inspiration.

"I ordered the flowers for my mom's birthday party. I decided on the irises." Like most days, Ilene and Cheryl begin by catching up on one another's news. For them, such exchanges serve to recognize and renew the trust they developed over the past several months so they can safely begin the writing that often exposes their vulnerabilities.

"OK, where were we?" Ilene and Cheryl consult the notes attached to their most recent draft and the comments they left on the computer for their next writing session.

"Today we need to finish addressing the comments from the second reviewer. It says a chart would make this section clearer. What do you think that would look like?" As Ilene and Cheryl consider a range of ways to organize their chart, they look through professional journals for examples to support their writing.

Early on, Ilene and Cheryl discovered their common and deep commitment to teacher preparation. Their ongoing discussions, questions, and involvement in teacher preparation guided their teacher research projects. For them, developing a productive professional relationship required an initial and sustained effort.

Together they reviewed and refined the theoretical foundations for their research, and then they analyzed and organized their research for publishing. Ilene and Cheryl's sustained engagement in teacher research was supported by four factors: (1) establishing a partnership, (2) developing a writing relationship, (3) addressing the intended audience, and (4) focusing on purposeful revisions. (To read the complete case study, go to this book's link on the IRA website at www.reading.org and click on Case Study #5: Sharing What We Learn in Teacher Research.)

Teacher researchers' voices are a welcome addition to the knowledge base on teaching. Part V of *Teachers Taking Action* provides a road map for disseminating teacher research findings. In chapter 11, the complexities of writing the manuscript are unraveled. Chapter 12 focuses on the publishing process while avenues for presentations are explored in chapter 13.

CHAPTER 11

Effective Writing
for Teacher Researchers

Janet C. Richards, Sharon K. Miller

BEFORE-READING QUESTIONS

▪ How can you integrate your personal and professional selves as you compose your research reports?

▪ How does the intended audience determine the structure a research report will follow?

▪ How can you determine and document your professional writing strengths and areas of writing that need improvement?

Nancy Jones is a first-year teacher of third-grade students in a low socioeconomic elementary school. Her school's staff development objectives state that during the fall semester, teachers will conduct a research project designed to determine how to enhance low-achieving students' reading abilities. At an annual faculty retreat in the spring, teachers are required to distribute copies of their completed research initiatives to their colleagues for small-group discussion.

As a graduate student, Nancy had learned about the benefits and power of teacher research. She also learned some methods for conducting rigorous classroom research projects. However, Nancy is concerned about writing her report for peer distribution because she believes academic writing is not her strong point. She is unfamiliar with invention strategies that could help her make decisions about how to begin her research report and determine what data to include in the report. Nancy also is apprehensive about actually sitting down to author a first draft. She wonders if it is appropriate to write in first person and whether she should use active or passive voice. She also is confused about whether her writing should reflect an integration of personal and professional experiences.

Teachers Taking Action: A Comprehensive Guide to Teacher Research, edited by Cynthia A. Lassonde and Susan E. Israel.
© 2008 by the International Reading Association.

Introduction

As a teacher researcher, you probably share some of Nancy's concerns and confusions about writing your research initiatives. In this chapter we offer specific suggestions based on our experiences as teacher researchers to help you enhance your abilities to write about your classroom research projects.

As a teacher, you speak and act from experience and authority. You know what occurs in your classroom, and you are an expert at conducting informal research projects. Perhaps you've begun to formalize your teacher research interests through graduate-level studies or districtwide professional development programs. Throughout your research processes, writing will help you gain insights, clarify what you already know, and determine what you still need to know about a teaching dilemma. You might write about your research to keep track of your efforts and progress. In the end, if you have graduate or professional development requirements to meet, you may be expected to write some type of report about your research, or you may wish to publish your work in a journal as a means of sharing your research with a larger audience.

We offer this chapter for teacher researchers who expect to write about their research projects—and those who don't. We want you to know why you *should* write about your classroom-research initiatives, even when writing isn't required. We want you to approach writing with confidence and an awareness of what diverse audiences will require. We want you to understand the writing process and to know how important it is to link the personal to the professional so your stories are told authentically in your voice. In addition, we provide ways to document your writing strengths and needs. We end the chapter by offering some basic writing tips that will simplify your composing efforts.

The Importance and Benefits of Writing Reports That Document Your Research

In 1983 when Calkins wrote *Lessons From a Child: On the Teaching and Learning of Writing*, no one could have imagined the impact this small book would have on classroom teachers everywhere. As the personal story of two years of her classroom research, Calkins not only provided numerous instructional strategies for teaching writing but also offered a model of inquiry that teacher researchers have imitated and refined in the intervening years. Her work proved that classroom teachers could do relevant and significant research and influence change in educational theory and practice. She also proved that doing such research was not something the teacher does *in addition* to teaching, but something that is *integral to* teaching practice.

Teachers who write about their research add to the knowledge base about teaching and, therefore, they should not hesitate to share their insights with other educators at all levels through publication. In addition to practitioner journals, teacher research stories are increasingly accepted and encouraged in scholarly journals. In fact, the fourth edition of *Handbook of Research on Teaching* (Richardson, 2001) highlighted teacher research; this was the first time this important volume acknowledged the potential contribution of teacher research to the field. By taking themselves and their teaching stories seriously, and offering them for publication, teachers reach new and diverse audiences that include other practitioners as well as local and national scholarly groups. Thus, by writing about their research efforts, teachers have opportunities to make a positive change to their profession.

Connecting Teachers' Personal and Professional Selves

One common quality of exemplary teacher research reporting is authentic voice. In a piece of writing by a teacher researcher, the force of an authentic voice is evidenced in a number of ways. By using **first person** (i.e., writing as the narrator of the story, using the personal "I") the teacher researcher is an active participant in the story. The researcher's voice is the powerful vehicle through which the struggle and the issues faced in the course of the inquiry illustrate the specific events in the tale. Readers can identify with the teacher and with the students as the progress of the inquiry leads the teacher researcher to further questions or to conclusions that benefit both instruction and learning. For this reason, we urge you to allow the passion with which you pursue your classroom inquiries to be evident in your texts. You undoubtedly chose inquiries based on the needs of your students and the context of your teaching situation. Your goals, in all likelihood, are to remove obstacles to learning and resolve instructional issues so your students' understanding and your teaching practices will be enhanced. Just as we cannot separate our personal selves from our teaching practices, we should not seek to separate our personal selves from our teaching stories. As teachers, we care too deeply about our students, our profession, and our teaching lives to hide or deny ourselves a voice.

Saul (2006), former editor of the *Thinking Classroom/Peremena*, an educational journal published in English and Russian, advises teachers who write for the journal to consider three notions: authenticity, autonomy, and community. Authenticity, she says, is "saying something you care deeply about to someone, an audience, to whom you really want to say it" (p. 3). "The best articles," Saul asserts, "have both reflected and inspired [a] sense of autonomy" (p. 3). The teacher/writer's story reflects his or her sense of agency, of decision making on behalf of students, and, at the same time, inspires a sense of autonomy in readers. If readers are eager to go back to the classroom and use the strategies described in the article, or if they are compelled to think differently about a topic, or if they wish to engage the author in a conversation, or possibly to begin writing or investigating the topic themselves, the article is a success. Finally, by choosing to share our stories with a broader audience through publication, we join a larger community of teachers with whom we share our perspectives on teaching and learning.

At the beginning of her second book, *Invitations: Changing as Teachers and Learners K–12*, Routman (1994) describes her earlier efforts at getting her first book, *Transitions: From Literature to Literacy* (1988), published. She was driven by her success in the classroom and a desire to share her story with other teachers. As she puts it, "I didn't consider myself a writer, and I was an 'unknown.' I was—like so many teachers...largely isolated from other teachers. Still something inside me persisted, telling me to at least try" (p. 1). The success of both of her books demonstrates the power of teacher voices in the conversations about teaching and learning. As teacher researchers, we do have stories to tell and audiences waiting to hear them.

The Intertwined and Recursive Stages of the Writing Process

To write well and publish their work, teacher researchers need to understand the widely recognized stages of the writing process. These are inventing, drafting, revising, and editing. However, not all writers follow these stages in perfect linear order. In fact, many writers compose according to what works best for them. For example, some may begin composing without using any invention strategies, and many do not wait until they have completed a draft before they revise and edit their work. "The writing process is recursive; that is, it is a cyclical, overlapping process" (Richards & Miller, 2005, p. 65). The various stages of the writing process are generally described as follows:

- **Inventing** involves brainstorming and thinking about a topic of your choice. Some writers invent as they write. Other writers make notes, or outlines, or talk into a tape recorder before they begin writing. Others draw or sketch their ideas, or they explain their thinking to colleagues.

- **Drafting** is a considerable challenge for some writers. It takes courage to actually sit down and begin writing. However, once authors start to write, the writing process becomes easier. Think of drafting this way: It's a beginning—not an ending. You don't have to let anyone read your draft. You can always throw your work in the garbage and start over. The important thing is to begin.

- **Revising** is the heart of all writing. Exemplary authors revise many times. They think like visual artists who step back from their work and look with a critical eye at what they have composed. Exemplary writers move paragraphs. They delete sentences. They may add new sections.

- **Editing** is the final stage of the writing process. This is when authors look carefully at their work to determine how they might make their writing more reader friendly. When authors edit, they consider their audience. They vary vocabulary, delete excess words, devise subheadings, omit clichés and professional jargon, and correct spelling and punctuation. It is at this point that the writing is ready for readers.

Again, not all writers move sequentially through these stages of composing. You will develop your own process to approach your writing tasks.

Writing for Diverse Audiences

If you are enrolled in a doctoral program, you have no doubt discovered that you have a variety of audiences for your work. As part of a school or districtwide professional-development requirement, you might need to write one kind of report to meet that expectation, but an entirely different model will be necessary if you choose to propose your teacher research to a dissertation committee as part of your doctoral program. Moreover, if your teacher research was conducted within a writing-project inquiry community that encourages local publication, you may find yourself writing for an audience of practicing teachers in your local area.

Revising your written approach through the lenses of these geographically close audiences might give you more confidence in your writing and you may choose to submit your work to a professional journal, reaching out to more distant readers. Considering the diversity of these audiences, and others you may identify, you must understand that your writing will be developed in different ways. How should you alter your writing style for these varied audiences? Should you adopt formal language or opt for a more informal voice? Should you use active or passive voice? In each case, your choice will depend on the audience for whom you write.

Research Reports Directed at Academic Audiences

As a graduate student seeking a doctoral degree, you are undoubtedly aware that the report of your research will need to meet some very specific requirements depending on the academic audience for whom you are writing. Although there may be no strict regulations on what to include in a research report, your graduate professors and your dissertation team may offer some specific guidelines. Generally, such audiences require the more formal, objective researcher stance, which means that a first-person perspective is inappropriate. Also, the students, who are critical to the research, may be defined as subjects or participants. As for voice, consult models to determine whether to use **active voice** (i.e., where the verb represents the action of the subject, as in "I analyzed the data") or **passive voice** (i.e., where the subject receives the action, as in "The data were analyzed").

TABLE 11.1
Organizational Pattern of Academic Reports

Title

Abstract (100–120 word summary of the study)

Two–three page overview of the inquiry

Context for the inquiry (teaching setting, grade/class level, important issues)

Study participants

Rationale for the research (why this was important, the goals of the study)

Literature informing the inquiry (prior research and established theory)

Questions asked in the inquiry

Data sources

Data analysis

Limitations of the inquiry (what issues interfered and could not be overcome)

Implications or conclusions (what the outcomes suggest for instructional practice)

References

Appendixes

Furthermore, the common organizational pattern in academic reports is fairly standardized. (See Table 11.1. Also, chapter 12 in this volume provides more information on publishing for academic audiences in professional journals.)

Research Stories for Practitioner Audiences

However, when written for practitioner audiences, that is, practicing classroom teachers, a report or article becomes a **practitioner narrative**, generally telling the story of the inquiry and following a narrative format, which integrates research citations into the story rather than presenting them in a separate section. These citations identify related research that supports or informs the research design, data analysis, or findings. They may be included at any point in the narrative where the specific research supports a description of the teacher researcher's beliefs, data, or findings. Put simply, the overall format for a practitioner's teacher research story is, This is where I was; This is what I wondered about; This is what I did; This is what I learned; So what? (See Table 11.2.)

The teaching context is clearly described, providing insight on the students, the school, and the community as appropriate to understanding the challenges and expectations in your classroom. System constraints with curriculum expectations are often defined to the extent that they have an impact on the study. The researcher's beliefs, curiosities, and wonderings about the students and their learning provide the framework for the genesis of the research question.

Aimee Rogers, a teacher researcher with the Southern Arizona Writing Project at The University of Arizona, completed an inquiry on reading for social action with her

<table>
<tr><td colspan="1">

TABLE 11.2
Organizational Pattern of a Practitioner's Teacher Research Story

</td></tr>
</table>

TABLE 11.2
Organizational Pattern of a Practitioner's Teacher Research Story

Description of teaching context (who the students are, the local issues that affect the instructional program)

Research question and its genesis (how did this question arise—usually out of a discrepancy between what the teacher desires for the students and what is happening in the classroom)

Expectations or goals for the study (what the teacher researcher hopes will be the outcomes)

How the data were collected

Analysis of data

Outcomes or findings

Implications for teaching

Next steps (what the teacher researcher will do next; often such a study leads to additional questions and future pursuits)

References

Appendixes, as appropriate

---

charter high school students. Her paper, which was published in the annual teacher research anthology, provides an excellent model of how to integrate background theory into the narrative. As Aimee describes her process of working with her students, she cites the research that informed her practice throughout the study:

> While introducing these texts and reading strategies, I would also encourage my students to participate in Freire's (Wink, 1997) problem-posing approach and Ada's (Wink, 1997) creative reading method. In addition, I wanted to begin to engage my students in critical literacy. Freire's problem-posing approach is ideal for the classroom. This approach has three phases: "to name, to reflect crucially, to act" (Wink, 1997, p. 105). The teacher's role in problem posing is to create a safe place for reflection and action, to help students think about the problem by asking difficult questions, and to help students organize their thoughts and actions (Wink, 1997). As I exposed my students to different and difficult issues of social justice, I wanted to be able to support them as they grappled with these issues and possibly undertook some of the steps of the problem-posing approach. I did not want to force my students into this approach, but I wanted to support them and push them in this approach if they entered into it on their own. (Rogers, 2006, p. 55)

You can see how the theoretical background, rather than appearing separately in its own section, was integrated among the descriptions of the classroom, the students, and the issues the teacher researcher confronted. Aimee's work also demonstrates how student data, both individual and collective, can be integrated into the narrative where appropriate; data, which support the assertions the researcher makes, should be included in the narrative at the point where these assertions are made. Qualitative data include excerpts from student work, student quotations, and illustrations of recurring patterns in student work. Quantitative data appear as charts or tables in the context of the narrative rather than in a separate section.

Always, the tone of the writing carries the personalized voice of the researcher. It should be engaging and interesting, revealing the dynamics of classroom life. The students come alive through the telling and through the data that are presented. Although both data and factual reporting are important, there is little evidence of the "detached" researcher's voiceless presentation of data and facts.

Other information may be included in appendixes as needed (e.g., copies of tests, surveys, questionnaires, and so forth) as long as sufficient information is included in the text to make clear the use of these instruments.

Assessing Your Writing Strengths and Needs

Writing your research report for many audiences may lead you to explore your own insecurities as a writer. How can you overcome your own problems and attack the writing with confidence? One primary avenue we recommend is to seek out trusted colleagues and friends who can provide support. The University of South Florida Round Table (Richards & Miller, 2005) is an example of such a collegial community. This is a group of "advanced graduate students, new professors, and those who [wish] to extend their academic writing skills" (p. 24). Through the support of a caring community, you will find opportunities to share your initial writing efforts and receive advice on how to improve your manuscripts.

A strategy that came out of the Round Table's work is "think-writing" (Richards & Miller, 2005). "Think-writing is talking to yourself in writing, thinking as you write" (MacLean & Mohr, 1999, p. 13). Many of the graduate students in the Round Table who are conducting teacher research projects use this strategy when it is time to begin writing their projects. They keep a journal called a **think-writing log**, in which they consciously jot down their thoughts as they compose. For example, Heather, one of the teacher researchers in the group, shared her log so others could see how it works. (See Figure 11.1.)

You can see that Heather began her think-writing log by using self-talk—that is, talking to herself about her own insecurities before she actually began her draft. Next, you see that when Heather actually began drafting her manuscript within her think-writing log, as she wrote she realized that she needed to explore one topic more fully. Instead of getting sidetracked by trying to do that exploration, she simply made a note to herself (in capital letters) to come back to that part later. Doing that enabled Heather to maintain her writing momentum and continue with the narrative. Later, when she reflected on her writing, she was able to understand more about her own writing process and her need for heavy planning. You can see how Heather learned more about herself as a writer by recording her thoughts before, during, and after writing a draft, and then reviewing her writing reflections (Richards & Miller, 2005). Afterward, Heather was able to take advantage of the cut-and-paste feature to extract her draft from the log and continue

IMMEDIATELY <u>PRIOR TO WRITING</u>

2/22 AT 2:30 P.M.

OK, here it goes. I think I might just type out what I am thinking, and revise later.... I haven't completed the research, but I do have an idea of what I am looking for, what I expect to see, and what I hope will occur in my classroom as a result. I have read some texts, so I have something to say at this point.... (Richards & Miller, 2005, p. 107)

HEATHER'S <u>DRAFT</u> WITH NOTES TO HERSELF

2/22 AT 2:40 P.M.

It is a difficult balance to assume responsibility for learning and at the same time attempt to scaffold students' abilities as they begin to assume some of their own responsibility to learn (Oyler, 1996, p. 25). Over the past four years, I have attempted to shift my teaching practices from a teacher-centered, transmission model, to a more transformative model.

[I NEED TO EXPLAIN WHAT THIS MEANS.]

HEATHER'S ENTRY INTO HER THINK-WRITING LOG <u>AFTER</u> SHE WROTE A DRAFT

2/22 AT 3:39 P.M.

Forcing myself to write helped me to solidify my ideas. I noticed that I had a lot of asides inserted in brackets.... But, back to the writing. Looking at it again, I realize it is less of a draft and more of an outline in prose form. I guess I really can't get away from that planning (Richards & Miller, 2005, pp. 107–109).

---

revising it. If you are hesitant about beginning a draft, looking at Heather's think-writing log may help you overcome your hesitancy.

There are other ways to help yourself take charge of your writing besides using a think-writing log. With a collaborative group to provide support, you may begin to recognize and note the problems you most often have when writing. Posting a list of your common problems above your computer and referring to them as you write, revise, and edit can help you to become a more effective writer.

We advise you to spend time in the university library searching out various scholarly and practitioner journals for articles by other teacher researchers. Recognize that some journals have more strict expectations, not unlike your graduate professors' requirements, while others are more welcoming of the informal, narrative structure with which you may be more comfortable.

Synthesis and Concluding Thoughts

When teachers become involved in teacher research and want to write a report or a teacher research story for some particular audience, they need to become comfortable not only with the writing process but also with themselves as writers.

Too often, those of us who write for the teaching profession depend upon others' ideas and obscure our own voices. If you put yourself into your writing and allow your voice to be heard, you usually will find that you are the author of new insights and understandings about your teaching concerns and dilemmas.

This idea—writing for yourselves—even when doing the required work of your profession, is critical for making certain that you are indeed in the text, that you are, in fact, personally connected to what you write. Your passion and commitment to writing up your research will be clear (Richards & Miller, 2005).

Once you have developed confidence that comes from writing accounts of your research, you will have the motivation and desire to pursue professional publication of your work and your readers will engage with your ideas and insights. You will also look for opportunities to disseminate your research to large national audiences.

PROBLEM-SOLVING VIGNETTE FOR DISCUSSION

Nancy, whose story we read about in the chapter-opening vignette, conducts her research project as required. She believes she has discovered several reading comprehension strategies that are helpful to her students' reading development, and she is eager to share her ideas and her students' success. What should Nancy know and what steps should she take to achieve her goals? She knows what she must do to satisfy her graduate professors' requirements. She has to follow their requirements very carefully to earn the grade (and the degree) she seeks. But she also knows that to share her story with a practitioner audience—her peers in classrooms everywhere—she will need to select a journal and write her teacher research narrative in such a way that others would identify with her struggles, her commitment, her passion, and her students. She wants to let others know what she has learned so that they may also help their students become better readers. As she becomes more comfortable with herself as a writer, she begins to understand aspects of the writing process that she can use to support others in her Round Table writing group. What would you do if you were Nancy?

TIPS FOR TEACHER RESEARCHERS

Here are some hints to help you as you work toward becoming an exemplary writer of research:

■ Think and write about your research project every day.

- Read exemplary research articles to become familiar with academic writing and effective prose.

- Read practitioner journals to determine what kinds of articles they regularly accept.

- See yourself as a writer—someone who cares deeply about a subject and has something important to say about it.

- Know your audience and keep it in mind as you write.

- Don't be afraid to write a weak first draft. You can always make it better.

- Share your writing with a critical friend; join or start a writing group.

- Identify your writing weaknesses, and pay attention to them as you write.

- Step back from your writing and determine if it says what you want it to say. Remember that time spent revising is time well spent and that good writing is good thinking.

- Use simple language and avoid jargon. Limit use of weak *-ing* verbs and excessive adverbs and adjectives.

- Know when to use passive or active voice. Decide in what voice you will write and stick to that voice.

- Invest in a writers' handbook and style manual. We recommend those by Hacker (2004, 2007) or Lunsford (2008). Spend time reviewing them and updating your writing knowledge.

- Finally, remember that successful academic writing should inspire your readers to question, to explore, to want to write themselves.

QUESTIONS FOR REFLECTION

- How can you find the time to write about your research?

- How can you learn to separate your teacher persona from your writer and researcher personas? Or should these selves be separated at all?

- How do you work through the writing process? What do you see as your strengths and needs as a writer?

REFERENCES

Calkins, L.M. (1983). *Lessons from a child: On the teaching and learning of writing.* Portsmouth, NH: Heinemann.

Hacker, D. (2004). *Rules for writers* (5th ed.). Boston: Bedford/St. Martin's.

Hacker, D. (2007). *A writer's reference* (6th ed.). Boston: Bedford/St. Martin's.

Lunsford, A. (2008). *The St. Martin's handbook* (6th ed.). Boston: Bedford/St. Martin's.

MacLean, M.S., & Mohr, M.M. (1999). *Teacher-researchers at work.* Berkeley, CA: National Writing Project.

Oyler, C. (1996). *Making room for students: Sharing teacher authority in room 104.* New York: Teachers College Press.

Richards, J.C., & Miller, S.K. (2005). *Doing academic writing in education: Connecting the personal and the professional.* Mahwah, NJ: Erlbaum.

Richardson, V. (Ed.). (2001). *Handbook of research on teaching* (4th ed.). Washington, DC: American Educational Research Association.

Rogers, A. (2006). Reading for social action: How do youngsters respond? In S.K. Miller (Ed.), *Voices in the village: Two years of tales* (Vol. 7, pp. 52–71). Tucson: The Southern Arizona Writing Project. Retrieved July 31, 2007, from sawp.web.arizona.edu/Anthology05_07.pdf

Routman, R. (1988). *Transitions: From literature to literacy.* Portsmouth, NH: Heinemann.

Routman, R. (1994). *Invitations: Changing as teachers and learners K–12.* Portsmouth, NH: Heinemann.

Saul, W. (2006, October). Touchstones for reflection: Authenticity, autonomy, and community. *Thinking Classroom/Peremena,* 7(4), 3.

Wink, J. (1997). *Critical pedagogy: Notes from the real world.* New York: Longman.

CHAPTER 12

Preparing and Submitting Your Research Manuscript for Publication

Kathy G. Short, Tracy L. Smiles

BEFORE-READING QUESTIONS

- How do you decide on possible manuscripts to submit for publication and to what types of journals?

- How do you select and prepare a specific manuscript to submit to a particular journal?

- How does the process of submission and review work within a refereed journal?

Teaching and research are integral to Tracy's work with children, adults, and schools. Recently, Tracy conducted a study of a phenomenon that has interested her for many years. Several groups of students in Tracy's seventh-grade writing/literature classroom asked to read *1984* by George Orwell in their literature circles. Skeptically agreeing to their request, Tracy realized that she had underestimated their commitment to reading and understanding a book that she judged as difficult. Using transcripts of their discussions and student interviews about those discussions, Tracy explored how students engaged with one another and with literature within peer-led literature discussions (Smiles, 2005). The knowledge Tracy gained about student engagement and the complexity of classroom talk, along with the encouragement of mentors and colleagues and feedback from audience members at presentations, increased her desire to share with other educators. This desire to share, combined with a deep-rooted belief in the importance of teacher voice as part of the public discourse about education, fed her desire to expand her participation in the professional conversation, and so she considers submitting her work to a journal.

Teachers Taking Action: A Comprehensive Guide to Teacher Research, edited by Cynthia A. Lassonde and Susan E. Israel.
© 2008 by the International Reading Association.

Although Tracy has experienced the ways that writing helps her think more deeply about her work through writing research papers for courses and conferences and the ways her practice has been enlightened and transformed by teachers who publish their research, the thought of actually submitting a manuscript based on her research papers is overwhelming. Tracy thinks, Where do I begin with a process that seems elusive? What do I write and for whom? Where do I send it? Tracy feels unsure about how to begin and has tremendous anxieties about exposing her work to virtual strangers who she worries will scrutinize and critique not only her writing but also her teaching.

Introduction

Teacher researchers express their voices and share with others in many ways, including conducting workshops for other teachers, presenting at conferences, and participating in study groups with fellow colleagues (Stock, 2001). There are teachers who want to reach beyond these immediate audiences, however, and one option is writing for publication in journals. Nonetheless, teacher research continues to be underrepresented in professional publications, even though many educators recognize the potential of teacher inquiry for building knowledge and generating theory about teaching and learning (Mills, 2003).

This lack of representation is understandable, considering teachers lead hectic professional lives that require their full time and energy, leaving little time or incentive to write. Furthermore, teachers who do make the time to write sometimes have difficulty finding forms and forums to publish their work. Often their research does not take forms, many of which are based in an experimental research tradition, that are familiar to journal editors (Fleischer, 1994). In addition, many teachers are not familiar with and, as a result, fear the formal peer-review process of most educational journals. Yet teachers do publish their research in journals and books. Classroom teachers such as Nancy Atwell, Bobbi Fisher, Karen Gallas, Linda Christensen, Vivian Paley, and many more have authored seminal works of rich classroom descriptions and theoretical reflections. This body of work has had tremendous influence on the teaching community, some transforming the profession in important ways.

As a journal editor, Kathy struggled with the journal submission statistics that reflect the low number of submissions from teacher researchers and the even lower number of manuscripts accepted by reviewers. Many journal editors state their commitment to publishing the work of teacher researchers, but little changes beyond the publication of a few more articles a year. When we began working with the editorial team of a major journal in our field, we decided to go beyond commitment to taking action by establishing support structures for teacher researchers who were novice writers and wanted to publish. Through our interactions with many teacher researchers and their manuscripts, we gained insights on their struggles with the process of submitting a research manuscript for publication (Smiles & Short, 2006). The information in this chapter has grown out of these experiences, particularly Kathy's editorship of *The New Advocate* and *Language Arts* and Tracy's work as a research assistant with *Language Arts* to support teacher researchers through the journal submission process. We also write out of Kathy's experiences as an author submitting her work to professional journals and Tracy's current efforts to revise existing papers and submit several journal manuscripts. The chapter is organized around our practical suggestions for preparing and submitting a manuscript for publication but begins with the theoretical frame for the role of publication and audience within writing and teacher research.

The Role of Writing in Teacher Research

As with all research, writing plays a vital role in conducting and sharing teacher research, particularly to support researchers in discovering new insights and sharing with others (Hubbard & Power, 1999). Teachers who write for publication have the opportunity to reflect deeply on their practice by exploring the beliefs, values, and images that guide their work. Writing also offers the opportunity to document how ideas evolve and belief systems change (Shubert, 1991).

Although writing is generative for researchers, we agree with many proponents of teacher research who say that writing is not essential to this inquiry. Hubbard and Power (1999) point out that some teachers do not want to write about their findings for a larger audience—informing their own practice fulfills their need to "go public." Other teachers want to challenge assumptions about teachers and classrooms that have been shaped by fragmentary perspectives on the complexity of practice within published research. They recognize that teacher inquiry offers an important point of view into the everyday drama of teaching by presenting more complex understandings of classrooms and classroom life (McCarty, 1997).

Murray (1982) points out that once a writer has chosen a topic, "information about that subject seems to attach itself to the writer" (p. 34). He believes that the writer's entire world becomes potential material while writing about a particular topic because of heightened awareness for that topic in the writer's conscious mind. Teachers have documented the role of writing in increasing their understandings about their teaching. Five (1992) states, "It seems I am not really sure what I've learned in my classroom until I write about it" (p. 50).

Murray (1982) also notes that "the more a writer knows about a subject, the more a writer begins to feel about that subject," and this feeling leads to a desire to organize and share those ideas with others (p. 34). Teachers find that their commitment to their topic is intensified through writing about their research, and they come to care deeply about that focus. This, in turn, creates an awareness of a waiting audience, or what Murray (1982) describes as "an act of arrogance and communication," meaning that, once writers develop a feeling that there are potential readers who want or need to know what the writer has to say, they cannot resist their desire to impart that knowledge. They develop audience awareness— the ability to both understand the experiences and beliefs of the audience they are addressing and use the language of the text to cue readers and invoke a particular stance (Ede & Lundsford, 1984).

In addition, and perhaps most important, writers, including teacher writers, are compelled to write when there's an approaching deadline. Deadlines, whether imposed by others or by the writer, are critical. Few writers ever publish without them.

Even given these professional benefits or external reasons for writing, combined with the internal forces that compel writers, the journey from writing for oneself to publishing for others is an intimidating one. Our goal is to demystify the process through concrete suggestions for systematically approaching the move from writing to publication.

Selecting a Manuscript and a Journal Audience

The first step in submitting a manuscript for publication is moving beyond a desire to publish by making decisions about a specific focus for a manuscript and a journal to consider for submission. As an editor, Kathy knows that the most common reason manuscripts are rejected is the lack of a central focus. Teacher researchers typically spend a great deal of time living with their research and gathering a wealth of data. As a result, this research often goes in multiple directions, reflecting the complexity of classrooms and learners. Writing about all of those directions fails to provide enough discussion about any one of these foci to give depth within a particular manuscript. We suggest that, instead of trying to write about an entire project in any one manuscript, the writer searches through projects for the different possible perspectives from which to view the data and findings, both in terms of what might be written about and who might be interested in that focus.

For example, Tracy listed the possible manuscripts that she might write based on her study of her students' engagement in peer-led literature circles:

- Organizing literature circles within a middle school classroom (practical article)

- Children as coresearchers (journals with teachers or researchers as audience)

- The use of multiple frames for data analysis (journals for researchers)

- Scholarly focus on different aspects of the findings (a research report for researchers or a reflection on research for a broader educator audience)

This process gets even more complicated when there are multiple research projects. Kathy grapples with this problem and has created a list of the possible foci and audiences for each project to figure out which manuscript to work on next. Once a list is generated, the next step is to search for specific journals that might be an appropriate fit for those manuscripts. A target audience and format are needed to bring focus to revising a particular manuscript for submission and to become motivated to work through this process. The desire to publish has to take on a specific form and goal to actually occur.

Peer-review refereed journals, as defined in chapter 10 in this volume, are journals in which the submitted manuscripts are sent for blind review to two or three reviewers from a board of experts in the field. The reviewers critique the manuscript and send their comments about its value for the field and their revision suggestions to the journal editors, who make the final decision regarding publication. These editors are typically respected members of that scholarly field, serving a term of service while continuing their positions in universities or schools.

These journals usually have large national or international audiences of educators and are associated with professional associations, such as the National Council of Teachers of English, International Reading Association, National Council of Teachers of Mathematics, National Council of the Social Studies, and the National Association for the Education of Young Children. There are also smaller peer-reviewed journals published by a particular university or scholarly press that have a more specific focus, such as curriculum theory or international education. These smaller journals often receive fewer submissions and so offer a stronger possibility of publication than the larger journals that receive hundreds of manuscripts.

An important distinction in peer-reviewed journals is between professional journals and research journals. Although both are scholarly in nature, their audience and written format are quite different (Mitchell & Reutzel, 2006). **Professional journals** have a broad target audience of school-based educators, teacher educators in universities, and undergraduate and graduate students. Their major focus is on improving practice and raising critical issues of theory and research as connected to practice. Instead of publishing reports of research, they publish reflections on research where the researcher discusses the findings in relation to practice in classrooms. In contrast, **research journals** publish reports of original and rigorously conducted studies that advance the knowledge of a particular field and so are primarily read by other researchers. Research journals publish fewer, longer manuscripts and have a rigorous review process that makes acceptance for publication more difficult. The International Reading Association, for example, publishes *The Reading Teacher* as a professional journal focused on literacy in elementary grades and *Reading Research Quarterly* as a research journal for scholarship on literacy among learners of all ages. Many teacher researchers submit to professional journals because the voice, format, and focus are accessible to classroom teachers—these journals let them speak to the audience they most want to inform.

Conversely, some write for research journals because of their desire that teacher research influence the knowledge base and scholarly community of the field.

Another group of educational publications and magazines, such as *Educational Leadership*, *Phi Delta Kappan*, *The Instructor*, and *Teaching K–12*, follow a journalistic tradition, but the articles do not go through blind peer review. Some do review submitted manuscripts, but many primarily contain invited articles, solicited and published at the discretion of a full-time professional editor. Their articles tend to be shorter and offer timely information on a topic or invite debate and differing perspectives around an issue (Mitchell & Reutzel, 2006).

Local state or regional journals may or may not be peer-reviewed but are often associated with professional organizations such as a state reading or language arts council. These journals typically want short, focused articles on practice that speak to their audience of teachers within that state. Editors of these journals usually publish both submitted and solicited manuscripts and actively seek submissions from teacher researchers. They also have a shorter turn-around time for publication and often provide a more supportive context for novice writers.

Other sources of publication include electronic journals, some of which have a specific focus on teacher research. Several of these journals are listed in Appendix A.

Selecting a Journal

Figuring out which journals might be interested in a manuscript involves familiarity with the field as well as effective search strategies. The journals that most educators consider first are those associated with the professional organizations that are significant to their professional growth. The problem with focusing only on these journals is that they often receive a high number of submissions and so can publish only a small percentage of what is submitted. Twelve to 20% is a typical acceptance rate. We keep those journals as possibilities but engage in strategies such as the following to locate other sources for publication:

- Seeking recommendations from professional colleagues who are well read in the field

- Examining articles that informed our research to see where they were published

- Checking the references cited in these articles and their publication sources

- Doing a subject search of the study focus on a professional database, such as ERIC, and noting the journals in which articles on this topic are published

Once a list of possible journals is created, we go to the journals' websites to read descriptions of each journal's focus and content, audience, submission guidelines, and calls for manuscripts. **Submission guidelines** provide the specifics about how to submit, including where to send the manuscript, page count, style and format, and cover page information, while the **call for manuscripts** provides information on the scholarly content, focus, and audience for that journal, including whether the journal has an open call for any manuscript on their focus or requests manuscripts on specific themes. For example, *Language Arts* is a themed journal and the articles in each issue focus on that one theme, while *The Reading Teacher* is unthemed and so each issue has articles on a range of literacy themes and topics.

We read through the journal descriptions and calls for manuscripts and note the journals that seem to be the best fit with our list of possible manuscripts. Once a narrowed list of possible journals is generated, we skim through an issue or two of those journals on the Internet or at the library to see if there is a connection between our voice and study and the voices and contents of those journals. We especially consider which journals reach the audiences that we see as significant for a particular aspect of our study.

Our list of possible manuscripts and "short list" of the best journal options support us in making a decision about which manuscript to work on first for submission. This choice is based on a range of criteria:

- A themed call for manuscripts that fits our study and has an impending deadline
- The findings we are most passionate about or committed to
- What speaks to the audience we most want to reach
- What we feel most ready to write about
- An existing paper that could easily be revised for submission to a journal
- Presentations on the study that we have made to a range of audiences

There is no one way to make this decision; we simply weigh these factors and move forward with selecting a particular journal and manuscript focus. Our experience is that the decision involves reflecting on our lists and then taking a deep breath and selecting a manuscript and a journal. We are not eliminating the other possibilities, just selecting a place to begin.

We initially resisted spending this amount of time researching journals and considering publication sources but found that without this background knowledge, we wasted a great deal of time in writing and submitting the wrong manuscript to the wrong journal. This research process also allowed us to see our writing of a particular manuscript as part of a program of writing from our work, instead of thinking that we were writing "the" article based on our study. Kathy found that once she went through this process several times, the process became shorter because she notes possible journals as she reads other educators.

Revising and Editing a Manuscript

Having selected a focus and journal, we take the time to read several issues of the journal to get a good feel for the tone and format of articles within that journal and the specific nature of the journal audience. Once a range of articles from several issues of the journal have been read and a sense of length, style, and audience has developed, we move back into our work to write or to revise an existing paper (see chapter 11 in this volume for a detailed discussion of the recursive nature of the writing process). If possible, a strong draft should be completed several weeks before the deadline to provide time to get responses from colleagues and to make final revisions and copyediting. (We admit that this is a goal and not always a reality.) Asking colleagues who are a close fit with the audience of the journal or who are readers of the journal to respond to the draft is especially useful—otherwise, their advice can be in direct contradiction to that of reviewers for the journal. The final check is for copyediting errors and style formatting (e.g., American Psychological Association). Although reviewers primarily focus on the content, copyediting errors signal carelessness and lack of professional respect on the part of the writer, which might affect reviewers' recommendations.

If the manuscript is being submitted to a peer-reviewed journal, the writers need to remove any direct references to their identities because the manuscript must undergo blind review. **Blind review** means that the peer reviewer evaluates the manuscript without the bias of association with a particular person. Writers can put "Author" instead of their name if referring to themselves in the draft and mask citations by putting "Author, 2006" instead of the actual reference.

Taking time away from a draft allows a writer to view that draft with fresh eyes and to consider other ways to organize and word particular sections. Kathy finds that she makes more effective revisions when she gets some distance from a draft than when she writes up to the deadline. Drafting is only the initial step in writing a manuscript, but most course papers stop at this point and so teacher researchers often have not experienced revision beyond editing changes. Drafting focuses a writer's attention on exploring ideas, while revision allows for crafting the wording and shaping ideas, as well as for shifting attention to a particular audience.

Each journal has guidelines for submitting a manuscript in terms of the cover page and author contact information, the number of paper copies to submit, whether to send an electronic file, and so forth. These final details need careful attention because they can delay a manuscript from being sent out for review. We also write a brief submission letter to indicate if we are submitting to a particular theme and to provide a brief introduction about ourselves and our manuscript. This letter only goes to the editor but provides important contextual information that frames the manuscript in that person's mind.

The Editorial Review Process

Some teacher researchers hesitate to submit to a professional journal because they are unfamiliar with the review process and are not sure how to proceed or what to expect. Others have sent a submission, but received a rejection, and are not sure how to respond to the comments of editors and reviewers. Many are surprised at being asked to make revisions beyond a few fix-ups of conventions and clarifying details and do not realize that revision is the norm, not an exception (Jalongo, 2002). In addition, teacher researchers are surprised at the length of the publication process for a peer-reviewed journal.

Kathy's editorial experiences indicate why the **editorial review process**, the process that manuscripts go through once they are received by an editor, is often more lengthy than writers expect. When the manuscripts arrive, they are entered into a database and distributed to an editorial team who reads them, determining whether that manuscript should be sent out for review. Manuscripts that are obviously not a fit for the journal's content, style, or format are often not sent to reviewers. The majority is sent out for review and so the initial editorial reading involves considering which reviewers from the Editorial Review Board have a professional expertise and interests that match a manuscript.

Reviewers usually have three to four weeks to respond to a manuscript, but, given busy schedules and the need for at least two reviews per manuscript, that length of time is often doubled. Once all the reviews are in, editors read the reviews and reread the manuscript to make a decision. It is not uncommon to receive contradictory revision and publication recommendations, and so making editorial decisions can be difficult. Also, if the journal is themed, the editors have to make decisions for the issue as a whole and frequently cannot decide on an individual manuscript without knowing how reviewers are evaluating the other manuscripts submitted for that theme. The time between submission and receiving editorial response can, therefore, be several months longer for themed journals. In general, the time between submission and response is four to six months.

The publication decisions used by most editors are to accept a manuscript with minor revisions, to ask for revisions and resubmission for a second round of reviews, or to reject the manuscript. A rejection indicates that the author is not invited to revise and resubmit that manuscript. Sometimes editors suggest more appropriate journals, and other times they indicate the need for major reorganization and revision that would lead to a new manuscript, in which case that manuscript could be sent as a new submission at a later time. An accept decision usually includes the request for minor revisions and copyediting that are submitted directly to the editor. An accepted manuscript will not go out for further comments from reviewers but may involve working through several additional drafts with the editor.

Many novice writers are surprised to learn that the most frequent publication decision is to revise and resubmit, which adds another three to four months to the process. Only a few of the manuscripts that Kathy eventually published as an editor were immediately accepted. Most received a revise and resubmit decision, which specified the types of revisions the author needed to consider. Once the authors revised the manuscripts, they were sent back out to reviewers, often one original reviewer and one new reviewer.

In our work with teacher researchers, we found that some viewed a revise and resubmit decision as a rejection. Other times, they decided to resubmit but did not attend closely to the due date given by the editors, because they did not realize the reality of the tight deadlines, particularly in a themed journal. A letter from an editor inviting an author to revise and resubmit a manuscript by a particular date signifies a strong interest in that manuscript and the possibility that it might be published. If the due date is problematic, we recommend immediately corresponding with the editors to see if the date is negotiable, instead of either not resubmitting the manuscript or sending it late without notifying the editor.

The editor's letter is accompanied by the reviews. Reviewers often make contradictory recommendations or suggestions that would result in a substantially different manuscript. Having written hundreds of editorial letters, Kathy knows that the editor carefully decides on the most significant revisions from those suggested by reviewers to highlight in the editorial letter. When Kathy gets an editorial letter about her own writing, she carefully reads that letter and focuses primarily on those suggestions. Typically, when the editor does not comment on something raised by a reviewer, either the editor does not agree with the reviewer or is leaving that particular suggestion to the author's discretion.

Sometimes an editor or reviewer will ask for revisions that violate the intent of the manuscript or involve wording that does not fit the voice or meaning of the author. When she disagrees with an editor, Kathy first tries to understand the issue or problem and find an alternative solution. If there is no alternative, she has the right to not make that revision and to explain her reasoning to the editor. No matter what, a letter should be sent to the editor, explaining point by point what was revised.

We know from experience that rejection hurts. When we receive a rejection, we read quickly through the editorial and reviewer comments and then give ourselves a couple of weeks to get over the sting. Kathy has published many articles, but receiving a rejection is still unpleasant for her and initially difficult to process. After several weeks, she pulls out the editorial and review comments and reads them closely and then goes back to her list of possible journals to determine which journal to submit to next. She uses the reviewers' comments to make the manuscript stronger before submitting it to the next journal. Well-published authors often have stories about articles that have received major recognition in the field, but that were initially rejected by more than one journal. Authors who get published are persistent.

If a manuscript is accepted, we know that we still revisit the manuscript multiple times. Editors usually ask for minor revisions in the content and for copyediting changes. Most journals also send the page proofs from the publisher for a final review before printing. At that point, the manuscript has been typeset and no major revisions can be made. The review of the page proofs is only for small copyedit corrections.

Copyright and informed consent are another aspect of the publication process. The publisher of the journal asks authors to sign a **consent to publish form** that gives the rights of publication to the publisher for that article, including future reprinting. If, for example, the writers later want to publish that article as a chapter in a book, they have to request permission from the journal publisher. Most publishers routinely provide that permission when the author of the piece requests it. Publishers can also give permission for reprinting an article somewhere else, such as an edited book, without getting the author's permission. Kathy finds that the publisher usually notifies her, but sometimes her work has been reproduced in another source without her knowledge. An additional aspect of the paperwork process is that an **informed consent form** has to be provided for any artifacts (e.g., drawings, writing) included in the article and for any talk that is directly quoted. Journals are not allowed to publish the actual words or work of a child or adult without a signed permission from the person or his or her guardian. Journals do provide their own forms, but teacher researchers usually have already gathered forms as part of their research and so provide copies of those to the journal.

Synthesis and Concluding Thoughts

The process of writing a paper for a university course or conference presentation is a familiar one to most teacher researchers. Surrounding oneself with books, papers, and data and working extensively to produce a coherent analysis and discussion of the data is an exhausting process that most have repeated over and over. We meet the deadline with relief and, in the exhilaration of that moment, consider revising the paper for submission to a journal. Those good intentions, however, rarely result in an actual submission, primarily because a long process of preparing, submitting, and revising a manuscript still lies ahead without any assurance of actual publication.

Given the time-intensive process of preparing and submitting a manuscript for publication, it is easy to understand why most teacher researchers choose not to involve themselves in this process. In fact, the difficulties of submitting a manuscript and getting it published can easily lead to questioning whether the benefits are worth the cost of time and effort. Demystifying the process and developing concrete research and revision strategies can decrease frustration and increase the probability of successful publication; therefore, the first step in moving toward publication is to become familiar with the process and develop strategies for systematically approaching the move from writing to publication.

The question of why anyone would choose to write for publication still remains. The thrill of seeing our names in print and the recognition of peers is clearly a motivation but is not enough to sustain us through the process. What does sustain us is the greater clarity and increased understandings we gain when we write about our work for a broader audience and the commitment we feel to influencing professional conversations in the field. Ultimately, we publish because we accept the challenge of exercising our voices beyond our local contexts out of a sense of professional responsibility to other educators and students and, in the process, of transforming ourselves as well.

PROBLEM-SOLVING VIGNETTE FOR DISCUSSION

For Tracy, the thought of submitting her work to a national audience evokes powerful feelings of vulnerability. She wonders if such an effort is worth her mental and emotional energy. At the same time, she believes that the voices of teachers need to be part of the professional and public discourse about education now more than ever. Such perspectives can work to dispel pervasive notions that quick fixes and increased accountability can reform education. The problem of how to deal with conflicts of time, motivation, and support for writing is one that she, along with other teacher researchers, must find a way to solve.

Tracy knows that the process of submitting a manuscript for publication will be challenging, requiring hard work, patience, and perseverance. However, she believes that the range of strategies and plan of action presented in this chapter can work to optimize her chances of successfully writing for and publishing in a professional journal. Tracy has generated a list of possible manuscripts and audiences, and she is considering a paper that she presented recently at a conference about the ways in which her students' use of argument reflects broader notions of what it means to be educated and possess business savvy. This paper has been presented in various forms, and the work has been well received. In addition, the paper itself, although not ready for submission to a major journal, is fairly complete, and a colleague who has done notable research on classroom talk has urged her to try to get this work published.

Tracy needs to choose a potential journal and use that decision to craft an appropriate piece to submit. She is considering *Voices From the Middle* and the *Journal of Adolescent & Adult Literacy* because her research offers practical insights on how a teacher might facilitate peer-led literature circles in middle school and how a classroom teacher might interpret the talk within that instructional context. *Teaching Today for Tomorrow* is another potential journal because of its focus on both research and the improvement of practice.

We invite you to locate and read articles from these journals in order to determine the foci, voices, and structures of their published articles. Based on your review of these three journals, how would you identify their major audience and the types of articles they publish? What advice would you give Tracy on which journal to select and what kind of voice and structure to use in revising her manuscript?

TIPS FOR TEACHER RESEARCHERS

Submitting a manuscript for publication is a process of research, decision making, and revision. The following guidelines provide a framework to support your decisions as you work toward your goal of successfully getting a manuscript accepted for publication.

- Brainstorm possible manuscripts that could be written from your study.
- Create a "short list" of journals to which you could submit.
  - Get recommendations from colleagues who are well read in the field.
  - Examine the publication sources of articles that informed your study and the references cited in those articles. Do an ERIC topic search.
  - Go to the journal websites and read their descriptions, submission guidelines, and calls for manuscripts.
- Choose the specific manuscript you want to submit to a particular journal.
  - Find a themed call with an impending deadline that fits your study.
  - Consider the findings you are passionate about or feel most ready to write.
  - Revise an existing paper or presentation.
- Revise and edit your manuscript before submission.
  - Read through several issues of the journal to get the tone and format of articles and the specific nature of the journal audience. Then revise your manuscript.
  - Ask colleagues who know the journal to respond to your draft.
  - Reread the submission guidelines and check style and length requirements.
  - Create the cover page and write a submission letter
- Deal with the long editorial review process.
  - If you receive a rejection, revise the manuscript based on the reviewers' comments and send it out to another journal.

- If you receive a revise and resubmit, closely read the editorial letter to guide your consideration of the reviewers' suggestions.

QUESTIONS FOR REFLECTION

■ Why do you want to write for publication? Which findings or ideas do you find most interesting or significant from your study and want to spend more time thinking about? What might other educators find of most interest from your study?

■ Whom do you want to inform or think with? Who is your audience, and what journals publish articles for that audience?

■ Do you care enough about these ideas and audience to invest the amount of time and effort needed to go through revision and the editorial review process?

REFERENCES

Ede, L., & Lunsford, A. (1984). Audience addressed/audience invoked: The role of audience in composition theory and pedagogy. *College Composition and Communication, 35*, 155–171.

Five, C.L. (1992). Teacher research: Catalyst for writing. In K.L. Dahl (Ed.), *Teacher as writer: Entering the professional conversation* (pp. 44–51). Urbana, IL: National Council of Teachers of English.

Fleischer, C. (1994). Researching teacher-research: A practitioner's retrospective. *English Education, 26*, 86–124.

Hubbard, R.S., & Power, B.M. (1999). *Living the questions: A guide for teacher researchers*. York, ME: Stenhouse.

Jalongo, M.R. (2002). *Writing for publication: A practical guide for educators*. Norwood, MA: Christopher-Gordon.

McCarty, T.L. (1997). Teacher research methods in language and education. In N.H. Hornberger & D. Corson (Eds.), *Encyclopedia of language and education: Volume 8: Research methods in education* (pp. 227–237). New York: Kluwer Academic.

Mills, G.E. (2003). *Action research: A guide for the teacher researcher*. Englewood Cliffs, NJ: Merrill/Prentice Hall.

Mitchell, J.P., & Reutzel, D.R. (2006). Publishing in professional journals. In S. Wepner & L. Gambrell (Eds.), *Beating the odds: Getting published in the field of literacy* (pp. 56–71). Newark, DE: International Reading Association.

Murray, D.M. (1982). *Learning by teaching: Selected articles on writing and teaching*. Montclair, NJ: Boynton/Cook.

Shubert, W.H. (1991). Teacher lore: A basis for understanding praxis. In C. Witherell & N. Noddings (Eds.), *Stories lives tell: Narrative and dialogue in education* (pp. 207–233). New York: Teachers College Press.

Smiles, T.L. (2005). *Student engagement within peer-led literature circles: Exploring the thought styles of adolescents*. Unpublished doctoral dissertation, University of Arizona, Tucson.

Smiles, T.L., & Short, K.G. (2006). Transforming teacher voice through writing for publication. *Teacher Education Quarterly, 33*(3), 133–147.

Stock, P.L. (2001). Toward a theory of genre in teacher research: Contributions from a reflective practitioner. *English Education, 33*, 100–114.

CHAPTER 13

Preparing and Presenting Your Research Findings

Nithya Narayanaswamy Iyer,
Suzanne Wegener Soled

KEY TERMS

Colloquium

Panel

Paper presentation

Poster presentation

Professional conferences

Proposal

Seminar

Symposium

Works-in-progress

Workshop

BEFORE-READING QUESTIONS

■ How do you select which conference to submit a proposal to or what type of format would be the best for the presentation?

■ How do you write a successful proposal to submit for a conference presentation?

■ How do you prepare for the conference presentation?

S   uzanne and her university colleagues have worked with secondary-grade science and
    mathematics teachers to help them find ways to connect engineering and technology
    with their content areas. Suzanne has collected what seems like tons of data over the
past five years that includes information about what the teachers have experienced about
their participation in her work, the attitudes and interest of their students regarding
science and mathematics as well as achievement data about their learning, and even
information about the graduate engineering and science students who worked in their
classrooms demonstrating engineering applications.

Suzanne and her colleagues, as a collaborative group of educational researchers, know
the importance of sharing their research so others might benefit from what they have
learned. But the questions they ask include the following: Who are the others? Do we have
something to share with other faculty researchers? Are these researchers from the field of
education or the discipline of engineering? Should we present alone, with our colleagues,
with the teachers, or with the graduate students? We want to make sure we are reaching
the right audience, with the appropriate message, and in a way that is satisfying.

Teachers Taking Action: A Comprehensive Guide to Teacher Research, edited by Cynthia A. Lassonde and Susan E. Israel.
© 2008 by the International Reading Association.

This collaborative educational research group begins to contemplate the merits of presenting at a really large conference, where they could share with education researchers and teachers, as well as at small professional conferences, where there will be many other engineering faculty interested in K–12 outreach. They consider presenting a paper by just talking to an audience, and they think of having a more interactive poster session where they could talk to fewer folks more intensely. They also contemplate with whom they could present. One possible collaboration consists of a faculty member, a teacher, and two graduate students presenting together. Another possibility is a teacher presenting independently at a local conference. Another presentation could be done by a pairing of teachers and graduate students. The various combinations of collaborators would present a different perspective of the research.

Introduction

As teacher researchers, we (Nithya and Suzanne) believe that if you are looking for avenues to share your work, you will find that one of the best ways to share new ideas, creative pilots, curricula, learning activities, and results of teacher research is to present at professional conferences. **Professional conferences** are meetings designed for professionals in their disciplines to come together to share information, ideas, and research as well as for professional development. Conferences often have shorter lead times than publications. (As described in chapter 12 in this volume, the journal review process can be quite time-consuming.) This means less time passes between the time you complete your research and the time you share your results at conferences. Also, conferences provide quick dissemination of your latest ideas or scholarly work. Conferences are offered at the local, state, regional, national, or international level. They may range in size from gigantic venues with thousands of participants covering a huge array of topics over the period of a week to intimate gatherings of fewer than 100 participants working with a single focus during a day.

Usually a conference is organized into many sessions, and each session has several presenters or speakers. Most often, speakers have to apply to present their findings. They are given time slots during which to present. In some cases these slots can be highly competitive, meaning there are many people who want to present and not enough time for all of them to do so. Conferences typically require presenters to submit a proposal. A **proposal** is an idea or a plan of the research findings or ideas that you want to present and the way in which you want to do so. The success of a proposal depends on more than just a quality idea or sound research findings. Once the proposal has been accepted, the next step is to prepare and execute an effective presentation. This chapter discusses the process of selecting an appropriate conference, the various types of conference formats, how to write a proposal, how to prepare for the presentation, and how to execute it.

Selecting an Appropriate Conference

Many college departments routinely organize colloquia, which are an excellent venue for presenting in front of a local audience (*colloquium* is defined later in this chapter, along with other conference formats). The local audience may be aware of some of the issues pertinent to and affecting the area and will be able to provide sound feedback. School districts also organize colloquia and workshops for professional development of its employees and may provide an avenue for presentations.

Beyond college departments and school districts, conferences are offered at the regional, state, national, and international level. In an academic year, there are numerous conferences from which to choose. (See Appendix A, Table A.1, for a chart of a number of conferences, their websites, and conference dates.) Choosing a conference depends on a number of factors such as whether the conference accepts papers in your field of study, the time of the year the meeting is held, the location of the conference, and the reality of the cost of attending.

Investigate the conference to find out if there is a match between your paper, the organization's discipline, and the conference theme. Usually the organization hosting the conference will provide information on its website regarding the mission of the conference and whether there is a particular theme for any given year. The American Educational Research Association (AERA), for instance, accepts papers from a broad range of disciplines such as education, psychology, statistics, sociology, history, economics, philosophy, anthropology, and political science. If your paper is based in a different discipline, submitting your paper to another conference would be more beneficial due to a better fit with the purpose of the conference. The paper may have an increased possibility of being accepted. Investigate your options broadly. For example, Suzanne submits papers about her research with secondary math and science students to the American Society for Engineering Education (ASEE) because the work involves engineering applications. The ASEE has a specific section devoted to K–12 educational outreach.

Because there are so many conferences in an academic year, and considering the increasing cost of attending conferences, we recommend choosing a conference that best fits your schedule and location. Most conferences require a registration fee, which can typically range from $50 to $500. This fee does not include travel or lodging expenses but may include some meals. Sometimes, school districts have professional development funds to support teachers and other staff to present their research, especially at local and regional conferences. In addition, there may be other sources of funds available through the institution or external grants and awards such as the International Reading Association (IRA) Teacher as Researcher Grant. (See Appendix A, Funding Research—Grants, for more information on grants.) Some conference presenters limit costs by choosing locations that are close to home to save money and time.

Types of Conferences

By first identifying the professional associations in the disciplines of interest to her, Suzanne was able to find associations oriented for science teachers, math teachers, specific fields of science such as physics and chemistry, as well as engineering. Figuring out the audience you want to communicate with through the professional associations helps to identify the best conferences to choose.

We believe that choosing the best avenue to present one's findings is crucial. In any academic year there are hundreds of conferences that one can attend. There are discipline-specific conferences that are organized regularly and annually as well as general or cross-disciplinary events. Even within one professional association, there may be larger national conferences and smaller regional conferences. For example, AERA offers a national conference with attendance as large as 15,000 people. There are numerous smaller regional and state conferences such as the California, Eastern, Michigan, Midwest, and Southwest Educational Research Associations with attendance from 100 to 1,000 people. Some organizations such as ASEE even have international global colloquia, an annual national-level conference, and smaller regional area conferences around the United States.

Conference Roles

One of the main reasons for attending conferences is to engage in intellectual conversations with attendees (Barton, 2005) for networking purposes. Further, Barton explains that conferences provide an opportunity to hear about and present recent research. This can be accomplished by just reading books and journals, but a conference provides a mode of discourse unlike any other academic genres. Additionally, conferences are a great source for meeting like-minded scholars interested in your area of study and can pave the way for future collaborations. Once you decide to attend a conference, we suggest you determine the extent to which you would like to be involved in it. There are a number of opportunities to participate by taking on specific conference roles. Organizations' websites typically list and describe various conference roles. The roles of chair, discussant, and audience participant are described here.

Large conferences have sessions in which papers with similar topics are grouped together. These sessions will require a session chair or a discussant. Chairs introduce the session and the session speakers. This involves welcoming the audience and introducing speakers in the order in which they will speak. Chairs may also briefly explain the content of the session, for example, if the session is a symposium or a themed session with papers based on a particular topic (Academy of Management [AOM], 2004; Barton, 2005). In addition, chairs are responsible for keeping time during presentations. In any session of AERA, for example, there are approximately four presenters, each presenting for 15 minutes. If there are five presenters, the presenter's time is limited to 12 minutes. Chairs have to make sure that the participants stay within the time limit (AOM, 2004; Barton, 2005). They do this by holding cards to remind participants of how many minutes remain. Finally, chairs actively moderate the discussions at the end of the sessions by ensuring that audience members' questions are directed to the appropriate panelists. When questions are not directed toward any particular panelist, chairs may suggest which panelist may answer that question. The chair should also make sure the session ends on time. Exceeding the time limit may not only hinder audience members who are ready to leave but also attendees who have arrived for the next session (Barton, 2005).

Although session chairs introduce participants and moderate the session, the role of discussants is to discuss the papers, synthesize them, and balance praise and criticism. According to Barton (2005), discussants are selected because the symposium organizers think they are qualified to take on these responsibilities. Discussants need to spend time reading and reflecting on the papers to develop an analysis. Presenters want to know what the discussant thinks of their papers, and it is important for the discussant to mention each paper individually. Discussants must not only comment on the papers but also draw on them to arrive at an overall synthesis. For example, the discussant may show how the papers develop a common idea, present alternative perspectives, or collectively advance the field (Barton, 2005). The task is easier if the papers submitted have a shared topic. In a symposium, discussants can comment on the common theme and draw examples from each paper to demonstrate. However, if the topics are diverse, synthesis can be very difficult. In this situation, the discussant may have to spend time reviewing the papers and providing a brief overview of their similarities and differences. Discussants serve an important role by offering comments on papers that will assist authors in the steps toward publication. Such valuable commentary may include remarks made in the session, comments written directly on the papers, or discussions with the authors at the annual meeting. Discussants should conduct these activities in advance to prepare properly. The Academy of Management (2004) recommends discussants integrate the ideas by

- Identifying shared constructs, linking findings, and presenting any contradictory results that emerge across papers
- Identifying any ongoing debates, themes, and puzzles within the topic domain and how the group of papers contributes to or clarifies them
- Avoiding reviewing each paper individually

Conferences cannot succeed without audience members. Audience members not only listen actively but also ask questions to stimulate discussions that focus on the greater good of the academic community. Questions should be clear and concise and should move the conversation in a direction that encourages insightful understanding of the paper.

From a personal standpoint, we enjoy all of these roles—presenter, chair, discussant, and audience member. Sometimes, once one of us finds out that our conference proposal has been accepted, we will also try to participate in the conference as a chair or discussant. This increases our involvement at the conference and gives us more opportunities to interact with our colleagues.

How can you decide which roles you will commit to at various conferences? Factors that might influence your decisions include your expertise on the topic (i.e., whether you think you would have something to contribute to the synthesis of a group of papers), your comfort in speaking in front of groups of people, or whether or not you are already presenting or would have the time to devote to doing your best in the role. We would suggest you attend sessions that have discussants and chairs before attempting to take on these roles. Then you will see for yourself what the expectations are.

Knowing the Formats for Conference Presentations

Conference formats vary widely and include paper presentations and posters, seminars, colloquia, symposia, interactive sessions, workshops, and special sessions. Information on conference formats is usually available online. The most common conference format is the **paper presentation**, which refers to a formal presentation of a paper by a single author, often grouped with other papers on a similar topic. Each presenter offers an abbreviated version of his or her paper for 10 to 15 minutes, with a short time at the end of the presentations for discussant or audience questions. The paper presentation or roundtable, a highly interactive format, does away with the formal presentation. It allows audience members to discuss the topic extensively with the presenter and other interested participants often for as long as an hour.

Presentations well suited for graphic display may be given as **poster presentations**, which allow the participants to have individualized discussions with the presenter in a more informal session over 60 to 90 minutes. Interactive conversations take place based on who stops by to talk about your poster and work. Later in this chapter, we focus on poster presentations. As a novice presenter, you may have an increased chance of getting your proposal accepted for a poster presentation than if you propose other types of presentations. Think of it this way: A program chair has one large room to use for the conference. In that room, in one session, the chair could schedule a single speaker, four to five paper presenters with a discussant, 10–20 roundtable presenters, or 50 poster presentations. Poster presentation formats are a good place to begin to build your confidence, too. As mentioned previously, rather than speaking in front of a large group of people, you will interact more informally with interested colleagues in a poster presentation.

Combinations of presenters are seen more frequently in colloquia, symposia, panels, workshops, special sessions, or works-in-progress. A **colloquium** is a set of seminars that usually have a common theme and can be spread over several days to as long as a few weeks. A **seminar** is an event in which there is typically only one speaker focusing on one major topic. A **symposium** normally consists of three or four speakers, each of whom presents a different perspective on a related topic or addresses a specific problem. Interactive symposia are designed for active engagement of the participants with the topic using activities such as panels, small-group sessions, or discussion. Similar to symposia, a **panel** is usually composed of several short presentations by different speakers followed by an opportunity for discussion with the audience. A **workshop** involves a planned, formal presentation with participant involvement, usually for a longer period of time such as a three-hour block, entire day, or several days, and may occur just before the start of the conference. It emphasizes problem solving, hands-on training, and requires the involvement of the participants. A workshop can also involve a short presentation followed by the participants debating and discussing the topic (Kitchin & Fuller, 2005). Special sessions, such as performances, readings, off-site visits, or town meetings, may provide for nontraditional formats with the focus of actively involving the audience. Finally, **works-in-progress** (WIPs) are reports of the preliminary development of an ongoing project and include the initial results of the project in progress. WIPs may also include creative pilots, innovative curricula, or other nontraditional ideas.

As a teacher educator, Nithya has been fascinated by the different routes preservice teachers take to attain teaching certification. Using surveys, she has studied if teachers prepared in these different routes to certification feel prepared and have the disposition to teach. Knowing the various formats for presenting, Nithya understands that her work was data based, and she explores presenting her paper as a poster or paper presentation or as a roundtable. These formats are appropriate because Nithya can meet audience members and extensively discuss her paper with them. This would be beneficial for Nithya because she would be able to interact with other teacher researchers interested in her topic and get direct feedback.

Understanding the Proposal Process

Conference proposals are typically reviewed anonymously by a panel of peers. The proposal should contain enough information to allow the peer-review committee to make an accurate judgment on the content of the paper. Guidelines vary from conference to conference and usually can be found on the organization's website.

Potential presenters need to be familiar with the proposal process, and the first step is knowing your deadlines. For example, AERA meets every year around March or April but proposals are due to them by the beginning of August of the previous year. Proposals can be due anywhere from 2 to as many as 10 months before the conference date. Typically, large conferences and national or international conferences have long lead times. Small or local conferences have shorter times between the proposal due date and the actual conference presentation. For many conferences, the deadline for submitting proposals tends to be similar from year to year. Most organizations require that proposals be submitted electronically. You can find deadlines for conference proposals posted online.

After finding a match between your topic and the conference and deciding on the best format for your presentation, the next step is to identify the proposal criteria. Each conference provides information about what is to be contained in the actual proposal, the proposal length, and the areas to be addressed, such as the importance to the community or expected outcomes.

The guidelines and the review process for the proposal are typically posted online, too. For example, AERA requires a 200-word abstract, with a proposal of a maximum of 2,000 words (AERA, 2006). Then, conference proposals are blind reviewed by three peer reviewers. The reviewer ratings, comments, and recommendation for acceptance or rejection are funneled to a program chair. The chair then decides whether a proposal should be accepted and where it will fit.

Other conferences may have a multistep proposal and acceptance process. For example, Frontiers in Education initially requires a 300-word abstract in January and authors receive notification of their acceptance or rejection in February. If the abstract is accepted, the full paper must be submitted for review in March, and authors are notified of peer-review results in April. Modified papers are due in May. If the paper has addressed the concerns from the peer review, it is accepted, published in the conference proceedings, and becomes one of the presentations at the annual conference in the late fall.

It helps to understand the likelihood of having a proposal accepted. Sometimes each proposal has an equal chance of being accepted for presentation. Other times, certain types of proposals will have a greater chance of acceptance based on the presentation format as mentioned in our discussion of poster presentations. If the goal of the program chair is to bring many professionals together to present their work, roundtables or poster presentations will be preferred and accepted at a high rate.

Preparing for the Presentation

After a proposal has been accepted, it is important to prepare for the presentation. For example, paper presentations are usually oral in nature and limited to 10 to 15 minutes. Speakers can use a variety of technology to assist in their presentation. Most often, transparencies or PowerPoint slides are used.

Presenting your study to other people requires advanced preparation work and practice. It is important to relax and take deep breaths before presenting.

The more prepared and familiar you are with your material, the more comfortable and confident you will feel. You may want to make some minor changes as you listen to other people present, but overall your presentation should be complete and rehearsed well in advance of the event.

Presenters have limited time to present. Times vary depending on the conference and the format. Paper presenters at national conferences may be given 12 minutes with 3 additional minutes for questions, while workshops may be longer—for example, at the New York State English Council's annual conference, workshops are one-hour long.

We recommend that you keep your presentation simple and use a minimum amount of educational jargon. Because the presentation time is limited, decide on a limited number of main ideas you want the audience to know. Also, write out your presentation as a minilecture, starting with an outline that you want to expand into a narrative. It is very important for you to practice your presentation and make sure its length fits within the allocated time. Further, do not read your paper. Speak your ideas directly to your audience, referring to an outline of key points and transitions, if necessary. Finally, state your final conclusions and end on time. See Table 13.1 for more information from Psi Chi, The National Honor Society in Psychology (2006) on how to prepare your paper presentation.

Distribution of the paper you are presenting will vary. For some conferences, all of the papers for the entire conference are given to conference participants in the form of booklets or compact discs. For others, papers may be downloaded from a

---

TABLE 13.1
Tips for Preparing Your Paper Presentation

1. Decide on a limited number of significant ideas you want your audience to code, comprehend, and remember.
2. Minimize details (of procedure, data analysis, and literature review) when highlighting the main ideas.
3. State clearly in simple, jargon-free terms what the point of the research is, what you discovered, and what you think it means—its conceptual, methodological, or practical value.
4. Employ some redundancy in repeating important ideas to enhance comprehension and recall.
5. Write out your presentation as a minilecture (with a listening audience in mind), starting with an outline that you expand into a narrative.
6. Practice delivering it aloud to learn it well, to make its length fit in the time allocated, and to hear how it sounds.
7. Get feedback from tape-recorded replay of your delivery and from critical colleagues who listen to it.
8. Do not read your paper. Speak your ideas directly to your audience, referring—if necessary only—to an outline of key points and transitions.
9. Try to speak loudly enough, clearly enough, and with sufficient enthusiasm to hold the attention of your audience despite distractions (internal and external).
10. State your final conclusions and end on time.

designated online conference site. If the conference organizers are not distributing papers, it is appropriate to bring approximately 25 copies of your paper or a summary of your presentation for distribution and a sign-up sheet for attendees to request the paper. In your paper make sure to indicate your name, the date of the presentation, and the conference name. It is helpful to include your e-mail address in case people want to contact you for more information after the conference.

Executing the Presentation

Presenting your paper in front of a live audience requires practice. Rehearsing your presentation with coworkers, family, and friends helps you keep time and practice the use of visual aids. Practice not only ensures you know your material well but also builds confidence in speaking about aspects that are not directly related to your study but may come up in conversation. Be prepared not only to perform your presentation as practiced but to field questions that may challenge your ideas. Sharing your presentation ahead of time with familiar colleagues will help you anticipate your audiences' responses and give you time to think about your responses.

Knowing your audience is very important. To make sure your presentation is geared to your audience, find out exactly who will be in your audience. Is the presentation geared toward practitioners such as teachers or counselors? Are they researchers in the field of study such as university faculty? Are they administrators from various school districts such as principals or central office staff? If you start by knowing who will be in attendance, you are more likely to meet their needs and expectations.

A Look at Poster Presentations

Poster presentations are a commonly used format in conferences. One benefit of poster presentations is the opportunity for the presenters to interact with the audience. A physical arrangement similar to an exhibit area is used for this interaction. Each presenter is provided with a freestanding bulletin board on which to display the poster, a table, or both. Check to make sure the poster adheres to the requirements of the conference at which it is being presented. Bring pushpins or tacks in case they are not provided.

Poster instructions are usually provided by meeting organizers. Usually a relatively large number of posters will be displayed during each poster session. Attention to the design and display of the poster is key to making the poster interesting and attractive to the audience. Information vital to poster presentations include planning, size, location, length of time for viewing, information to be included, and layout suggestions.

For planning, it is essential to know the size of the poster. This may vary from conference to conference. Most posters are $4' \times 6'$, but some may be $4' \times 4'$. Others might allow freestanding tri-fold posterboards. The size of the poster determines the amount of information to be included as well as the layout. The length of time for viewing varies. One hour is the typical minimum amount of time. If the poster is up for more than one hour, the presenter may not be expected to be there the entire time. AERA (2006) provides the following recommendations regarding posters:

> The poster should be as self-explanatory as possible so that your main job is to supplement the information it contains. The poster format provides a mechanism for in-depth discussion of your research, but this is possible only if the display includes enough information to have a sketch pad and drawing materials available to help you make your points. It is also strongly recommended that the author have available a number of copies of the full paper to distribute to interested parties. (n.p.)

When working on your poster's display, it is preferable to assign the materials in columns rather than rows. It is easier for an audience member to scan posters from left to right than to skip around the entire display (AERA, 2006). Additional poster recommendations from Psi Chi (2006) are shown in Table 13.2. Also, Figures 13.1, 13.2, and 13.3 show sample layouts for poster presentations.

Synthesis and Concluding Thoughts

With planning, a successful proposal is within reach. If you are considerate of your audience, the type of conference, and the format of the conference presentation,

---

TABLE 13.2
Tips for Preparing Your Poster Presentation

1. Construct the poster to include the title, the author(s), affiliation(s), and a description of the research, highlighting the major elements that are covered in the abstract.

2. Minimize detail and try to use simple, jargon-free statements.

3. Remember that pictures, tables, and figures are amenable to poster display.

4. If you can, use color in your visuals.

5. Make sure your lettering is neatly done and is large enough to be read from a distance (i.e., do not simply pin up a set of typed pages—reserve these for your handout).

6. Consider using a flow chart or some other method of providing the viewer with a guide to inspecting your display.

7. Don't overwhelm the viewer with excessive amounts of information; rather, construct a poster display that enhances conversation.

8. Be ready to pin up and take down your poster at specified times.

9. Be sure to bring thumbtacks with you.

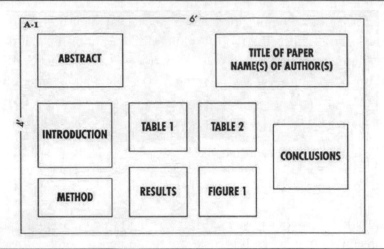

FIGURE 13.1
Sample Poster Presentation Layout #1

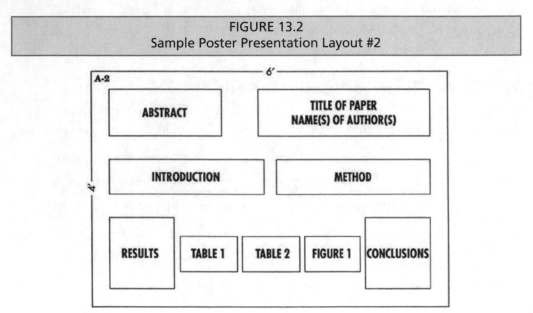

FIGURE 13.2
Sample Poster Presentation Layout #2

and if you practice your presentation before you go to the conference, sharing your work in this venue can be fruitful and fulfilling. Being present to see and hear immediately how others react to your work can be challenging and exciting. Presenting your work is similar to publishing your work (see chapter 12 in this volume) in that it can help you achieve increased clarity of your ideas. Conference

FIGURE 13.3
Sample Poster Presentation Layout #3

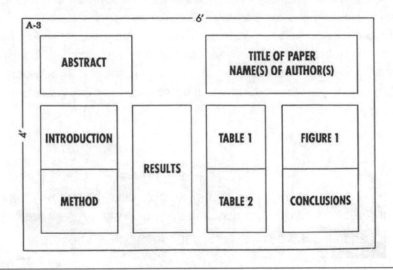

presentations offer the added benefit of spontaneity through audience feedback and flexibility of conference formats.

We have often found that the real challenge of conference presentations is the mental effort expended in thinking about writing the proposal, rather than the actual writing of it. So, we suggest you just jump in and try. As you gain experience with the process, you will develop an instinct for determining which professional association you are interested in participating in and the audience with whom you want to speak. We have found more satisfaction in small interactive sessions than in presentations that involved "talking at" a large group of people. We have learned to pace our work, to accomplish our proposal writing at several points during the year, and to spread out our conference attendance. We find ourselves reenergized and rejuvenated as we connect with our colleagues, stretch our thinking through their questions, and share our work.

PROBLEM-SOLVING VIGNETTE FOR DISCUSSION

Although presenting her work at a conference is something Suzanne wants to do, she wonders if it is worth all the energy and time she expends. She has to match the ideas she wants to share with an audience and research organizations, due dates, and conference themes. And it takes time to write the proposal. After all her work, her proposal may even be rejected. Then she thinks of all the exciting mathematics and science lessons that have been created as a result of her research, and she thinks of how she wants others to become as enthused and excited about this work as she is. The results of her work are worthwhile and valuable. Suzanne wants others to know about them and to use them because she believes they improve learning.

Suzanne considers the following key questions: Who is my audience? At what type of conference do I want to present? Do I present by myself or with others? What kind of session format do I want? What conference roles should I consider? If you were Suzanne, how would you figure out the answers to each of these questions? What factors would you consider as you made your decisions?

TIPS FOR TEACHER RESEARCHERS

The following tips may be helpful as you make decisions about how to prepare and present your research findings and disseminate your work.

■ Understand and read the guidelines for submitting your proposal.

■ Decide the type of format in which you would like to present your work.

■ Think about the audience you would like to present to and then create a list of conferences to which you would like to submit and present your proposal.

■ Check for resources and funding options available.

■ Practice your presentation in front of critical friends.

■ Pace your presentation while presenting.

■ Connect your visuals with your speaking topic.

QUESTIONS FOR REFLECTION

■ Are you ready to share your research results with other teachers?

■ What is the best possible way for you to disseminate your work?

■ What format should you choose to present your work?

REFERENCES

Academy of Management. (2004). *The role of presenters, discussants, and session chairs.* Retrieved January 15, 2007, from meetings.aomonline.org/2005/Roles.html

American Educational Research Association (AERA). (2006). Presentation tips and information: Instructions for the preparation of posters. Retrieved January 9, 2007, from www.aera.net/meetings/Default.aspx?menu_id=22&id=664

Barton, K.C. (2005). Advancing the conversation: The roles of discussant session chairs, and audience members at AERA's annual meeting. *Educational Researcher, 34*(9), 24–28.

Kitchin, R., & Fuller, D. (2005). *The academic's guide to publishing.* London: Sage.

Psi Chi, The National Honor Society of Psychology. (2006). *Tips for convention presenters and attendees.* Retrieved January 4, 2007, from www.psichi.org/conventions/tips.asp

Wikipedia. (n.d.). *Workshop.* Retrieved January 15, 2007, from en.wikipedia.org/wiki/Workshop

PART VI

Where Do We Go From Here?

Part Opener: Final Reflections
Cynthia A. Lassonde

In each of the part openers and their corresponding online case studies, you read about educators learning and practicing the craft of teacher research. We hope you can apply these cases to your situation and circumstances and learn through the narrative nature of each context.

Whether you work in a high-needs urban school as Kira in part I or with English-language learners as Elaine in part IV, teacher research can help you find solutions to instructional stumbling blocks that you meet every day. As Belinda tells us in part II, "If one person could develop a recipe for all other teachers to follow and get the same results, teaching would be easy!" There are no teaching recipes; however, integrating teacher research methods into your classroom can have a positive influence on teaching and learning. Remember how Jill learned to maximize her students' learning through teacher research in the part III opener? Good teaching doesn't happen overnight, but critical and reflective practices can help it happen.

Now that you are better equipped to design and manage a teacher research project, we'd like to share with you these final reflections about the future of teacher research. Chapter 14 provides a look at what is ahead.

The Future of Teacher Research

Susan Davis Lenski

BEFORE-READING QUESTIONS

▪ What will teacher research look like in the next decade?

▪ How will new teachers be trained as teacher researchers?

▪ What topics for teacher research in literacy will be especially salient in the near future?

Tamara is in her first year of teaching reading in an urban middle school. Her teacher training had included intense work on teacher research, including completing two work samples. When she meets her colleagues, she asks them about their current research projects, and she wants to know how she can become involved. Tamara tells her colleagues about her experiences with teacher research, especially how to look at students' achievement, and she is invited to join the teachers who are developing research lessons using the lesson study approach. Tamara is able to invite her university methods instructor and a young adult author to be virtual research partners of the lesson study team. Tamara's first year is not without difficulties, but her work on collaborative teacher research helps her develop a sense of efficacy that will remain with her throughout her long teaching career.

Introduction

As we learned in chapter 1, teacher research has come of age in the past two decades. As the field of education began to experiment with qualitative research methodologies in the 1980s, teachers found that they could formalize teacher inquiry through systematic research. Two important books were published in the 1990s: *Teachers Are Researchers: Reflection and Action* (Patterson, Santa, Short,

Teachers Taking Action: A Comprehensive Guide to Teacher Research, edited by Cynthia A. Lassonde and Susan E. Israel.
© 2008 by the International Reading Association.

& Smith, 1993) and *Inside/Outside: Teacher Research and Knowledge* (Cochran-Smith & Lytle, 1993), both showing how teacher research could be conducted in schools. Those teacher research pioneers who published their work in the early 1990s brought the idea of teachers researching their practice to the forefront of educational thought, and the research of individual teachers began to gradually influence classroom practice.

Theoretical Issues

During the early years of teacher research, the most common goal was to provide teachers with the tools and the motivation to improve their professional practice (Lytle & Cochran-Smith, 1994). Teacher research at that time was mostly characterized as one teacher investigating his or her own instructional practice to become a more effective teacher. Rarely would the effects of teacher research spread to a regional or national arena.

Times have changed. By the first decade of the 21st century, teacher research has become an integral part of many graduate and teacher preparation programs. Teacher researchers now collaborate more frequently, and as presented in Part V in this volume, they have many venues to publish and present their work. An additional change in teacher research is the change of purpose—from investigating teacher practices to examining student outcomes.

Political Influences on Teacher Research

Teacher research has not been exempt from the political pressures that have been recently heaped on teacher education (see Cochran-Smith, 2005). Educators in the 21st century have been pressured to "prove" that their teaching practices positively influence student learning. So instead of teacher research focusing on instructional improvement, teacher research is now including ways to determine how instructional interventions affect student achievement. Several influential organizations are encouraging these efforts, particularly in teacher education. Many colleges of education are accredited by the National Council for Accreditation of Teacher Education (NCATE), which now requires colleges of education to demonstrate that teacher candidates have a positive impact on P–12 learning (NCATE, 2002). The Carnegie Corporation of New York, the Annenberg Foundation, and the Ford Foundation are also working to reform teacher education through the Teachers for a New Era project. One of the major components of this reform is that teachers learn rigorous methods of collecting data on student-learning gains.

As all teacher researchers know, it is extremely difficult to find correlations between teacher behaviors and student learning through teacher research. To determine whether it was even possible to attribute student gains to teacher interventions, my colleagues (Lenski et al., 2001) and I surveyed 10 respected literacy researchers to determine how they envisioned making the link from instruction to achievement. The findings from this study indicated that researchers should be cautious about making claims about causation, and that teacher research that describes classroom situations are a valuable addition to the knowledge base in literacy. The authors also encouraged researchers to look for innovative ways to investigate teacher practice and student achievement. One new method for accomplishing both of these purposes is through the lesson study approach.

Lesson study is a systematic teacher research approach that has groups of teachers plan a lesson together and research the results of that lesson. The lesson study approach was introduced in the United States from Japan as a new way to think about professional development. A group of educators who were trying to understand why Japan's students scored so much higher than students in the United States in mathematics suggested that one of the reasons for Japan's successful schools could be their method of teacher research. These educators discovered that Japanese teachers had developed a way to create instructional lessons and examine student achievement in a process that was called lesson study (Yoshida, 1999). Stigler and Hiebert (1999) popularized lesson study in their book about international methods of instruction. Lesson study is now one of the fastest growing approaches to teacher research.

Lesson study is a "comprehensive and well-articulated process for examining practice" (Fernandez, Cannon, & Chokshi, 2003, p. 171). Lesson study has a number of features in common with the teacher research that is popular in the United States, but there are also distinct differences. In the lesson study approach, a community of teachers collaborates on a single **research lesson**. After considering how the lesson fits with the school's overall goals, a group of teachers then details possible teacher actions, predicts how students will respond, and develops evaluative measures. Sometimes, teachers communicate with virtual research partners to develop lessons. **Virtual research partners** are off-site teachers or experts who give input on the lesson under development. Then, one of the teachers implements the research lesson while the other teachers in the group observe the lesson and collect data on student responses. After the lesson, the group meets to discuss the lesson and to decide the extent to which the instructional goals were met. Then the teachers revise the lesson and reteach it using the revised form.

This microscopic approach to teaching produces exemplar lessons that are often published as models of instruction. The benefit of lesson study, however, is not merely the production of outstanding lessons. Teachers who participate in developing the research lessons learn from one another how to develop powerful lessons, and they work together to make a positive effect on student outcomes. A lesson study framework can be found in Table 14.1. (See Appendix B for a reproducible version of this form.)

TABLE 14.1
Lesson Study Framework

Steps of the Research Lesson	Teacher Actions	Student Actions	Evaluation
	What the teacher is doing or saying	What the students are doing or expected student responses	What data are you collecting? How will you collect it? What is the purpose for the data being collected?
Connect the lesson to goals, previous learning, and standards.	Tell students to spend five minutes rereading their journal entries from the story they read the previous day. Ask them to add any other comments they might have.	Students will open journals, read them, and make notes. Some talking among students is expected but shouldn't interfere with overall learning.	Record number of students who have journal entries from previous day. Collect entries to determine if students are prepared for the lesson.
Introduce the new concept.	Explain to students that they will be making connections among the story, their lives, other books, and other subjects.	Students will listen to the introduction. Students will raise their hands before speaking.	Record number of students who speak or act in ways that distract other students from learning the new concept. Collect data through observing and recording extraneous student comments.
Demonstrate, model, or explain the new concept.	Provide students with a Connections Chart, which has room for students to record connections to their lives, other books, and other subjects. Give examples of one or more connections in each category.	Students will listen to the teacher and read the categories on the Connections Chart.	Record number of students who speak or act in ways that distract other students from learning the new concept. Collect data through observing and recording extraneous student comments.
Engage the students in learning the new concept.	Tell students to turn to their partners and brainstorm connections. Give students 4–5 minutes to complete this task. Circulate around the room and answer questions. Share some of the connections with the entire group if there is time.	Students will talk about connections in pairs. Most students will be able to stay on task without difficulty. Questions should be brief.	Students stay on task during paired discussion. Observe by circulating around the room and listening to students talk.

(continued)

TABLE 14.1
Lesson Study Framework (continued)

Steps of the Research Lesson	Teacher Actions	Student Actions	Evaluation
Give students opportunities to practice or apply learning.	Instruct students to complete the Connections Chart individually.	Students will work independently for 5–10 minutes without talking. Students may look through the story or their journals.	Record on-task behavior by recording numbers of times students are not reading story, reading journal, or writing on Connections Chart.
Have students share new ideas and applications.	Have a blank Connections Chart projected on a screen. Ask students to volunteer to write one of their connections on the chart.	Several students will volunteer to come to the front and write their connections. Not all students will volunteer.	None
Summarize learning.	Tell students that making connections is a natural activity when reading. Remind students that they should make connections during times when they read independently. Have students record this strategy in their journals for future reference.	Students will listen to conclusion and will record the strategy in their journals. There should be very few questions.	List any questions students have about the lesson.

Teacher Candidates as Researchers

For teacher research to make its way into mainstream thought, teacher candidates need to be socialized into the ways of teacher research. Teacher research can be beneficial for teacher candidates in a number of ways. It can help new teachers learn about their community, school, and students; it can help new teachers understand what it means when an administrator states that an idea is based on research; and it can help new teachers learn from their practice and the practice of their mentors. As teacher candidates enter the profession as teacher researchers, they have a head start on those who do not have this background.

A great number of teacher candidates like Tamara are being trained to become teacher researchers in their preparation programs (Green & Brown, 2006). Teacher research will be standard practice for many future teachers. The shift from teachers as consumers of research to producers of knowledge began almost two decades ago (Richardson, 1994). Since that time, educators have been convinced that teacher candidates should come to their first teaching job with the tools for researching their practice. To illustrate this point, a survey conducted at the end of the 20th century indicated that nearly half of the teacher preparation institutions surveyed by the

American Association of Colleges for Teacher Education (AACTE) required their candidates to participate in action research (Henderson, Hunt, & Wester, 1999). In many cases, the action research followed the same steps as those that were taught in graduate programs. In other institutions, however, teacher educators developed special models to teach candidates how to research their practice during student teaching. One such example is the work sample methodology.

Work sample methodology is a way for teachers and teacher candidates to prepare units of study that focus on student achievement. Work sample methodology was developed at Western Oregon University for teachers to examine ways in which they could connect teaching and learning (Girod, 2002), and it is currently being implemented in many teacher preparation programs across the United States. Work sampling was developed so that teacher candidates could learn "systematic connections between their teaching actions and the learning of each student in their classrooms" (Girod & Girod, 2006, p. 482). They learn about these connections through the teacher research that is part of the work sample.

Work samples are instructional units that include a rigorous investigation of learning. Work samples for teacher candidates contain the following components and are typically evaluated by student teaching supervisors with a rubric:

- Description of school and classroom context
- Articulation of the learning goals
- Rationale statement defending the goals and pedagogical decisions
- Lesson plans
- Plans for data collection
- Pre- and posttest assessments
- Analysis of teaching results and student learning gains
- Reflections on the connections of teaching efforts, student learning, and personal professional growth

As teacher candidates develop work samples, they think of research questions, develop pre- and postassessments, learn how to collect and analyze data, draw conclusions from the data, and reflect on the effectiveness of their teaching. This type of activity educates teacher candidates on ways to embed teacher research naturally in their instruction.

Topics for Future Teacher Research in Literacy

Teacher research can make an important contribution to the field of literacy by providing rich, layered studies that investigate topics to inform instruction and make an impact on student achievement. There have been a number of syntheses on scientifically based research published in the first decade of the 21st century that report on the quantitative research on reading, early childhood learning, and English-language learning. These reports describe the research that has been done in the past; what's needed now is a look to the future. Teacher research can break new ground on topics that have not yet been investigated in larger contexts, and it can provide a detailed picture on subjects from larger studies. In addition, teacher research can contribute important information on topics that are difficult to research in experimental studies. Topics for future teacher research can be identified by referring to the national literacy trends as represented by the "What's Hot, What's Not" list that is published in *Reading Today* (the newspaper of the International Reading Association) each year along with innovative thinking by teaching communities.

"What's Hot, What's Not"

For the past 10 years, Jack Cassidy and Drew Cassidy (2007) have surveyed prominent leaders in the field of literacy to determine which topics are "hot." The Cassidys construct a list each year by asking literacy educators and researchers with national and international perspectives to contribute ideas for the survey. They use that information to make informed decisions about what topics to include on the year's survey. The survey respondents are selected to represent various geographical regions of the United States and Canada as well as countries outside North America. The respondents are given the list of topics and are asked which topics are "hot," or are most heard about, and which topics are "not hot." The respondents are also asked whether, in their opinion, the topic "should be hot" or "should not be hot." The results of the surveys are compiled and reported in *Reading Today*.

The list of "**What's Hot, What's Not**" is an interesting indication of the opinions of leaders in the field and can be used as ideas for teacher research, especially the topics that are labeled "should be hot." These topics are the ones that literacy leaders believe should be given more attention by educators. For example, as a new, middle school reading teacher, Tamara wants to begin a teacher research project with her colleagues. Because she worked at the school as a student teacher, she knows the community and student population and is aware of some of their needs. As Tamara and her colleagues discuss topics for research, they refer to the "What's Hot, What's Not" list and notice that the topic of informational text is "very hot." All of the teachers in the research group agree that students in their schools have difficulty reading textbooks and that a lesson study on teaching informational texts would be beneficial for the teachers and students.

Foundational Skills and Future Trends

During the past decade, teachers have been focusing on certain aspects of student achievement, especially as they relate to the No Child Left Behind legislation. There has been a renewed emphasis on meeting the literacy needs of students who have

not met state benchmarks and a targeted look at lessening the achievement gap between white students and students from other ethnic and cultural backgrounds.
Despite the standards-based emphasis in the last decade of the 20th century and the
first decade of the 21st century, the number of fourth- and eighth-grade students
who could read at a basic level improved slightly in the past 15 years, but there was
no change in the percentage of students who could read at the advanced level according to the National Assessment of Educational Progress (Perie, Grigg, &
Donahue, 2005). This trend is troubling to many and has called into question the
direction of education in the United States. For example, a recent report from the
National Center on Education and the Economy (2007) suggests that the focus on
standards is not sufficient for the needs of the global economy. Instead, education
should keep a strong emphasis on foundational skills and also renew its focus on
helping students achieve at the highest proficiency levels and teaching students
how to think flexibly and creatively.

There will be a continued need for teacher research in the foundational skills
that influence student achievement. Teacher researchers need to look at the ways
they can improve their instruction and also at how students respond. Some of the
foundational skills that need continued teacher research include the following:

- Motivation: What motivates students to read? How can teachers develop
  motivational strategies and programs that increase the intrinsic motivation
  of students? What teacher qualities foster motivated students?

- Phonemic awareness: What is the optimal amount of time that teachers
  should devote to phonemic awareness instruction? Should phonemic
  awareness be taught in all grades to English-language learners (ELLs) who
  are newcomers to the United States? How and when should the transition
  be made from phonemic awareness to phonics instruction?

- Phonics instruction: Can phonics be effectively taught through literature-
  based reading approaches? How can phonics instruction be taught in
  needs-based groups? How much do students learn from systematic phonics instruction?

- Word analysis: How can word analysis be taught in content area classes
  such as science and social studies? What word analysis approaches should
  be taught in intermediate grades, middle school, and high school?

- Strategy instruction: How are strategies used as instructional tools? How
  do students internalize strategy instruction?

- Assessments: How much time do teachers spend on large-scale assessments? How are assessments used by classroom teachers? How much time
  do teachers spend preparing for assessments?

- Fine-grained assessments: How do teachers use informal assessments to modify instruction? How can running records and miscue analysis help teachers learn about students as readers?

- Informational text reading: What percentage of informational text is read at the various grade levels? How do teachers instruct students to read informational texts? How are textbooks used in elementary grades?

- Comprehension instruction: In what ways do teachers actually instruct students in comprehension? What does the instruction look like? How do students apply comprehension instruction in their individual reading?

- Independent reading: How have teachers adapted Sustained Silent Reading in independent reading programs? Does independent reading motivate students to read more? How does the volume of reading affect overall student achievement?

Teacher research can also contribute to the field of literacy by conducting classroom and school-based research on the topics that are critical for schools in the 21st century. Teachers are uniquely positioned to conduct research on these topics because they are typically the first to notice changes in student characteristics and backgrounds. Some of the following topics could be important to the future of literacy education:

- Out-of-school literacies—Students are reading and writing in new ways outside school (e.g., text messaging). How do out-of-school literacies affect reading achievement? How can (or should) out-of-school literacies become incorporated into the school curricula?

- Response to intervention—School teams are collecting data on how students respond to literacy interventions. How can these teams best serve students with literacy needs? What kinds of interventions increase student achievement?

- Reading specialists and literacy coaches—The role of reading specialists and literacy coaches have changed in the past decade. What impact do literacy coaches and reading specialists have on teachers? What impact do they have on student achievement?

- Community and parent involvement in schools and classrooms— Communities are changing, especially because of the increasing number of immigrants in the United States. How should teachers communicate with families who do not speak English? What can teachers expect of families? What effective methods draw families and communities into working with schools?

- Technology—Technology has changed considerably in the past decade and the changes will continue through the foreseeable future. How do teachers use technology in classrooms? What backgrounds do students have in technology when they come to school? How effective are computer-based reading programs? How does the digital divide affect student learning across regions of the United States and the world?

- ELLs in mainstream classes—More teachers than ever before will have ELLs in their classrooms. How should mainstream teachers instruct newcomers in their classrooms? What methods for teaching reading to ELLs are most effective? How do state laws about home languages affect students in schools?

- Achievement gap—The national trends in the United States indicate that students who are white are most successful in school. How can teachers find ways to decrease the achievement gap in their classroom? What reading methods work best with students from various ethnic and cultural backgrounds?

- Workplace literacy—The ability of students to use reading and writing to solve problems in the workplace will be a future topic of interest. How do students use reading and writing to solve problems? What kinds of literacies are necessary in the workplace? How can teachers integrate literacy instruction in subject areas so that students improve literacy achievement while learning?

- Advanced reading in the disciplines—The number of students who graduate from high schools in the United States and still need remedial reading courses is increasing. How can advanced reading practices be incorporated in middle and high school subjects? What kinds of reading and writing abilities are needed for college? What kinds of critical reading skills are needed for the next generation?

Synthesis and Concluding Thoughts

Teacher research has become an important part of the work that teachers do. Teachers have always looked for ways to improve their practice and student achievement; teacher research, however, has provided educators with the tools for systematically conducting investigations in these areas. Teacher research can change school systems, classroom instruction, and student learning. It also changes teachers by helping them realize the power they have over their own actions. Teacher research can empower teachers to take action and make changes based on informed decisions.

Teacher research also makes an important contribution to the knowledge base in literacy, but readers of research need to understand what questions teacher research can answer and which questions need to be answered by experimental or large-scale studies. Teacher researchers need to guard against overgeneralizing their work and need to have a clear idea of the role teacher research plays in the larger conversation about research.

New methods of teacher research are being developed as more and more educators look to teacher research as a way to continue professional learning. Methods such as lesson study and work samples are among those that have made their way into many teachers' lexicons; others surely will follow.

Teacher research will continue to gain influence as educators show the difference they are making in their students' literacy lives. As politicians demand more from teachers and teacher educators in the future, additional methods for researching what helps students learn and become contributing members of society will be developed. As teacher research moves to this new level, it will grow into an increasingly respected method for generating knowledge about teaching.

PROBLEM-SOLVING VIGNETTE FOR DISCUSSION

The principal of an elementary school orders all Sustained Silent Reading programs to cease. He states that he hears that research does not support any type of independent reading in any classroom because students do not spend their time reading. The teachers at the school collectively rebel at the directive, saying that they will conduct research to show the principal the ways that independent reading can benefit students' literacy achievement.

Fourteen of the teachers decide to use independent reading as the topic for their next teacher research project. Six of the teachers decide to use the lesson study approach. A team of primary teachers and a team of intermediate teachers design research lessons that can be used in their independent reading programs. Four of the teachers decide to use work sample methodology to develop units that rely on the independent reading of informational texts. Four other teachers decide to develop teacher research projects in conjunction with virtual research partners at a nearby university.

The teachers in this school are proactive when faced with an administrative recommendation. They develop teacher research projects to determine what is best for the students in their school. How can you use teacher research to respond to federal, state, district, and school mandates?

TIPS FOR TEACHER RESEARCHERS

As you conduct teacher research throughout your career, you will find that some research topics remain the same through the decades but many change. To keep abreast of the new ideas in literacy, it is important that you learn what other scholars and teacher researchers have contributed to the field and that you consider how you can conduct research on these new ideas. To keep current in the field, you will want to join professional organizations; attend state, regional, and national conferences; and read as many professional journals as you can. Watch for new approaches and ideas in teacher research and develop new ideas yourself. These actions will help you grow as a teacher researcher, will contribute to the body of knowledge, and will shape the future directions of teacher research.

QUESTIONS FOR REFLECTION

- How can teacher research become more accessible to practicing teachers?

- Should teacher research focus on improving instruction or on student performance?

- How do new approaches of teacher research contribute to the existing methods for research teacher practice?

- How will technology affect teacher research?

REFERENCES

Cassidy, J., & Cassidy, D. (2007, February/March). "What's hot, what's not for 2007?" *Reading Today*, *24*, 1, 10–11.

Cochran-Smith, M. (Ed.). (2005). The politics of teacher education [Special issue]. *Journal of Teacher Education, 56*(3).

Cochran-Smith, M., & Lytle, S. (1993). *Inside/outside: Teacher research and knowledge.* New York: Teachers College Press.

Fernandez, C., Cannon, J., & Chokshi, S. (2003). A U.S.–Japan lesson study collaboration reveals critical lenses for examining practice. *Teaching and Teacher Education, 19*(2), 171–185.

Girod, G. (Ed.). (2002). *Connecting teaching and learning: A handbook for teacher educators on teacher work sample methodology.* Washington, DC: American Association of Colleges for Teacher Education.

Girod, M., & Girod, G. (2006). Exploring the efficacy of the Cook School District simulation. *Journal of Teacher Education, 57*, 481–497.

Green, S.K., & Brown, M. (2006). Promoting action research and problem solving among teacher candidates: One elementary school's journey. *Action in Teacher Education, 27*(4), 45–54.

Henderson, M.V., Hunt, S.N., & Wester, C. (1999). Action research: A survey of AACTE-Member Institutions. *Education, 119*, 663–668.

Lenski, S.D., Grisham, D.L., Brink, B., Mahurt, S., Jampole, E., Cohen, S., et al. (2001). Researching the relationship between school–university partnerships and students' literacy learning. *Journal of Reading Education, 26*(3), 23–28.

Lytle, S.L., & Cochran-Smith, J. (1994). Inquiry, knowledge and practice. In S. Hollingsworth & H. Sockett (Eds.), *Teacher research and educational reform* (pp. 22–51). Chicago: University of Chicago Press.

National Center on Education and the Economy. (2007). *Tough choices or tough times: The report of the new commission on the skills of the American workforce.* San Francisco: John Wiley & Sons.

National Council for the Accreditation of Teacher Education (NCATE). (2002). *Professional standards for the accreditation of schools, colleges, and departments of education.* Washington, DC: Author.

Patterson, L., Santa, C.M., Short, K.G., & Smith, K. (Eds.). (1993). *Teachers are researchers: Reflection and action*. Newark, DE: International Reading Association.

Perie, M., Grigg, W.S., & Donahue, P.L. (2005). *The nation's report card: Reading 2005* (NCES 2006-451). Washington, DC: National Center for Education Statistics.

Richardson, V. (1994). Conducting research on practice. *Educational Researcher, 23*(5), 5–10.

Stigler, J.W., & Hiebert, J. (1999). *The teaching gap: Best ideas from the world's teachers for improving education in the classroom*. New York: Free Press.

Teachers for a New Era. (n.d.). *About Teachers for a New Era*. Retrieved July 31, 2007, from www.teachersforanewera.org/index.cfm?fuseaction=home.aboutTNE

Yoshida, M. (1999). *Lesson study: A case study of a Japanese approach to improving instruction through school-based teacher development*. Unpublished doctoral dissertation, University of Chicago Department of Human Development.

APPENDIX A

Favorite Resources for Teacher Researchers

Teachers Taking Action: A Comprehensive Guide to Teacher Research, edited by Cynthia A. Lassonde and Susan E. Israel.
© 2008 by the International Reading Association.

eacher researchers who want to develop professionally, increase their knowledge about doing teacher research, and improve their level of teaching effectiveness will benefit from the following annotated list of resources. The contributors and editors of this book have compiled a list of their favorite resources, and we present them here organized by topic area. This feature can be valuable to readers in many ways. Readers can use resources related to their areas of interest that they feel need further development prior to beginning a research project. Study groups can use the resources by having each member of the study group select resources of interest, be responsible for reading and learning about the topic, and share important details with the study group. Administrators who are working with teachers on a research project will also save time locating resources for teachers.

Conducting Research

Researching, Designing, and Planning a Study

Duke, N.K., & Mallette, M.H. (Eds.). (2004). *Literacy research methodologies*. New York: Guilford.

> This book is a helpful resource for teachers who are in the planning stages of the research project. The contents of the book include 13 methodologies, such as case studies, ethnographic research, and survey research. Each chapter highlights sample research studies that use the methodology discussed in the chapter, which will give teachers a helpful guide when planning their method of research.

Hubbard, R.S., & Power, B.M. (1993). *The art of classroom inquiry: A handbook for teacher-researchers*. Portsmouth, NH: Heinemann.

> This text offers practical ideas for conducting classroom-based research with students, including suggestions for organizing materials and strategies for data collection.

Johnson, A.P. (2003). *What every teacher should know about action research*. Boston: Allyn & Bacon.

> This guide is for teachers interested in solving real classroom problems. Included are helpful suggestions for defining a problem, developing a plan, evaluating the plan, and sharing it with others.

Power, B.M. (1996). *Taking note: Improving your observational notetaking*. York, ME: Stenhouse.

> This practical resource explains how to take accurate observational notes and how to code and use the information for assessment and research purposes. Lots of helpful examples from all grade levels are included. This resource is a must-have for anyone who wants to get organized before starting a research project. Powers offers numerous note-taking strategies.

Robinson, V.M., & Lai, M.K. (2006). *Practitioner research for educators: A guide to improving classrooms and schools*. Thousand Oaks, CA: Corwin Press.

> This helpful book offers practical suggestions for teacher researchers. It also addresses how teachers might strengthen the culture of inquiry in their schools.

Strauss, A.L., & Corbin, J.M. (2007). *Basics of qualitative research: Techniques and procedures for developing grounded theory* (3rd ed.). Thousand Oaks, CA: Sage.

> This is a popular resource available for those who want to engage in qualitative research using the grounded theory method. This step-by-step guide is easy to use with examples provided for a variety of research designs. The highlights of the book include resource design tips, strategies for and examples of research projects, and evaluation recommendations.

Action Research Network: actionresearch.altec.org/

> This website provides an online template to encourage teachers to record information about various aspects of their research. Researchers can describe all aspects of their teacher research projects, take notes and keep them all in one place, upload their research instruments and data, make a first draft of their final paper and bibliography (if doing this for a class), and share this information with others of their choice (e.g., the public, their professor, outside reviewers, someone at their school). The archive of projects is searchable by grade level, student achievement, type of research, type of teaching, subject matter, and so forth as search terms.

Teachers Network: teachersnetwork.org/

> This website focuses on teacher professional development and networking and includes teacher research as a valuable form of professional development. The site includes samples of studies and other print resources that can help teachers new to this form of embedded professional development think about how to frame their own research. The site also includes information about grants that can support the work teachers do in their classrooms.

Teacher Research: TeacherResearch.net

> This website shows how teachers in schools can initiate and sustain educational research within their everyday work in their classroom. Teachers as researchers are often supported by a process of mentoring that integrates mentoring into action inquiry. Teachers and research mentors are experts whose skills, values, and understandings complement and enrich one another's practice.

Engaging in Teacher Research—Professional Groups

California Science Project—Science Education Network Academy: www.accessexcellence.org/21st/TL/AR

> At this site, teachers investigate ways to increase inquiry-based instruction in the science classroom.

The National Reading Research Center School Research Consortium: www.teach .virginia.edu/go/clic/nrre/ques_r30.html

> This is a teacher research community of 35 teachers across grade levels from the Athens, Georgia, area.

The National Writing Project: www.nwp.org

> This network creates a structure to pool resources for teacher inquiry and to disseminate research findings. It also sponsors teacher inquiry grants.

The Teacher Researcher Network of Fairfax County (Virginia) Public Schools: www.fcps.edu/plt/tresearch.htm

> This site provides institutional support for more than 200 teacher researchers in the form of experienced teacher researchers to lead school-based inquiry groups; opportunities to

collaborate within school groups and across school groups; and support for networking, writing, and publishing.

Finding and Evaluating Professional Literature

Education Resources Information Center (ERIC): www.eric.ed.gov/

This database, sponsored by the Institute of Education Sciences (IES) of the U.S. Department of Education, houses full-text research articles and documents designed specifically for educators.

Google Scholar: scholar.google.com

This is a specialized Web-based search engine that enables users to search a wide array of scholarly works, although it is not limited to education-related topics.

International Reading Association (IRA): www.reading.org

The website of this nonprofit literacy organization offers teachers a database of teacher research tools. In addition, topics by other teacher researchers are listed. Using the keyword term "teachers as researchers," users can find tips on how to get started with teacher research, where to find grants, and other valuable information related to teacher research.

Funding Research—Grants

American Educational Research Association (AERA): www.aera.net/

At this website, large and small research grants and links to other research grants are available. Grants support English-language learners, Head Start programs, Early Head Start programs, literacy research, and dissertation support.

The Barbara Bush Foundation for Family Literacy: barbarabushfoundation.com

The Barbara Bush Foundation offers grants for research in the area of family literacy, early childhood development in literacy, and early childhood innovative literacy programs.

Grantsalert.com

This helpful link provides a wealth of resources on writing grants, making it unnecessary for teachers to spend money on publications that focus on this topic.

International Reading Association (IRA): www.reading.org/association/awards/index.html

This website has nearly 400 awards and grants available for educators involved in reading and literacy. Research grants include the Elva Knight Research Grant, Helen M. Robinson Grant, Nila Banton Smith Research Dissemination Support Grant, and Teacher as Researcher Grant.

National Council of Teachers of English (NCTE): www.ncte.org/about/grants

This website provides information related to funding available in the areas of Early Literacy, Professional Development, Adolescent Literacy, Teacher Quality/Teacher Education, English-language learners, and English as a Second Language.

National Education Association (NEA): www.nea.org/earlychildhood

This site provides information about grants available in the area of urban school development to increase literacy achievement and performance, as well as suggestions for funding related to youth literacy projects.

National Reading Conference (NRC): www.nrconline.org

> This site provides suggestions for grant opportunities available through literacy constituents. A summary of awards and opportunities is available for literacy researchers.

Teachers.net

> This is a grant-writing chatboard that teachers can use to obtain recommendations from their peers about available grants, apply for free Federal Grant Kits, and review award-winning grants.

Sharing Research

Writing and Publishing Resources

Hillocks, G. (1995). *Teaching writing as a reflective practice*. New York: Teachers College Press.

> Hillocks asserts that writing is at the heart of education. By learning about the theories that drive writing, teachers can apply them to their academic and professional writing efforts.

Murray, D.M. (1991). *The craft of revision*. Fort Worth, TX: Holt, Rinehart and Winston.

> Murray organizes this book around the following revision principles: (a) Revise to consider the information communicated, (b) revise to illuminate your voice, (c) revise to delete superfluous information, and (d) revise to provide form and order.

National Writing Project: Teacher Inquiry Communities: www.nwp.org/cs/public/print/resource_topic/teacher_research_inquiry

> This national network links to sites interested in developing leadership and inquiry resources for teacher inquiry, providing a means for sharing information and disseminating practices.

Richards, J.C., & Miller, S.K. (2005). *Doing academic writing in education: Connecting the personal and the professional*. Mahwah, NJ: Erlbaum.

> As a model of academic prose, this book demonstrates how teachers can combine the two languages of their profession—the personal and the professional—by presenting authentic teacher experiences with academic writing.

Teacher Research: Graduate School of Education: George Mason University: gse.gmu.edu/research/tr/

> This website has information on developing and implementing a teacher research study as well as how to write a draft and submit it for publication.

Wepner, S.B., & Gambrell, L.B. (Eds.). (2007). *Beating the odds: Getting published in the field of literacy*. Newark, DE: International Reading Association.

> This edited volume is accessible with useful suggestions on getting started, writing for journals and books, and responding to revise-and-resubmit and rejection decisions.

Scholarly Journals for Article Submission

English Education
Conference on English Education

Michael Moore, Editor
COE Building, Room 3140
Georgia Southern University
Curriculum, Foundations and Reading
PO Box 8144
Statesboro, GA 30460
912-486-7268
Fax: 912-681-5382
E-mail: Englisheducation@georgiasouthern.edu
www.ncte.org/pubs/journals/ee

Research in the Teaching of English
Melanie Sperling, coeditor
School of Education, Sproul Hall
University of California–Riverside
Riverside, CA 92521-0128
E-mail: RTE-Submissions@ucr.edu
www.ncte.org/pubs/journals/rte

Practitioner Journals for Article Submission

English Journal
NCTE Secondary Section
Louann Reid, Editor
English Department, 1773 Campus Delivery
Colorado State University
Fort Collins, CO 80523-1773
E-mail: English-Journal@ColoState.edu
www.ncte.org/pubs/journals/ej

Language Arts
Language Arts Editorial Office
School of Teaching and Learning
The Ohio State University
333 Arps Hall, 1945 N. High Street
Columbus, OH 43210
614-292-7559
Fax: 614-688-3980—Mark: Attn: Language Arts, Room 227
E-mail: langarts@osu.edu
www.ncte.org/pubs/journals/la

Additional Journals for Article Submission

The ALAN Review: scholar.lib.vt.edu/ejournals/ALAN/

Council for Exceptional Children: www.cec.sped.org/AM/Template.cfm?Section=Publications1

Exceptional Children & Teaching Exceptional Children: escholarship.bc.edu/education/tecplus

Journal of Adolescent & Adult Literacy: www.reading.org/publications/journals/jaal/index.html

Language Arts: www.ncte.org/pubs/journals/la

National Middle School Association: www.nmsa.org/

Reading Research Quarterly: www.reading.org/publications/journals/rrq/index.html

The Reading Teacher: www.reading.org/publications/journals/rt/index.html

Online Journals

Action Research International: www.scu.edu.au/schools/gcm/ar/ari/arihome.html

AR Expeditions: arexpeditions.montana.edu

Journal of Curriculum and Instruction: www.ecu.edu/cs-educ/joci/about.cfm

Networks: An Online Journal for Teacher Research journals.library.wisc.edu/networks

Teaching Today for Tomorrow: www.7oaks.org/teaching_today_for_tomorrow_an_on_line_journal.aspx

Voices From the Field: www.alliance.brown.edu/pubs/voices

Conferences for Presentation

Table A.1 on pages 201–203 identifies the professional association or conference names that are of interest to teacher researchers, the conference website address, the approximate date that conference proposals are due (when available), and the approximate date when the conference is held annually.

Teaching Practice and Research in Practice

Girod, G. (Ed.). (2001). *Connecting teaching and learning: A handbook for teacher educators on teacher work sample methodology*. Washington, DC: American Association of Colleges for Teacher Education.

This handbook provides a rationale for the inclusion of teacher work sample methodology in preparation and licensing programs; describes how student learning is the central concept within teacher work samples; explains how to teach students and teachers about work samples; and supports teacher educators in reviewing, adapting/adopting, and implementing the methodology.

Lambros, A. (2002). *Problem-based learning in K–8 classrooms: A teacher's guide to implementation.* Thousand Oaks, CA: Corwin Press.

Lambros, A. (2004). *Problem-based learning in middle and high school classrooms: A teacher's guide to implementation.* Thousand Oaks, CA: Corwin Press.

These two texts provide scenarios that require teacher intervention, and the author suggests solutions. These situations may provide starting points for teacher research projects.

Pappas, C.C., & Zecker, L.B. (2001). *Teacher inquiries in literacy teaching-learning: Learning to collaborate in elementary urban classrooms.* Mahwah, NJ: Erlbaum.

This text is a series of class research studies by urban elementary teachers working with university researchers, and it details inquiry projects focused on literacy topics.

Robinson, R.D., Wedman, J.M., & McKenna, M.C. (2008). *Issues and trends in literacy education* (4th ed.). Boston: Allyn & Bacon.

This text comprises readings by notable literacy researchers, teacher educators, and classroom teachers on research studies in literacy education.

Short, K.G., Harste, J.C., & Burke, C.L. (1996). *Creating classrooms for authors and inquirers.* Portsmouth, NH: Heinemann.

The book focuses on inquiry learning. It may offer you a different perspective from which you can evaluate your classroom practices.

Stigler, J.W., & Hiebert, J. (1999). *The teaching gap: Best ideas from the world's teachers for improving education in the classroom.* New York: Free Press.

This book discusses the differences between students' achievement in the United States and students' achievement in other countries. One difference is in teaching practices. The authors suggest ways teachers can use the lesson study approach to improve their practices and student achievement.

Wiburg, K.M., & Brown, S. (2007). *Lesson study communities: Increasing achievement with diverse students.* Thousand Oaks, CA: Corwin Press.

The authors explain how to connect lesson study to classroom, school, and district instructional goals. They also provide case examples and step-by-step guidance in designing research lessons.

Professional Conferences to Promote Teacher Research

Fairfax County Public Schools (Virginia) Teacher Researcher Network Conference: www.fcps.edu/plt/tresearch.htm

At the annual conference in late April/early May, attendees can share ideas; hear how teacher research increases student learning across departments, grade levels, and disciplines; and learn how teacher research increases teacher dialogue, collaboration, and sharing of instructional issues. The conference features teacher leaders and administrators from across all grade levels and throughout the district and surrounding districts. The research topics are varied, featuring a wide range of disciplines and student populations. The conference consists of roundtable discussions by teacher researchers and workshops by teachers, panels of teachers, and administrators.

International Conference of Teacher Research (ICTR): www.nl.edu/academics/nce/ictr.cfm

> Operating since 1992, this small conference brings classroom teachers and university teachers together to talk about their own teacher research and the effects of teacher research on their practice. It is unusual for its friendliness and the power of the conversations between participants, and for the fact that the participants are usually about 50% classroom teachers and 50% university faculty. Teacher voice, as shown by the centrality of classroom teachers in the conversations, is a key component, both in this conference and in the philosophy behind teacher research. This conference is teacher research in action.

Helpful Tips and Technological Resources for Researchers

Brainstorming Software

Some computer software facilitates the process of breaking down research problems into subcomponents. Programs such as Inspiration allow researchers to construct graphic or semantic webs of interrelated ideas. The resulting web contains both the subcomponents and the organization of interrelated ideas. Inspiration software and a free trial version can be found at www.inspiration.com.

Databases

An electronic database allows teacher researchers to organize and access a large collection of information. Some researchers may want to develop a database for a specific purpose, such as for reference or bibliographic information, while others may want to develop a database for multiple purposes. Many databases are commercially available. Bibliographic database information, including a free trial version, may be found at ProCite at www.procite.com/pcpurchase.asp. Statistical Packages for Social Sciences (SPSS) may be found at www.spss.com/products/.

Electronic Planners

An electronic planner, similar to a paper-and-pencil planner, can prevent researchers from being overwhelmed and can assist them in developing a research schedule or writing log. Many electronic planners are available. One of the most popular is developed and marketed by Franklin Covey and is found at www.franklin covey.com/fc/get_organized/electronic_planning.

Human Subjects Certification

In order to pursue research on human subjects, researchers must be certified as ethically competent in managing educational research with human subjects and especially with children who are vulnerable. Modules on issues related to human subjects can be found on the Collaborative Institutional Training Initiative (CITI) website: www.citiprogram.org. Once the online modules have been reviewed and studied, researchers can take an online test. Passing the multiple choice questions results in issuance of a certificate qualifying the researcher for completing research with human subjects.

Project Management Software

Project management software has been very popular in the business world. One example of such software is found at www.aecsoftware.com/products/fasttrack/. This software, called "FastTrack" helps to organize and coordinate various aspects of a research project. It can be especially helpful with projects that have separate pieces, each needing to be laid out, coordinated, and monitored.

Spreadsheets

An electronic spreadsheet is a software program that allows teacher researchers to manipulate large amounts of data within a grid format. This data can then be reviewed and analyzed as each researcher desires. Many different spreadsheet programs are available commercially. The most popular for statistical purposes in education are Microsoft Excel and SPSS (v.14).

Statistical Packages

Statistical packages that are commercially sold are designed to assist researchers by performing needed calculations on available data. Other than Microsoft Excel and SPSS, other, smaller statistical packages are commercially available to perform calculations. One such program, designed for education, is Minitab, and that can be found at www.minitab.com/education/.

TABLE A.1
Associations and Conferences of Interest to Educators

Name of Association or Conference (Abbreviation)	Website	Proposal Due*	Conference Date
American Association for the Advancement of Science	www.aaas.org	November	February
American Association of Colleges for Teacher Education (AACTE)	www.aacte.org		February
American Association of Physics Teachers (AAPT)	www.aapt.org	March	July
American Educational Research Association (AERA)	www.aera.net	August	April
American Educational Studies Association (AESA)	www3.uakron.edu/aesa/index.html	April	November
Annual Conference of the American Reading Forum	americanreadingforum.org	December	January
Arizona Educational Research Organization	www.azedresearch.org	September	October
Association for Science Teacher Education (ASTE)	theaste.org		January
American Society for Engineering Education (ASEE)	asee.org	January	June
Association for the Advancement of Computing in Education (AACE)	aace.org	December	March
Association of Educational Communications and Technology (AECT)	aect.org	February	October
Association of Mathematics Teacher Educators (AMTE)	amte.sdsu.edu		January
Association of Teacher Educators (ATE)	ate1.org	March	July
California Educational Research Association	www.cera-web.org	October	November
The Council for Exceptional Children	www.cec.sped.org		April
Eastern Educational Research Association	www.govst.edu./eera	October	February
European League for Middle Level Education	www.elmle.org		January
European Society for Engineering Education (SEFI)	www.sefi.be		July
Florida Educational Research Association	www.feraonline.org	June	November

(continued)

Name of Association or Conference (Abbreviation)	Website	Proposal Due*	Conference Date
Frontiers in Education (FIE)	www.fie-conference.org	January	October
Georgia Educational Research Association (GERA)	www.gaera.org/	September	October
Hawai'i Educational Research Association	www.hawaii.edu/hera/	February	February
Hawaii International Conference on Education	www.hiceducation.org	September	January
International Association of Special Education	iase.coe.nau.edu/index3.html	August	June
International Conference of Teacher Research	(ICTR website) www.nl.edu/academics/nce/ictr.com	November	March
International Conference on Learning Disabilities	www.cldinternational.org/	January	October
International Reading Association	www.reading.org/association/meetings/annual.html		May
International Study Association on Teachers and Teaching	www.isatt.org	January	July
Iowa Educational Research & Evaluation Association	www.ierea.org/		December
Kentucky Council of Teachers of English/Language Arts (KCTE/LA)	www.kcte.org/	November	February
Louisiana Education Research Association	www.LERAWEB.homestead.com	January	March
Michigan Educational Research Association	www.mera.net		May
Mid-South Educational Research Association	www.msera.org/	June	November
Mid-Western Educational Research Association (MWERA)	www.mwera.org	May	October
NAFSA: Association of International Educators	www.nafsa.org		May
National Association for Alternative Certification	www.alt-teachercert.org/index.asp	December	April
National Association for Gifted Children	www.nagc.org		Dates throughout the year
National Association for Research in Science Teaching (NARST)	www.narst.org	August	April

(continued)

Name of Association or Conference (Abbreviation)	Website	Proposal Due*	Conference Date
National Council of Teachers of Mathematics (NCTM)	nctm.org		Dates throughout the year
National Middle Level Science Teachers' Association (NMLSTA)	nmlsta.org		March
National Middle School Association	www.nmsa.org	December	November
National Network for the Study of Educator Dispositions	www.educatordispositions.org		November
National Reading Conference	www.nrconline.org/		November
National Science Teachers Association (NSTA)	www.nsta.org		Dates throughout the year
New England Educational Research Organization	faculty.education.uconn.edu/edlr/ccobb/neero/index.html		April
North American Association for Environmental Education	naaee.org	January	November
Northeastern Educational Research Association	www.nera-education.org/		October
Northern Rocky Mountain Educational Research Association	www.nrmera.org/	May	October
Ohio Association of Elementary School Administrators (OAESA)	oaesa.org		February
Ohio Technology Education Association	www.otea.info/		March
School Science and Mathematics Association (SSMA)	ssma.org	May	November
Science Education Council of Ohio (SECO) (Southwest chapter of NSTA)	www.secoonline.org		February
Society for Information Technology & Teacher Education (SITE) (an arm of AACE)	site.aace.org/conf/	December	March
South Carolina Educators for the Practical Use of Research	www.midnet.sc.edu/scepur		February
Southeastern Association for Community College Research	www.saccr.org/		July
Southwest Educational Research Association	www.sera-edresearch.org/		February
Washington Educational Research Association	www.wera-web.org/	June	December

*Months that proposals are due have been taken from the association's website where available. Proposal deadlines and conference dates may change yearly. Visit the association's website for details.

APPENDIX B

Reproducible Forms

Teacher Research Organizing Worksheet

		Notes
Identification of inquiry	Statement of purpose(s) and inquiry questions	
Theoretical framework	Research support	
Research plan design	Description of the proposed activities	
	Specification of project timelines and hours	
	Goals for project(s)	
	Cooperating members and their roles	
Data collection and analysis	Organization of representative artifacts	
	Labels that clearly specify the nature of the artifacts	
	Introductory material and examples of work	
	Quantitative forms	
	Qualitative forms	
Results	Journal entries and log sheets	
Conclusions and implications	Discussion of results	
	Educational importance	
	Challenges	
	Further research needs and ideas	

Visualizing Key Decisions in Framing Your Study Chart

Research Focus

Research Question(s)	Data Sources
Q1-	
Q2-	
Q3-	

Description of Data Sources

Literature Review Matrix

	Overview	Context	Methods	Findings	Other Notes
Study #1					
Study #2					
Study #3					
Study #4					

Data Collection Checklist

Directions: This chart will help you plan for data collection as you consider multiple sources for data. Consider the strategies and associated tools that best get at answers to your research question, then check sources that seem most applicable.

Observing (observational data)	Asking/Reflecting (inquiry data)	Examining (document data)
__ Field notes	__ Informal interviews	__ Student work samples
__ Anecdotal records	__ Formal interviews	__ Student tests
__ Log, diary, journal	__ Questionnaires and surveys	__ Student self-assessments
__ Checklists	__ Attitude scales	__ Portfolios
__ Videotapes and audiotapes	__ Sociograms	__ Standardized test scores
__ Photographs	__ Focus group interviews	__ Lesson plans
__ Behavior scales	__ Conferences	__ Peer reviews
	__ Reflective journal	__ School records

Adapted from Arhar, Holly, & Kasten. (2001). *Action research for teachers: Traveling the yellow brick road.* Upper Saddle River, NJ: Prentice Hall. p. 137.

Family Call Log Sheet

Student _____ Per_____ Date _____

Reason for call _____

Time of call _____ Who was reached _____

Outcome of call (circle all that apply): Message left on machine? Conversation with person?

If so, with (name) _____

Details of message/conversation _____

_____

_____

_____

_____

_____

_____

_____

_____

_____

_____

_____

_____

_____

_____

_____

Teachers Taking Action: A Comprehensive Guide to Teacher Research, edited by Cynthia A. Lassonde and Susan E. Israel.
© 2008 by the International Reading Association. May be copied for classroom use.

Student Referral Form

Name of student: _____ ID # _____ Grade _____

Referring faculty member _____ Date _____ Period _____

Counselor _____ Telephone _____ Course _____

REASON FOR REFERRAL: Item(s) checked indicate infraction(s)

01 ___ Disruption in class
02 ___ Excessive tardiness to class
03 ___ Failure to obey staff member
04 ___ Forgery/cheating
05 ___ Inappropriate affectionate behavior
06 ___ Inappropriate behavior
07 ___ Inappropriate language
08 ___ Radio/Walkman/headgear offense
09 ___ Teacher detention cut
10 ___ Being in an unauthorized area
11 ___ Computer code (Internet use agreement)
12 ___ Disruption in study hall/hallway
13 ___ Disruption in assembly/cafeteria
14 ___ Dress code violation
15 ___ Excessive tardiness to school
16 ___ Drugs/alcohol/use/possession/exchange
17 ___ Failure to sign in when late
18 ___ Fighting
19 ___ ID infraction

20 ___ Inappropriate language/gesture to staff
21 ___ Insubordination, inappropriate behavior
22 ___ Intimidation/treatment to student/staff
23 ___ Other infractions not mentioned
24 ___ Saturday detention
25 ___ Sexual harassment/contact of pupils/staff
26 ___ Smoking
27 ___ Staff assaults
28 ___ Study hall cut # _____
29 ___ Theft/extortion/gambling
30 ___ Truancy
31 ___ Unauthorized departure from school
32 ___ Use of cell phone/beeper/pager
33 ___ Vandalism
34 ___ Verbal confrontation
35 ___ Weapons policy violation

PREVIOUS ACTION(S) TAKEN BY STAFF MEMBER

Conference with student (date) _____ Assigned teacher detention (date) _____

Family member contacted (date) _____

Description of infraction:

Administration action taken: _____ Filed warning _____ Saturday detention

_____ Out of school suspension _____ Conference with student (dates)

_____ Family member contacted (dates) _____ Other action: _____

Comments:

Signature of Administrator/Dean of Students: _____

Cc: Case Manager _____

Student Referral Form, Montclair High School, Montclair, NJ. Used with permission.

Teachers Taking Action: A Comprehensive Guide to Teacher Research, edited by Cynthia A. Lassonde and Susan E. Israel.
© 2008 by the International Reading Association. May be copied for classroom use.

Understanding and Applying References Outline

General Bibliographic Information

Title of article:

Location:

Author(s):

Journal information:

Page numbers:

Publisher:

Keywords:

Relevance to Research Problem or Question

General research area explored:

Rationale:

Quality of study design (if applicable):

Importance of study:

Research Study Details

Hypothesis:

Type of research:

Subject(s) characteristics:

Procedures:

Results/conclusions:

Criticisms and comments:

Unexpected findings (if applicable):

Developed by Moira A. Fallon for use in Survey of Research with Special Populations, State University of New York, College at Brockport.

Self-Evaluation Checklist

Mark each item using the following rating scale: 0 = poor or not developed, 1 = meets expectations, 2 = exceeds expectations. Any item marked with a zero should be revised to meet minimum expectations.

Research Problems

___ Problem is defined
___ Subproblems defined
___ Source is considered
___ Potential for change identified
___ Goals of problem set
___ Data available
___ Diverse sources used

Review of Literature

___ Key words identified
___ Databases identified
___ Advanced search complete
___ History defined
___ Concepts synthesized
___ Multiple viewpoints included
___ Data valid

Methodology

___ Action plan
___ Subject identified
___ Instruments defined
___ Procedures set
___ Proposal approved
___ Data reliable
___ Unexpected discussed

Analysis

___ Multiple sources
___ Analysis supports evidence
___ Evidence described
___ Inferential statistics
___ Patterns of change used
___ Contribution to field
___ Sampling valid

Conclusions

___ Objectives met/not met
___ Generalizations made
___ Implications discussed
___ Future research discussed
___ Impact of change noted
___ Short-/long-term effects

Comments:

Total points _____

Developed by Moira A. Fallon for use in Survey of Research with Special Populations, State University of New York, College at Brockport.

Teachers Taking Action: A Comprehensive Guide to Teacher Research, edited by Cynthia A. Lassonde and Susan E. Israel. © 2008 by the International Reading Association. May be copied for classroom use.

Lesson Study Framework

Steps of the Research Lesson	Teacher Actions What the teacher is doing or saying	Student Actions What the students are doing or expected student responses	Evaluation What data are you collecting? How will you collect it? What is the purpose for the data being collected?
Connect the lesson to goals, previous learning, and standards.			
Introduce the new concept.			
Demonstrate, model, or explain the new concept.			
Engage the students in learning the new concept.			
Give students opportunities to practice or apply learning.			
Have students share new ideas and applications.			
Summarize learning.			

AUTHOR INDEX

Note. Page numbers followed by *f* or *t* indicate figures or tables, respectively.

SUBJECT INDEX

Note. Page numbers followed by *f* or *t* indicate figures or tables, respectively.

CALL LOGS: Family Call Log Sheet, 106–107, 209
CALLS FOR MANUSCRIPTS, 153
CAMPUS-BASED RESEARCHERS, 94
CARNEGIE CORPORATION OF NEW YORK, 178
CASE STUDY RESEARCH, 46*t*, 50–51; aim of, 76;
   Alexandra's story, 109; instrumental, 54;
   intrinsic, 54; methodology, 76; stumbling
   blocks, 109
CCA. *See* Constant comparative analysis
CERTIFICATION: human subjects, 200
CHRISTINE'S STORY, 93–95
CITATIONS, 18
CITI. *See* Collaborative Institutional Training
   Initiative
CLASSROOM APPLICATIONS, 114–115
CLASSROOM-BASED RESEARCHERS, 94
CLASSROOM INQUIRY, 71–72
CLASSROOM OBSERVATIONS, 82, 84*f*
CLASSROOM RESEARCH, 32; resources for, 192
COACHES, LITERACY, 185
CODES, 75; adjusting, 79–80; artifact-action, 80;
   common sources of, 82; emergent, 82;
   professional development case, 82; sample
   transcript dialogue, 79; with too much
   detail, 79
COLLABORATION, 89–100; Christine's story, 93–95;
   complexity of, 96–98; Donna's story, 90–92;
   Elizabeth's story, 92–93; Jim's story, 95–96;
   problem-solving vignettes, 98; reflections
   on, 90–91, 92–93, 93–95, 95–96; tips for,
   98–99; with virtual research partners, 179
COLLABORATIVE AUTHORSHIP, 97
COLLABORATIVE INSTITUTIONAL TRAINING INITIATIVE
   (CITI), 200
COLLABORATORS, 10
COLLOQUIUM, 163, 167
COMMUNITY INVOLVEMENT, 185
COMPARISON GROUPS, 19
COMPREHENSION INSTRUCTION, 185
CONCEPTUALIZING, 58–60
CONFERENCE PRESENTATIONS: executing, 170;
   formats for, 166–167; panel presentations,
   164–165; paper presentations, 166; poster
   presentation layouts, 172*f*, 173*f*; poster
   presentations, 166, 170–171; preparing for,
   168–170; tips for preparing paper
   presentations, 169*t*; tips for preparing poster
   presentations, 171*t*; tips for teacher
   researchers, 174
CONFERENCE PROPOSALS, 162; problem-solving
   vignette, 173–174
CONFERENCE ROLES, 164–166

CONFERENCES, 201*t*–203*t*; for presentations, 197;
   professional, 162, 198–199; proposal
   process, 167–168; selecting, 163–166; types
   of, 164
CONFIDENTIALITY, 117
CONSENT TO PUBLISH FORMS, 157
CONSTANT COMPARATIVE ANALYSIS, 75–76; first-pass,
   77–79; mechanics of, 75; supporting
   conclusions, 80
CONSULTING LITERATURE, 60–62
CONTEXTUAL ISSUES, 32–33
COOPERATIVE WORK GROUPS (CWG), 37–38
COPYING, 128
CORRELATIONAL RESEARCH, 46*t*, 48
COUNCIL FOR EXCEPTIONAL CHILDREN, 201*t*
COUNCIL FOR EXCEPTIONAL CHILDREN, 197
CRITICAL FRIENDS, 10
CRITICAL ISSUES, 113–115; managing, 115–120;
   tips for teacher researchers, 121
CRITICAL REFLECTIVE PRACTICE, 7, 9–10
CURRICULAR CONTEXTS, 80
CURRICULUM DESIGN CASE, 77–80
CWG. *See* Cooperative Work Groups

D

DAILY PRACTICES AND ROUTINES, 114–115
DATA: forms commonly used, 19–20; hard-copy,
   82–84; housing data, 81; organizing, 19–20;
   qualitative, 73–88; sample interview data,
   82, 83*f*; themes resulting from triangulating
   data, 84–86, 86*t*; triangulating, 84–86; types
   of, 63
DATA ANALYSIS, 20; constant comparative
   analysis, 75–76, 77–79; planned inferential
   analysis, 116; qualitative, 73–88; Self-
   Evaluation Checklist, 212; tips for teacher
   researchers, 87
DATA CHECKLISTS, 22
DATA COLLECTION, 19–20, 21–22; context and
   time restraints for, 19; effective principles
   of, 25; selecting appropriate strategies for,
   63–64
DATA COLLECTION CHECKLIST, 63, 64*f*, 208
DATA SOURCES, 33, 39*f*
DATA STORAGE, 22–23
DATABASES, 199
DESCRIPTIVE RESEARCH, 46*t*, 47–48
DEVELOPMENTAL RESEARCH, 48
DI. *See* Direct Instruction
DIRECT INSTRUCTION (DI), 37–38
DOCUMENTATION: paper presentations, 166, 168,
   169, 169*t*; poster presentations, 166,
   170–171, 171*t*, 172*f*, 173*f*; reports, 136–137;